## Date Due

# A PILGRIMAGE TO PALESTINE

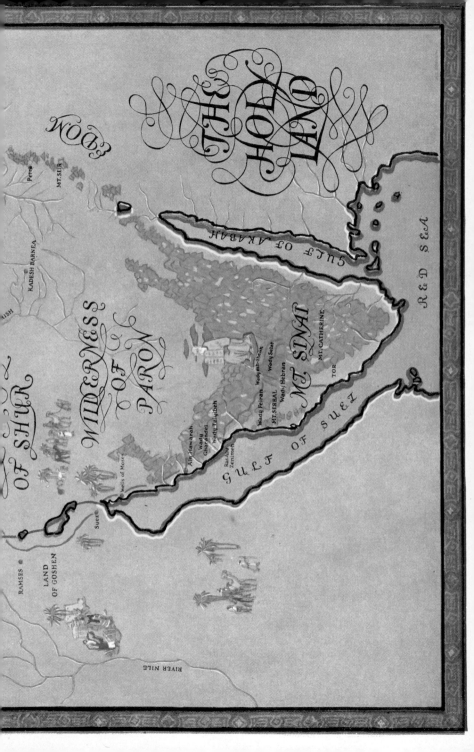

MT. HERMON
BAALBEK
DAMASCUS
MT. LEBANON
Cae sarea Philippi
BEIRUT
WATERS OF
MEROM
Bethsaida
SEA OF GALILEE
SIDON
Safed
Chorazin
Capernaum
Bersa
Tiberias
Sepphoris
TYRE
Nazareth
Cadara
GILEAD
Jerash.
AMMON
RIVER JABBOK
HESHBON
MEDEBA
Callirrhoe
MOAB
RIVER ARNON
el-Kerak
ACRE
HAIFA
MT. CARMEL
Athlit
MT. TABOR
Shunem
ESDRAELON
JEZREEL
MT. GILBOA
Beisan
Samaria
MEGIDDO
DOTHAN
SHECHEM
MT. EBAL
MT. GERIZIM
BETHEL
JERICHO
Gilgal
RIVER JORDAN
DEAD SEA
PLAIN OF SHARON
JERUSALEM
BETHLEHEM
Tekoa
HEBRON
En-dedi
Masada
JAFFA
EKRON
ASHDOD
Gath
Beit Jibrin
GAZA
BEERSHEBA
ASHKELON

THE
GREAT
SEA

TRIPOLI AND CEDARS OF LEBANON

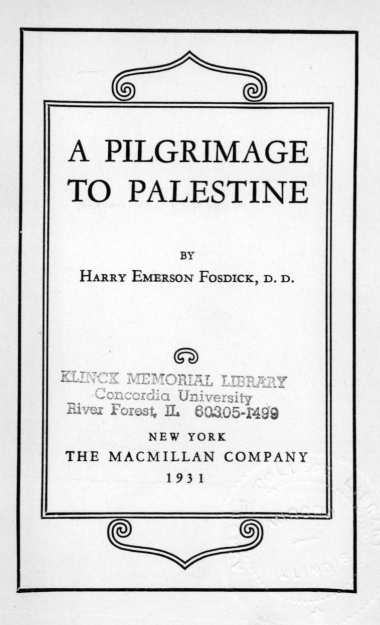

# A PILGRIMAGE TO PALESTINE

BY

HARRY EMERSON FOSDICK, D. D.

NEW YORK

THE MACMILLAN COMPANY

1931

PRINTED IN THE UNITED STATES OF AMERICA
BY THE CORNWALL PRESS

TO
MY FRIENDS
THE AMERICAN COLONY
JERUSALEM

# FOREWORD

Four months in Egypt, Palestine, and Syria were too stimulating to the mind and imagination not to find expression in a book and the present volume is the result. It has been written *con amore* for the sheer love of the land about which it tells. After years of studying the Bible I found the Book vivified and illumined by studying the country where it grew and where its major scenes were set. I have written down my impressions of this experience alike as a privilege—deepening the experience by expressing it—and as an obligation. I wish to share with others who may desire it as much of the pleasure and enlightenment of a pilgrimage to Palestine as I can convey in writing.

The method of organizing the material which here is used I chose after hesitation. Most books about Palestine are built on either of two patterns. Some are simply travelogues in which the successive experiences of the traveler furnish the strand for the narrative. Some are treatises, proceeding from one geographical district to another, "wiping up" each, as the soldiers would say, before going to the next, until the land is covered. In this book neither telling a travelogue nor districting the country has furnished the outline; history provides the strand on which the narrative is threaded. After two introductory chapters on the geographical setting and historical background of the country as a whole, I ask the reader to follow from the Hebrews at Sinai to the modern Zionists the successive eras of Palestine's story as they were illumined for us by our pilgrimage.

Our indebtedness for help, alike in making the journey and in understanding what we saw, is wide and deep. As for books, a selected list has been appended including a few of the more important volumes of which any traveler to Palestine may well confess himself to have been a pensioner.

As for people to whom Mrs. Fosdick and I owe gratitude for the success and happiness of our journey, they are too many to name and yet too much our creditors to be forgotten. To the editors of the Ladies' Home Journal, for their interest and cooperation, and to the members of the American Colony, Jerusalem, for their invaluable kindness and good-will, we are especially in debt. Nor may I neglect to mention my colleague, Professor Julius A. Bewer, who has taken pains to read the entire manuscript of the book, and my secretary, Miss Margaret Renton, who has combed it with painstaking care to substantiate the accuracy of its statements. Let me also bear witness to my personal appreciation of Mr. Henry J. Soulen's companionship. From among the many charming pictures which this accomplished artist drew in connection with our trip we have been compelled, for the purposes of this book, to restrict ourselves to the colored map.

In using footnotes we have confined ourselves to Biblical references. These references are made either to the American Standard Revised Bible or else to Dr. James Moffatt's New Translation, and when the latter is the case the letter M has been appended to the references.

Seldom have I enjoyed writing so much as in the preparation of this book. I am hoping that it may bring a corresponding pleasure to others who through its use may either make their own trip to Palestine more interesting or else enjoy vicariously a pilgrimage which they cannot take in person.

HARRY EMERSON FOSDICK.

New York, June 11, 1927.

# CONTENTS

# APPROXIMATE DATES FOR PALESTINE

| | |
|---|---|
| End of paleolithic age | 10000 B.C. |
| The cave-dwellers at Gezer | 3000 B.C. |
| The first Semitic invasion—the Amorites | 2500 B.C. |
| The Canaanites settle in Palestine | 1800–1750 B.C. |
| Egyptian domination — Ahmose I to Ikhnaton (Amenhotep IV) | 1580–1375 B.C. |
| The Hebrews come under Joshua | 1200 B.C. |
| The Philistines arrive | 1184 B.C. |
| David sets up his kingdom in Jerusalem | 1000 B.C. |
| The northern and southern kingdoms divide | 937 B.C. |
| The Assyrians take Samaria; northern kingdom ends | 722 B.C. |
| The Babylonians twice sack Jerusalem; the Exile begins | 597 and 586 B.C. |
| The Jewish community is reestablished in Judah under the Persians | 538–520 B.C. |
| Alexander the Great conquers Syria | 333 B.C. |
| Palestine ruled by the Syrian Greeks | 320–142 B.C. |
| The Maccabean age of Jewish independence | 142–63 B.C. |
| Pompey captures Jerusalem for Rome | 63 B.C. |
| Herod the Great becomes Jewish king, under Rome | 37 B.C. |
| Titus puts down the Jewish revolt and sacks Jerusalem | 70 A.D. |
| Hadrian crushes the Bar Khokhba revolt and destroys Jerusalem | 132–135 A.D. |
| Jerusalem, a Christian city, visited by Saint Helena | 326 A.D. |
| Chosroes II, the Persian, raids Palestine | 616 A.D. |
| The Moslems capture Jerusalem | 636 A.D. |
| The Crusader kingdom in Jerusalem | 1099–1187 A.D. |
| The Turks take Palestine | 1516 A.D. |
| Napoleon Bonaparte invades Palestine | 1799 A.D. |
| The British seize Jerusalem | 1917 A.D. |

# A PILGRIMAGE TO PALESTINE

enough for a child to throw a stone across—but a mystic boundary over which his dead have gone into the Promised Land. Siloam is not to him an actual pool— unsightly and malodorous, where soiled and thirsty men and animals drink and women wash their clothes—but a symbol of peace: "By cool Siloam's shady rill." Galilee, whose very syllables are musical, and whose memory is fragrant with Christ's life and work, has to him largely ceased to be geography and has become romance. And Jerusalem is the celestial city that comes "down out of heaven from God." With such idealizations in his mind the tourist, full of anticipation, starts for Palestine and if he knows Shakespeare tells his friends that he is going to see the

................holy fields
Over whose acres walk'd those blessed feet,
Which fourteen hundred years ago were nail'd
For our advantage on the bitter cross.

Then he is taken in hand by one of those abominations of the earth, a tourist ship which allows a day to see Athens and two days to see Palestine. He is hurried into the Holy City, hurried around it, rushed to Bethlehem and back; he is shown incredible impostures, from a dented stone on the Via Dolorosa where our Lord's Cross smote a wall, to the footprint that our Lord left in the rock on Olivet when he ascended. He is hastened through the Garden of Gethsemane; he is dropped in an automobile four thousand feet in an hour from Olivet to the Dead Sea and is hoisted straightway back again; and then he is carried off to his ship, often stripped of his old illusions, with the poetry of the Holy Land vanished and no new insight to take its place. It is a great pity. For to one who stays long enough to understand and who comes in the first place prepared to obey the law of all successful travel, "He who would bring home the wealth of the Indies must carry the wealth of the Indies with him," Palestine is a land of thrilling interest such as few other countries can claim and Jerusalem is still "the joy of the whole earth."

## II

To be sure, every Western visitor must at some points readjust his understanding of the Holy Land. From his youth he has thought of it as "flowing with milk and honey." [1] Ancient Hebrews, with nomadic life in the desert for their standard of judgment, wrote such grateful appreciations of their land that many a traveler expects a riot of fertility. Instead, even in springtime, when the rains just have ceased and the country is most beautiful, the land as a whole, and the Judean uplands in particular, are to Western eyes treeless, stony, barren, and uninviting. At the beginning of his visit the traveler must learn that a country's fruitfulness and beauty are relative; they depend on the previous experience of the visitor.

We proved this to our satisfaction during our stay.

[1] Exodus 3:8 (Note that the references are to the American Standard Revised Bible, published by Thomas Nelson & Sons, except those indicated by M, which are to the New Translation by Dr. James Moffatt, published by George H. Doran Company).

We came first into Palestine with memories of the Riviera and Sicily in our minds, and in comparison Palestine was dour and grim. But afterward we went down by camel caravan into the Sinaitic peninsula and spent two weeks in "that great and terrible wilderness" [1] where for years the nomad sons of Israel had battled for a precarious existence. There still the Bedouin live, baked by the heat, haunted by thirst, counting a succulent weed a godsend. We ourselves became so accustomed to the wilderness that for days after we came out our closed eyes saw sterile wadies, hot granite crags baking in the sun, plains of sand and gravel radiating heat, and in the torrid landscape hunted for some forlorn, half-withered palm tree that might promise shade.

Overnight by train we passed from that blistering, arid desert back into Palestine and found ourselves in the morning climbing up from the Philistine plain through the foothills of the Shephelah to the Judean ridge. I knew then why the Hebrews thought this new country they were conquering a paradise. To our eyes also it looked green and beautiful so that we could not easily imagine anything more lovely. The odor of orange blossoms drifted into the windows as we passed through the fertile plain. The harvesters were sickling golden grain on the Shephelah hills. The Judean valleys were luxuriantly covered with fig and olive trees.

That same day we went by the north road from

[1] Deuteronomy 1:19.

Jerusalem to Shechem, past old sites renowned in the earliest days of the Hebrew conquest—Ramah, Mizpah, Bethel, Shiloh—to the twin mountains, Gerizim and Ebal, where victorious Joshua pledged the people to Jehovah's service.[1] As I saw the overflowing fountains, the fertile valleys, the abundant olive groves of Ephraim, with ripe grain fields and freshly plowed ground lying side by side, fulfilling the prophet's picture of fertility, "the plowman shall overtake the reaper," [2] I understood what the eighth chapter of Deuteronomy meant: "a good land, a land of brooks of water, of fountains and springs, flowing forth in valleys and hills; a land of wheat and barley, and vines and fig-trees and pomegranates; a land of olive-trees and honey; a land wherein thou shalt eat bread without scarceness, thou shalt not lack anything in it." [3] We were seeing Palestine with eyes accustomed to the desert; one must so see it to understand what the Bible says about it.

### III

Nevertheless, there are some impressions which the country makes upon the Western visitor which should be frankly stated. According to our standards it is not a fruitful land. One understands why those who lived here should have told in one of their earliest traditions that God cursed the ground and said to man that in the sweat of his face he should gain his daily bread.[4]

[1] Joshua 8:30-35.
[2] Amos 9:13.
[3] Deuteronomy 8:7-9.
[4] Genesis 3:17-19.

There are, to be sure, some copious wells and fountains and some naturally fertile places which bear plenteous crops. But for the most part the scarcity of water is so grievous, the uncertainty of rainfall is so hazardous, so small a proportion of the land is fit for tillage, the soil must so be fought for by terracing hills and conserving every inch of arable space, that one who knows Western lands pities herdsmen and farmers alike for their hard toil with such small consequence.

As for the uplands, they look, as one traveler put it, as though they had been stoned to death. No stonier country than Palestine, I think, is to be found on earth. The Arabs have a legend that when God made the world he put all the stones which were to cover it into two bags and gave them to an angel, and while the angel was flying over Palestine one bag broke. I never understood the many passages in Scripture about stones until I went to Palestine. Readers of the Bible will recall many passages in Scripture where stones are sacred, but not every one will have noticed how frequently in Old and New Testament alike their commonness, cheapness, and troublesomeness are implied. "The king made silver to be in Jerusalem as stones" [1] is a meaningful picture of Solomon's wealth when one has lived even a little while on the Judean ridge. Dashing one's foot against a stone [2] is a symbol of trouble; having a stony heart [3] is a picture of impenitence; gathering stones out of the highway [4] or out of a vineyard [5]

---

[1] I Kings 10:27.
[2] Psalm 91:12
[3] Ezekiel 36:26.

[4] Isaiah 62:10.
[5] Isaiah 5:1-2.

—as needful now as ever—is a metaphor of spiritual preparedness. The Master pictured an unreliable life as stony ground [1] and described a disdained request as asking for bread and receiving a stone.[2] One does not notice until he goes to Palestine how common such figures are in Scripture, but, having been there, one can supply in imagination the very gesture and tone of voice with which John the Baptist must have said that God was able of these stones to raise up children unto Abraham,[3] and Jesus said of the multitude that welcomed him to Zion on the first Palm Sunday, "If these shall hold their peace, the stones will cry out." [4]

When first the children of Israel approached Palestine from the south and Moses sent out spies to investigate the land, a twofold report was brought back. "It floweth with milk and honey," said some; "a land that eateth up the inhabitants thereof," said the rest.[5] Both descriptions were true. In certain moods and aspects Palestine is beautiful. I do not understand what Dean Stanley meant by saying that it lacks variety of color. I never saw a country with coloring so obvious, rich, and changeable, where reds, browns, yellows, purples in such profusion stain bare hills and distant landscapes with ever-varying shades and tints. Moreover, in certain areas—notably the plain of Esdraelon, which cuts across the country between Samaria and Galilee, and the plain of Sharon by the sea—the land is fertile

[1] Matthew 13:5-6, 20-21.
[2] Matthew 7:9.
[3] Matthew 3:9.
[4] Luke 19:40.
[5] Numbers 13:27, 32.

and fruitful. But for the most part it suggests the psalmist's cry:

> My soul thirsteth for thee, my flesh longeth for thee,
> In a dry and weary land, where no water is.[1]

As for the herdsman's task, seeking pasturage for flocks, the Arabs say that the noses of the sheep on the uplands have to be filed to a fine point so that they can get at the grass between the rocks.

Whether or not there used to be more trees upon these hills than now has often been discussed, but I do not see how any one can doubt it. In this last war alone it is estimated that forty per cent of all the olive trees in Palestine were cut down for military purposes. To say nothing of the locusts, two great enemies of the trees have ravaged the land for centuries: militarists and goats. The first destroy trees wholesale when they are grown; the second prevent trees from growing at all. I have seen goats climb mature olive trees to crop the leaves, so that a man who cares for trees is sympathetic with the Scriptures' symbolism which always uses sheep for the saved and goats for the damned. As for militarists, their ruthless work is as destructive of forests as of human societies. When Pompey came to take Palestine for Rome, the record says that he cleared away the trees, and Josephus tells us that Titus cut down every tree within ten miles of Jerusalem. When one recalls the endless invasions which have crossed this land, one wonders that any woods are left at all. Away back in ancient Israel's time the meaning

[1] Psalm 63:1.

of war to the fruitfulness and beauty of the land was set down plainly in the Bible: "Every man threw a stone on every good field till it was covered, they stopped every fountain, and they felled every fruitful tree." [1]

It is not surprising, therefore, to read in our records, within the Bible and out of it, of forests growing where today no forests are. Even in the Lebanons they are finding boundary stones set by Hadrian's foresters—I saw one in Beirut—where today only bare mountains remain. The forest of Hereth, where David hid,[2] is gone; there is no forest of Bethel to shelter bears today;[3] Kiriath-jearim, which means "city of forests," would have no excuse now for such a name, and the woods of Sharon, which Strabo called "a great forest," and which once stretched from the valley of Ajalon up to Mount Carmel, now have few relics of their ancient glory. One must not exaggerate this matter. Probably, judged by Western standards, Palestine never was a well-wooded land, but one suspects that the ravages of war, unhealed for centuries by the laggard, barren rule of the Turk, have stripped these hills of a beauty that once was theirs and that may be theirs again. The Zionists, at least, are proceeding upon that assumption. Wherever there is a Zionist colony, the trees by tens of thousands are being planted again.

## IV

Another impression immediately made upon the visitor is that the land is small. How tiny and compact

[1] II Kings 3:25 M.      [3] II Kings 2:23-24.
[2] I Samuel 22:5.

it is, no description, however vivid, is likely to make clear to one who has not been there. Many factors encourage one's imagination of a larger country, even though one has memorized the statistics of distances and acreage. For one thing, our Bible-school maps naturally have made Palestine huge and central, with Egypt and Assyria hanging on the edge; for another, our modern life moves in continental areas and does business on a vast scale, so that where much has happened, as in Palestine, one instinctively imagines for it a large setting. From Dan to Beersheba, therefore, has come to sound like a long way; as a matter of fact, it is about 150 miles, and in a day one can traverse the whole length of Palestine in an automobile. The Mediterranean and the Dead Sea are barely fifty miles apart; and as one moves north the distance narrows until the Sea of Galilee is little over twenty-five miles from the Bay of Acre.

In comparison, therefore, with the spaces in which Western life habitually moves, the littleness of the Holy Land is difficult to picture. The state of Connecticut, with an area of 4965 square miles, is one of the smallest in the United States, and yet nearly all the events narrated in the Old Testament happened within an area no larger. Such comparisons, however, fail utterly to explain why Palestine feels so small to the visitor. Connecticut is comparatively flat; little though it is, you cannot see from one end to the other; but Palestine is one of the most dramatically broken countries in the world and there are many points of vantage from which one can practically see all over it. Not only is it small; it feels even smaller than it is.

Jordan rises in the fountains of the north as high as 1700 feet above the sea, born from the snows of Hermon and Lebanon, and, flowing down through the Waters of Merom and the Sea of Galilee, empties at last, nearly 1300 feet below sea-level, into the Dead Sea. That gorge of Jordan, one of the natural marvels of the world, extends from the latitude of Jerusalem on the south to lofty Hermon, which lies outside the northern boundaries of Palestine. But I well remember walking the shores of the Dead Sea, where the Jordan ends, and watching the noble snow-capped peak of Hermon, at whose base the Jordan rises. That is why Palestine seems small; one can see all over it.

When, therefore, the Bible tells us that from Mount Nebo's top Moses was shown the whole of the Promised Land, there is no exaggeration about it. Mount Nebo towers 4000 feet above the very spot on the Dead Sea shore from which I could see Hermon, and from that altitude the eye still can sweep the whole length of Palestine.

A trip to Neby Samwil helps to make clear this dramatic visibility of the Holy Land. The mountain stands nearly 3000 feet high, six miles northwest of Jerusalem, and two and a half hours on donkeys brought us, as comfortably as donkeys permit, to its summit. It used to be considered the site of Mizpah, where Samuel judged Israel,[1] and the reputed tomb of Samuel, a Moslem shrine, still is here.  Here the medieval pilgrims caught their first view of the Holy City and called the spot the Mount of Joy.  Here Richard the Lion-Hearted, forced to turn back from capturing the city by the disaffection of his allies, refused to look upon the sacred place which he could not seize. The view is glorious.  With one turn of the head we could see the whole breadth of Palestine, fifty miles, from Jaffa to the Dead Sea, and beyond that into Moab.  To the west the Mediterranean shone clear on the horizon and, moving eastward, the glance swept over the coastal plain with its palm trees and orange groves; then over the Shephelah hills, the old battleground of the Philistines, with their wheat fields and olive trees; then up the bare, rocky ridge of Judea, 2500 feet above the sea, with Jerusalem close at hand and Bethlehem beyond.  Then came the abrupt drop into the wilderness of Judea with its ghastly, spectral aspect as of a lunar landscape, until, beyond the abyss of the Dead Sea, Moab lifted its great plateau three to four thousand feet from the Dead Sea level, marking the eastern horizon with its towering wall.

From more than one height one thus can take in Palestine at a glance, with its amazing diversity, its unparalleled associations of history and sentiment, compact in a small compass.

The littleness of the land, accentuated by its brokenness and wide visibility, adds light and interest to many

[1] I Samuel 7:6.

a narrative in the Bible. When, in the story of Ruth, Naomi and her family in famine time moved from Bethlehem to Moab, I used to think they traveled a long way.[1] As a matter of fact, Moab can be seen from Bethlehem, the most conspicuous element in the eastern landscape, lifting its towering plateau from the Dead Sea gorge. Naomi went thirty miles to Moab, and Ruth the Moabitess, who came back with her, had often seen Bethlehem from her native hills.

I used to think that when Hannah, who lived at Ramah, took her son Samuel to Shiloh and left him there with Eli, visiting him once a year,[2] she was putting a great distance between them. It was really fifteen miles. One walks the heights about Jerusalem and looks down into the Philistine country as David must have done when he was king. Those chief enemies of his in Ekron and Gath were barely twenty-five miles distant. And when the Master, driven from Nazareth, went to Capernaum to make that the center of his ministry,[3] he walked some twenty miles across the hills. The modern lord of automobiles and airplanes has to readjust his idea of distances to fit this little land.

## V

A further impression sure to be made upon one who sees Palestine is its extraordinary diversity. Little as it is, there are as many kinds of climate and landscape

[1] Ruth 1:1-2.          [3] Luke 4:16-31.
[2] I Samuel 1:19-28 and 2:18-19.

there as one could expect to find in a whole continent. That one may swelter in the torrid heat of the Dead Sea while he looks at snow-crowned Hermon is typical. If a traveler starts at Beersheba and moves north along the spinal ridge of Palestine, he will begin on the border of a fiery desert, on portions of which rain never falls, and he will end among the pines and snows of Anti-Lebanon. On that short route—a possible day's trip in an automobile—he will have climbed from a parched wilderness to the cool ridge on which Jerusalem stands, where rains fall in the spring and the snows sometimes lie thick in winter. From that temperate height he will have looked on one side into the blazing, barren gorge of the Dead Sea and on the other into the wheat fields of the moderate Shephelah and the citron groves and palm trees of the hot Philistine plain. As he moves north he will leave the grim rocks of the Judean ridge for the more open and gracious country of Ephraim, with its green valleys, its fig trees and olive groves, and, crossing the plain of Esdraelon, will climb the central ridge again to pass through Galilee, with its oaks and sycamores, to the northern mountains, with their pines and cedars. Whatever else may be true of Palestine, it is never monotonous. In no other country in the world can you pass from thirteen hundred feet below sea-level to nine thousand feet above.

All this brokenness and diversity of the land is constantly reflected in the Bible, but I never felt it until I went there. When I read the Book now I am conscious that it was written in "a land of hills and

valleys." [1]  The central ridge is all cut up by valleys,
slashed into on every side by wadies dry in summer but
torrential when it rains.  This separation of Palestine
into innumerable small pockets helps to explain the
tribal nature of its old inhabitants.  Those many breeds
of Canaanites, from Jebusites to Perizzites, were scattered among these numberless natural pigeonholes along
the central ridge.  The tribes of Israel also were sun-
dered from each other by these abrupt, sharp boundaries, so that it took at least two centuries after their
arrival to make one nation of them, and then this unity
lasted at the utmost eighty-five years.  It is the easiest
country in the world, one traveler assures us, in which
to lose oneself.  Out of this chopped-up, irregular,
diversified land the Bible came.  In its pages mountains
and valleys are the boundary lines—"from the valley
of the Arnon unto mount Hermon" [2]—and the omnipresent wadies of the land enter constantly into the
figurative language of the Book.  Sometimes they mean
what crossing the Rubicon means to us—"the valley of
decision"; [3] sometimes they are retreats where revela-
tions are given—"the valley of vision"; [4] sometimes
they are symbols of difficulty—"the valley of the
shadow of death"; [5] and once, weary of so broken a
country, a prophet foretells the happy time when "every
valley shall be exalted, and every mountain and hill
shall be made low." [6]

[1] Deuteronomy 11:11.
[2] Joshua 12:1.
[3] Joel 3:14.
[4] Isaiah 22:1.
[5] Psalm 23:4.
[6] Isaiah 40-4.

To take only one illustration of the land's strange contrasts, we may go, as I have gone more than once, up
from the Philistine plain over the Jerusalem ridge
to the Judean wilderness upon the other side.  It is a
trip of hardly more than thirty-five miles, but it presents
an astonishing antithesis.  The plain reminds one of
southern California with its verdant fertility.  Its
oranges cannot be surpassed; its grain fields are fruitful, and in the season of its beauty even a Westerner
will reecho the prophet's praise for the excellency of
Sharon.  Then in an hour one has climbed a few hundred feet, has passed by the walls of Jerusalem, skirted
the flank of Olivet, driven through traditional Bethany,
and is plunging down that amazing fourteen miles
through the wilderness of Judea toward the Dead Sea.
Every vestige of life has vanished except, in the springtime, a few brilliant flowers—"a root out of a dry
ground," [1] as Isaiah said—and a sparse growth of thin
weeds, like down on a bald head.  By June even this has
gone and all is dead, dry, yellow rock and earth—a
landscape, I imagine, like the moon, if one could see it
at close range.

Somewhere into this arid waste, this weird desolation,
slashed by barren wadies and baked in merciless heat,
the Master went when he was tempted, [2] and down
through this wilderness from Jerusalem to Jericho the
victim in the Master's parable was traveling when he fell
among thieves. [3]  Even yet jackals and hyenas roam

[1] Isaiah 53:2.            [3] Luke 10:29-35.
[2] Matthew 4:1-11.

here, and many a night I have heard the yelping of
jackal bands that had come up from the wilderness
to scavenge under the wall of Jerusalem.

When Mark says that the Master during his temptation in the wilderness was "with the wild beasts," [1] he
is speaking literally.  Lions and bears are familiar
figures in the Bible and they lived in the copses beside
Jordan and in this wilderness which leads up from it
to the ridge.  Here prowled the lion and the bear that
David, the shepherd lad, slew;[2] and up from here
came the lion that Benaiah caught and killed in a pit
on a snowy day.[3]  "Where else than in Palestine,"
exclaims one commentator, "could lions and snow thus
come together?"

Such wild life was known in the wilderness well on
into the Christian era.  We hear of no lions there after
the crusades.  In Medeba, an ancient town of Moab,
celebrated in the taunt-song which the early Hebrews
chanted against their fallen foes,

> . . . we ravaged till war's fire
> was blown to Medeba,[4]

a large, mosaic map of Palestine was recently uncovered in the floor of an old church.  The map was made
in the fifth century A.D. and has already settled more
than one disputed site for the archeologists.  It is a
quaint, old-fashioned map with huge fish in the rivers
to show that they are rivers and huge ships on the sea
to show that it is sea, and up from the thicket of Jordan,

[1] Mark 1:13.
[2] I Samuel 17:34-35.
[3] II Samuel 23:20.
[4] Numbers 21:30 M.

through the wilderness, we could discern in the mosaic a lion chasing a stag.

Only the year before our visit two students, who should have known better, figuring that the distance from Jericho to Mar Saba through the wilderness was only a few miles, started off across the waterless, trackless waste. The distance was short as the bee flies, but before they had well started they were as lost as compassless sailors in a thick fog. The Bedouin found one of them unconscious and brought him to Jerusalem. All that was found of the other was a few bones and buttons in a jackal's den. And all this below the very gates of Jerusalem and within a few miles of orange groves as lovely as earth can boast!

Only one important qualification can I think of to the endless variety of Palestine: the Great Sea is always a stranger, alien to the life of the land. In Greece the sea is everywhere intimate and alluring: in numberless bays and estuaries of an infinitely broken coast it beckons and invites, and sprinkles its islands like stepping stones across the Ægean to tempt even landsmen to seamanship. But in Palestine the sea is always distant, strange, foreign. Long ago a psalmist stood on the Judean ridge and, looking westward, sang,

> Yonder the sea lies, vast and broad,
>     with its countless swarms,
>     with creatures small and great,
>     with fleets of the nautilus,
>     with leviathan at his play.[1]

[1] Psalm 104:25-26 M.

Always to the Jews the sea is thus a marvel, not a neighbor; they gaze from afar upon it but they do not sail it; and whenever the test of choice comes they still are Bedouin of the desert and not seamen.

Nor is the reason difficult to understand. Opposite Judea and Samaria there is not a harbor on the seacoast worthy of the name—only a long, straight, inhospitable lee shore with the prevailing southwest winds blowing in upon it. No maritime people ever could come from such a coast or ever did come. When, therefore, in the old allegory, Jonah flees from God by way of the sea to distant Tarshish,[1] perhaps in Spain, that is as desperate a venture as he could try, and when, in the prophets, the vision of God's kingdom becomes so comprehensive that "the isles shall wait for his law,"[2] that is the Jews' widest imagination of a universal reign.

Amazingly varied the Holy Land is for so small a country, but there is one limitation—the sea, while in the picture, is not of it. The Jew was a landsman.

## VI

One further impression stands out clearly about Palestine: it is only the out-of-doors that matters much. Almost everything that men have put under a roof they have spoiled for the intelligent visitor. They have fairly ruined Olivet, building churches all over it. In Jerusalem the so-called Church of the Holy Sepulcher,

[1] Jonah 1:3.     [2] Isaiah 42:4.

which covers the traditional site of Golgotha and the empty tomb, is the scene of such sectarian bitterness, riot, and mummery that one is thankful to believe the location false. They have not left even Jacob's well in peace, but that deeply impressive spot, one of the most certain identifications of site in Palestine, where, as the Fourth Gospel records, Jesus talked in out-of-door symbols about living water and fields white for the harvest, is enclosed in an ugly half-finished church.

One's regret and even indignation constantly are stirred by this ecclesiastical desecration of holy places. Across the centuries, whether for pious or for mercenary reasons, the competing churches have surrendered to the passion for identifying sites until they will show you at least three tombs of Jonah and preposterous identifications everywhere, from the pious blunders of ignorant crusaders to deliberate swindles, like Joseph of Arimathæa's summer home. And wherever they have found an excuse they have built a chapel or a church and ecclesiastical hangers-on have gathered there to live upon the benefactions of the pilgrims. This is an ugly side to Palestine, but it has one good effect: it drives the traveler out of doors.

The thoughtful visitor soon makes up his mind that nothing in Palestine under a roof is much worth seeing and nothing in Palestine out of doors is not worth seeing. Of course, there are exceptions—the Church of the Nativity at Bethlehem, which is extremely old, much of it as old as Constantine the Great; the Mosque of Omar, standing where the Jewish temple stood, which

is very beautiful; the new Franciscan church on Mount
Tabor, which is the loveliest modern building in Palestine.   But while in a few such cases antiquity lends
interest or beauty sanctifies, it is the land that invites the
pilgrim and rewards his stay.   One thing neither
ignorant piety nor ecclesiastical greed can alter—the
outline of the land.   The hills of Nazareth, the Sea of
Galilee, Esdraelon's plain, the heights of Ephraim, the
Jordan valley, the Salt Sea, and Jerusalem with the
mountains round about her, as the psalmist sang,[1]—
such unchanged elements in the landscape, fragrant
with our sacredest memories, are the true pilgrim's
Palestine.

From the summit of Mount Tabor, better than from
any other vantage point I visited, one can grasp the lie
of the land.   The hill rises out of the plain of Esdraelon,
sheer on every side, so that while the top is less than
1900 feet above the sea it commands a glorious view.
"Thabor rises up to heaven," said an old traveler, "like
an altar that the Creator built to Himself."

We wound up the serpentine road, to be greeted on
the top with cordial hospitality by the Franciscan monks.
The old tradition says that on this height our Lord was
transfigured,[2] and although it was on a shoulder of
Mount Hermon and not here that the transfiguration
probably took place, one in this case does not mind the
false location.   Tabor would be as worthy of the scene.
Ruins are here of old structures full of interest to the
historian: bits of the first church, said to have been built

[1] Psalm 125:2.                    [2] Matthew 17:1-8.

by Saint Helena, mother of Constantine the Great; ruins of the church of the crusaders, of a Benedictine monastery, of a Saracen fortress, with the chaste and beautiful Franciscan church now crowning all.

It is the view, however, which makes the visit forever memorable. Toward the west we saw Mount Carmel running its long ridge down the south of the Esdraelon plain, from the site of Elijah's sacrifice to the Mediterranean Sea at Haifa. To the east we could see far across the Jordan valley into Gilead. Northward we looked across the hills to the Sea of Galilee, the Lebanons, and the white dome of Hermon in the distance. Southward we could see far down into central Ephraim, well on toward the mountains that are about Jerusalem. The view swept practically the whole range of Palestine, from Judea to Hermon, and from Gilead to the Great Sea.

This outlook, splendid in itself, is, I think, in point of reminiscence quite without parallel in all the earth. Here, on the slopes of Tabor, Deborah and Barak gathered their forces, and down these precipitous sides they dashed to the discomfiture of Sisera and his army.[1] Here, after many centuries, the crusaders fought and Saladin captured the hill itself. In the shadow of the mountain Napoleon drew up his invading French against the Turks. In full view across the plain are Gilboa and the battlefield where Gideon defeated the Midianites [2] and where Saul and Jonathan died

[1] Judges 4:4-16.            [2] Judges 7:1, 19-23.

together.[1] To the southeast is Beisan, which for centuries guarded the pass from Esdraelon to Gilead, and where the excavators find ruins of every civilization from the cavemen to the crusaders. To the west is the brook Kishon, where Elijah slew the priests of Baal.[2]

I recall one full moonlight night we spent on Tabor. Across the plain one could see the dark shadow of Gilboa's mount fifteen miles away, while in the foreground, three miles across the valley on the slopes of Little Hermon, the Arab village of Endor showed its lights, where long ago had lived the famous witch. It was as easy as it was fascinating to reconstruct the scene: Saul in disguise leaving his army on Gilboa, perhaps on such a night as this, to slink in fear round the Philistines in the plain, reach Endor and consult the witch, only to return more frightened than he was before, to die the next day by his own sword.[3]

Above all other charms, however, of such a night on Tabor, was the view northwest toward Nazareth. Only five and a half miles away it nestled among the hills. Surely Jesus, who lived there all his youth and who loved the out-of-doors, must have climbed Tabor. Surely he, too, must have looked on this far-flung vista of the land he loved.

Many visitors leave Palestine disappointed, but I am sure the fault is not in Palestine. The traveler has not known how to make the trip or has been inwardly unfitted to make it or has been unable to take time.

[1] I Samuel 31:1-6.    [3] I Samuel 28:4-25 and 31:4.
[2] I Kings 18:40.

Surely he never lighted his camp-fire on the shores of the Dead Sea while the sun went down in glory behind towering Olivet. He never has spent a moonlight night on Tabor, or walked with memories of the Master over the hills of Nazareth, or at sunset heard a Bedouin shepherd piping to his flock above the Sea of Galilee.

# CHAPTER II

# THE BACKGROUND OF HISTORY

## I

IN no country that I ever visited do the old and the new so strangely jostle as in Palestine. We lunched one day by the roadside at Dothan, near the spot where, in the old story, Joseph's brethren drew him from the pit and sold him to the merchantmen. The camel-trail still runs close at hand, coming up the valley from beyond Jordan and crossing the central ridge to Jaffa. As we sat there meditating on that older day when Ishmaelites came from Gilead with camels, "bearing spicery and balm and myrrh, going to carry it down to Egypt," [1] the mayor of Bethlehem tore past in a high-powered motor car. He is a Christian Arab who had lived twenty-five years in America and amassed a fortune.

These strange juxtapositions of antiquity and modernity continually startle the visitor. The Zionists are raising wheat on the mound of Gezer, where thousands of years before Christ cavemen dwelt and first-born children were sacrificed to propitiate the gods. The up-to-date express train from Cairo to Jerusalem

[1] Genesis 37:25.

25

allows the incoming traveler his first glimpse of the valley of Ajalon where, in the ancient poem, the sun and moon stood still.[1]   One day on the Dead Sea we steered our boats toward the Arnon to row as far as possible and then swim farther up the historic river. Its beetling crags of red rock, like veined mahogany, make still a splendid gorge, once the boundary between Amorites and Moabites.[2]   As we entered the fresh river from the salt sea, our minds full of memories of Joshua and his conquests on the heights above, we heard the whir of motors and saw in the sky the Cairo-Bagdad airmail, three planes, headed east.

As between these two aspects of the Holy Land, its unique allurement lies, of course, in its antiquity. Palestine is the home of history.   One may intelligently see Geneva without knowing what Julius Cæsar did there to the Helvetians; one may even profitably visit Venice without knowing Henry Dandolo from Sargon; but how, with either profit or pleasure, one can visit Palestine without understanding the background of its long, amazing story, I do not see.

Acre, for example, ten miles north of Haifa on the seacoast, is a poor, shriveled town today with few visible reminders of its ancient glory, but what ghosts walk its narrow streets and sail its choked-up harbor! To these walls the Hebrew tribesmen came and here they stopped twelve centuries or more before our Lord —"Asher drove not out the inhabitants of Acco."[3]

---

[1] Joshua 10:12-13.                [3] Judges 1:31.
[2] Numbers 21:13.

Here walks the shade of Sennacherib, who seized the city before he marched on Jerusalem in Isaiah's day, and here came Alexander the Great conquering the world. From the heights a few miles to the north Jesus must have looked upon the town—called Ptolemais in Roman times—and perhaps he came here when he repaired to the coasts of Tyre and Sidon.[1] Paul walked these streets, tarrying here a day with his fellow Christians,[2] and before the second century was gone a Christian bishop had here his seat. Then came the Moslems, in 638 A.D., within six years of Mohammed's death; and when, centuries afterward, the crusaders drove them out, Acre was for long their capital, the center of bloody sieges and hairbreadth escapes. Here Richard the Lion-Hearted is said to have slain five thousand Moslem captives whose ransom was not quickly paid; here Saint Francis of Assisi prayed; here Napoleon Bonaparte turned back baffled from the walls. Was there ever such a summary of history as Palestine affords? He who sees the land without eyes to see the long, astounding play that has been staged upon it has not really seen the land at all.

## II

The story of Palestine as the modern scholar knows it goes a long way back into geologic time. Once, they say, the Jordan gorge was not a gorge at all but an inland sea that stretched from Mount Hermon southward. It may have joined the Great Sea across

---

[1] Matthew 15:21.                    [2] Acts 21:7.

Esdraelon in the north and across the lowlands in the south, so that the Judean ridge was once an island. At any rate, the Dead Sea now is a poor relic, the shrunken left-over of a greater day.

Even in the records of human life the story of the Holy Land has a far-off beginning.  If one would know how far, let him leave the Sea of Galilee a short distance from the small mud village of Mejdel, from which Mary Magdalene came, and walk in toward the hills. He will pass in springtime the black tents of the Bedouin and their pasturing herds of sheep and camels and come at last to the Wady el Hamam, the "valley of pigeons."  It is a wild, uncanny place, its narrowing ravine closed in by precipitous walls of rock that rise over a thousand feet.  Caverns on every side pockmark the cliffs, some of them intricate labyrinths not yet explored.  The inhabitants of the valley now are pigeons, but cavemen once lived here, and later, when Herod the Great was king, bandits held back an army here until soldiers from the heights were let down in cages to the caverns' mouths.

Most interesting of all these dens is one far up the valley where they found the "Galilee skull."  One can see yet the cross-section of strata through which the excavators dug, finding in one level below another the remains of Arab, Byzantine, Roman, Hellenistic, Jewish, and then prehistoric life; and far down—so far that it may represent a time twenty thousand years B.C.—they found the skull.  The visitor may see it in Jerusalem in the Palestinian Museum and judge for himself if it is not, as the experts say, the relic of a primitive man who, many thousands of years before Christ, lived beside Galilee.

One's imagination vividly is stirred as he lingers in the cavern where that ancient human being lived and died.  Who at that far-off time could have dreamed that humanity would climb from the Galilee man to the Man of Galilee?  Yet among these hills, perhaps in this valley, the Master retired to pray and knelt, it may be, in the cavern where this caveman had lived twenty millenniums before.  Paul's contrast between Adam and Christ, by many considered obsolete, is here presented in a modern form: "The first man, Adam, became an animate being, the last Adam a life-giving Spirit." [1]   I walked back to the Sea of Galilee, after a rememberable hour, reassured that a world in which such an ascent had occurred as these hills had witnessed, from primitive man to the Master, cannot be without spiritual significance at its very center.

### III

Palestine must have been a paradise for the cavemen.  Even one who has not been there but has read his Bible might guess that.  When Midianites swept down from the desert or Philistines proved too menacing, it was "in caves and holes and rocks and tombs and pits" [2] that the people hid.  These caverns and dens still are everywhere—once the homes of the cavemen, later

[1] I Corinthians 15:45 M.          [2] I Samuel 13:6 M.

the cells of the anchorites, and now the joy of the
archeologists. In the Old Testament retreat to them
is the symbol of distress and tragedy—"Men shall go
into the caves of the rocks, and into the holes of the
earth";[1] and in the New Testament they complete the
picture of the martyr's sacrifice—"wandering in deserts
and mountains and caves, and the holes of the earth."[2]
How many events in Scripture are associated with caves
one ordinarily does not notice until one sees the land.
Then one understands why Lot, after fleeing from
Sodom, lodged in a cave;[3] why the five kings at Mak-
kedah were captured in a cave;[4] why David's life is all
bound up with caves at Adullam and Maon and
En-gedi; why Obadiah hid the prophets in a cave;[5]
why the Gerasene demoniac abode in sepulchral caves
by Galilee;[6] and why to this day so many holy places
in the land, from the scene of the annunciation at
Nazareth and the grotto of the nativity at Bethlehem
to the shrines of the medieval saints, are caves.

The history of human life in Palestine begins in these
caverns. Even to an amateur they are intriguing places.
I shall not forget the day at Beit Jibrin—center of one
of the most amazing cave-cities in the world—when I
chose at random a hole upon a rough hillside, disappeared into the labyrinth below, wandered alone
through cavern after cavern, each bearing signs of
ancient habitation, and reemerged at last far down the
ridge through another opening. From away back in the

[1] Isaiah 2:19.
[2] Hebrews 11:38.
[3] Genesis 19:30.
[4] Joshua 10:17.
[5] I Kings 18:4, 13.
[6] Mark 5:3.

paleolithic age, before 10,000 B.C., flint instruments tell the tale of human beings in such subterranean dwellings, and as late as 3000 B.C. they left their remains unmistakably at Gezer.

Indeed, their vague record still is in our Bible. Behind the early races, whose antecedents and relationships the Hebrews thought they knew, are haunting memories of dim old peoples—Emim, Zanzummim, Zuzim, Rephaim, Nephilim, and Horites. They are prehistoric folk, sometimes giants, sometimes associated with an old mythology,[1] and occasionally used to explain some contemporary prodigy of size, like Og, king of Bashan,[2] or some strange survival of primitive ways. Perhaps not all of them were cavemen, but some were; scholars think that "cave-dweller" is what Horite means.

So far back does the story of Palestine go in the Book, and the land confirms it. What is written on the page is written also in the excavations of a mound like Gezer. First come those dim archaic peoples, of what race we know not, and then begin the great invasions— Amorite, Canaanite, Egyptian, Hebrew, Philistine, Assyrian, Babylonian, Greek, Roman, Moslem, Persian, Crusader, and British—which, with their swift and terrible recurrence, outline the tragic history of Palestine.

## IV

There are two ways of thinking about the Holy Land

[1] Genesis 6:1-4.          [2] Deuteronomy 3:11.

which help one to understand its history: it is an oasis and a bridge. With desert to the south of it, desert to the east of it, crowded by desert against sea save at its narrow northern neck, it has been, through all its known existence, the center of hungry eyes. The population of Arabia, from the early Bedouin to the Moslems, recurrently has overflowed into this inviting spot. "They would come up," says the old Hebrew record, "with their cattle, tents and all, swarming like locusts; they and their camels were past numbering, and their coming was the ruin of the country." [1] Of such an immigration from the desert the Hebrew conquest was one example, and so inevitable was this attraction of the Palestinian oasis for the desert-dwellers that from the beginning it was foredoomed to numberless invasions.

Moreover, Palestine is a bridge. The two great civilizations of the earliest days grew up around the Nile and the Euphrates, and the only roadway between the two lies over Palestine. During the long centuries, therefore, when Egypt and Assyria were at war, every invading army tramped across this little land. When Thutmose III of Egypt, in the fifteenth century B.C., wanted to strike his northern foes, he came up seventeen times through Palestine; and when Allenby, during the Great War, wished to crush the Turks, he followed the same route. With every other passage from Nineveh or Babylon to the Nile blocked by the Arabian Desert except this narrow bridge, Palestine was again foredoomed to be the world's most cruelly invaded land.

[1] Judges 6:5 M.

So far as we know, the Amorites came first—perhaps as long ago as twenty-five hundred years before Christ—and their remains are mostly underground, where archeologists must dig for them. Then came the Canaanites, the overflow, it may be, of the great Hittite empire to the north, and many a wall that they built may still be seen under old Jewish superstructures or standing in ruins, as at Jericho. Then Egypt, whose first known invasion had occurred eleven centuries before, decisively struck north under the great Thutmose, and the relics of long Egyptian domination are being continually exhumed. Then the Philistines came, a seafaring folk from Asia Minor or the islands of the Mediterranean, who ravaged the coasts of Egypt, and driven north, settled in the great plain between the Judean ridge and the sea.

Before the Philistines fairly were victorious, however, from the sea side, the Hebrews already had swept in from the desert side and in a series of swift and ruthless raids had seized the uplands of Ephraim. And after the Hebrews had crushed the old Canaanites, conquered the new Philistines, and organized their nation around its capital at Jerusalem, with shock after shock across the centuries the storm of invasion and conquest still beat repeatedly upon the people and the land.

Think, for example, what the inhabitants of Jerusalem have seen since David, about a thousand years B.C., made here the Hebrew capital. I have before me a list of thirty-eight sieges which the city has endured; and, interesting as it may be to read of them in print, it is far more vivid to walk the walls and picture on the spot the invading foes who, one after another, cast up their mounds and brought up their battering-rams against its gates.   The dwellers in this town have seen Assyrian invasions which wrecked everything in Judah up to the walls of Jerusalem and stopped.   They have seen Egyptian armies come to humiliate King Rehoboam and steal his treasures [1] or sweep north against Babylon, leaving good King Josiah killed on the way.[2] They have felt the terrific scourge of the Babylonians themselves, who seized the city twice,[3] sacked it utterly, and left it burned and empty, "a haunt of jackals."

Returning from exile, after long years, they saw the Syrian Greeks come up against them, sacrilegiously to desecrate their temple and forbid their sacrifices; and afterward they saw the Romans come, impatient at rebellious restlessness, who twice sacked the city and, where the temple had stood, built at last a shrine to Jupiter.

From these heights about Jerusalem the inhabitants have seen the gorgeous processions of the Eastern Christian churches move up to the holy places; they have watched Chosroes, the Persian, on his furious orgy of fire and slaughter; they have seen the Moslem conquest roll in its rising tide.   Before their eyes the crusaders came and went, the Turks swept in for four centuries of blasting rule, and far down across the coastal plain they saw the banners of Bonaparte sweep up and back again.   Last of all, they just have built

[1] I Kings 14:25-26.
[2] II Kings 23:29.
[3] Jeremiah 24:1 and 39:1-10.

a monument to celebrate the latest invaders, the British under Allenby.

Of course, a land whose history has been so laid down in successive strata of invasions bears everywhere the marks of its experience. To the traveler, newly come, every hilltop seems crowned with ruins, every valley a possible paradise for excavators. My friend, Professor Badé, while we were there, tackled one hilltop just north of Jerusalem and in a few weeks had uncovered part of an ancient Jewish city, probably the true Mizpah, built on Canaanitish foundations. There one could see the base of the old citadel with walls sixteen feet thick, with oil- and water-vats and storage chambers ready for a siege. There even was a great cistern, empty and sealed as though deliberately abandoned because ceremonially unclean, into which, it may be, in Jeremiah's day the treacherous Ishmael threw the bodies of Gedaliah and his friends.[1]

If ever there was a country with "sermons in stones" it is Palestine, so that the traveler who comes with no interest in history, no zest for memorials of a long-buried past, might better have stayed at home. As for folk like the recent traveler who said, "Why didn't somebody tell me that Palestine is talked of in the Bible? I would have bought one," what a pity that they cannot be sent to Monte Carlo or Atlantic City and forbidden to leave.

Daily, as one travels in the Holy Land, one runs on towns where memories of millenniums cluster. Kiriath-

[1] Jeremiah 41:1-9 M.

jearim, nine miles from Jerusalem, is a sample. Here
the Ark rested for twenty years [1] before David took
it up to his new shrine on Zion. Here are the remains
of a Byzantine church destroyed by Chosroes II, the
Persian, in the seventh century. Here is a beautiful
crusader church of the twelfth century and in its walls
an old stone from the days of Roman occupation. The
crusaders found it there and used it in building, and
one still can read the inscription, "Section of the Tenth
Legion, the Thunderer."

Palestine is thus a unique, sometimes a bewildering
salmagundi of historical allusions. You go to Gadara,
southeast of the Sea of Galilee, to follow the tour of
the Master through the Decapolis, and you recall that
Vespasian was camping there when he heard the news
of Nero's death and was hailed Roman Emperor by
his soldiers. You scout the country around ancient
Gaza to see what reminders you can find of the Philistines, and you land in Khan Yunis, where the Arabs
almost captured Napoleon Bonaparte, alone with his
personal staff, and just missed turning the course of
history into new channels.

## V

If I were to choose only two scenes out of scores
which so light up the history of Palestine, I should
select Samaria and Masada. The first lies less than
fifty miles north of Jerusalem, and the two hours' ride

[1] I Samuel 7:2.

by motor up the north road is an illustration of the compact historical wealth of Palestine. Some three miles out from the city's gate we pass Tell el-Ful, a bare hill now, but once Gibeah, the home and royal residence of King Saul.[1]   A few moments beyond we see the remnants of two ancient Roman roads, one leading north to Damascus, the other to the seacoast at Cæsarea.   A little over a mile farther we pass er-Ram, an Arab village, the old Ramah, where Samuel judged Israel.   Five miles beyond that we pass through the ancient Beeroth, now Bireh, one of the earliest towns that Joshua entered.   Leaving it, we see on the right Bethel, where Jacob prayed, the Ark once rested, Samuel held court, Elisha taught, Jeroboam set up his golden calf, and Amos prophesied.   Less than four miles beyond we run through Jifna, the ancient Gophnah, an important town in Roman days, seized by Vespasian in 69 A.D.  A mile and a half farther takes us to 'Ain Sinia, much knocked about by shell fire in the last war, when the front lines were here.

Seven and a half miles more and we can see Shiloh, with its memories of Eli, Samuel, and the holy Ark.  A half mile farther finds us passing Sinjil, named of old from Raymond de Saint-Gilles, Count of Toulouse, a crusader.  After sixteen miles we pass Jacob's well at Sychar, where Jesus rested, and, running between Mount Gerizim, where the Samaritans still worship, and Mount Ebal, where Joshua built an altar, we pass the ancient Shechem, famous in tradition and history

---

[1] I Samuel 10:26 and 15:34, etc.

from Abraham to the crusaders under Tancred. Six miles beyond we turn off to climb the great hill of Samaria itself, the capital city of the northern kingdom of Israel. Where else in the world does one sweep through such a panorama of history in forty-odd miles?

A long day spent at Samaria is well worth while, for this is one of the most thoroughly excavated sites in Palestine and from its foundation until now its history has been traced in its ruins. The ancient city stood on a noble hilltop with such breadth of view and such safety in its elevation and precipitous flanks that one understands Amos' picture of its proud inhabitants "secure in the mountain of Samaria." [1] Omri, king of Israel, about 875 B.C. bought this hill and built here his capital,[2] and the excavators uncovered his palace next the native rock and walked through his halls. After him Ahab and Jezebel, of infamous memory but of worldly pomp, built here their idolatrous temple to Baal [3] and their "ivory house." [4] The excavators found the latter above Omri's palace, faced with white marble, which explains its name. The palace of Jeroboam II was unearthed on the next higher level. Then came records of the Assyrian deluge, when in a three years' siege the armies from the Euphrates wrought the final ruin of the northern kingdom and sacked the city.

The Assyrian town, built in its place, the excavators found. Remains of a Greek city were over that—the

[1] Amos 6:1.
[2] I Kings 16:23-24.
[3] I Kings 16:32
[4] I Kings 22:39.

town which John Hyrcanus, the Jewish Maccabee, destroyed late in the second century B.C.   Then came the city which Herod the Great built and which Jesus looked upon, impressive ruins of which—notably the great basilica—are still above ground for all to walk among.   Here Philip preached the Christian Gospel while it was still in its earliest infancy;[1] here the crusaders had a bishopric; and here today is a little mudbrick Arab village, squalid, malodorous, and full of dogs, like a mean and tattered flag on a great masthead where once flew some of the noblest banners of the earth.

We walked for a long time over and around the ancient city gates, which still present a striking spectacle as they tower high above the sudden drop of the mountain to the green, flat plain below.   At these gates the four lepers lay that time Ben-hadad, the Syrian, besieged the town so closely that famine stalked its streets and women ate their children.[2]   From here they crept down into the camp of the enemy below, found it empty, and came back again to herald the good news that Ben-hadad's army had fled.   That famous story [3] has still its perfect setting on its ancient stage.

One cannot from this splendid height look over the landscape of the northern kingdom, so much more gracious and fertile than Judea's stubborn, stony ridge, without wondering why Samaria should have left so

---

[1] Acts 8:5.
[2] II Kings 6:28-29.
[3] II Kings 6:24-33 and 7:1-15.

little mark on history and Jerusalem so rich an influence. For Samaria in the day of its power was immeasurably stronger, wealthier, and more promising than its southern neighbor. Here was the obvious hope of the Hebrew people, not on that dry and barren hill of Zion. Yet Jerusalem has risen and still stands, potent in history and promising further influence to come, while Philistia, Samaria, and Trans-Jordania long since have faded without fruit. The geographical reason for this supremacy of Jerusalem in Palestine is clear: compared with any other city in the land it is hard to approach, difficult to besiege on its rocky, waterless ridge. The seacoast plain of Sharon is beautifully fruitful, symbolic in the Scripture of affluence and plenty, but it always has been open to world conquerors and their trampling hosts. Samaria and Esdraelon are much more fertile than Judea, but all through history they have been too accessible, too alluring to invasion and conquest. Trans-Jordania is prosperous and plentiful compared with the dour land about Jerusalem, and we can sympathize with the wish of Gad and Reuben to stay there rather than cross into Palestine itself,[1] but it has always been open to the pressure of attacking Bedouin when, as the prelude to Job says, "the Arabs made a foray."[2] Judea alone, austere, grim, forbidding, has stood aloof; has sustained her thirty-eight sieges, to be sure, but with preponderant advantage on the side of the besieged; has been given time to develop her tradition and make

[1] Numbers Ch. 32.      [2] Job 1:15 M.

her contribution—so that while Samaria has fallen from ruin into ruin, Jerusalem is the city of three faiths and the race's holiest shrine.

## VI

If Samaria vividly portrays the destruction of the northern kingdom, I should choose Masada to typify the disasters of Judah. It is, I think, one of the most tragic spots in the world, and it is seldom visited. We got at it by way of the Dead Sea, although it can be reached by land across the wilderness. A day's trip by boat from the north shore of the sea brought us at evening to our anchorage on the west coast with the portentous massif of Masada confronting us. It is a huge rock rising 1500 feet sheer out of the Dead Sea plain. Torn loose in some ancient cataclysm from its neighboring range, it stands now disengaged, a solitary precipitous block. It is ideally formed by nature for the purposes man once made it serve—a last, desperate refuge in the midst of the wilderness, to be defended when all other hopes had failed. The Maccabees fortified it in the brave days when the Jews were striking for liberty against the Greeks, and Herod the Great refortified and provisioned it as a possible resource in an emergency.

We slept that night by the shore of the sea and at five o'clock, as the sun came up over the plateau of Moab, we started for the ascent. An hour and a half of hard walking took us to the mountain's base. No

words can picture, no painting represent that desert
of salt marl through which we passed.  On the north
shore of the Dead Sea, near the Jordan's mouth, one
sees fantastic carving of the saline clay into all manner of bastions and battlements, but here, below
Masada, they are huge, weird, incredible.  The marl
has weathered into forts and temples, towers and terraces, gigantic and eerie, so that, as we passed among
them, surrounded by utter silence and sterility, we
could easily imagine ourselves in some old, dead world
whose architecture had outlasted its inhabitants.

Josephus writes that there was only one open path
up Masada, on the eastern flank, called The Serpent,
very steep and difficult.  "To slip is certain destruction," he says, "for on each side yawn precipices deep
enough to quell all courage by terror."  We saw traces
of that path still but, although a certain Captain War-
ren went up it with great risk a generation ago, it
looks quite inaccessible now.  Even when we felt our
way along the range and clambered up an abrupt wady
to the ridge's top and then across the old ramp which
the Romans built when they took the fortress nineteen
hundred years ago, the climb was fatiguing enough.

The top of Masada's rock, as Conder measured it, is
a plateau 350 yards one way by 690 yards another. The
walls, built by the Maccabees and Herod the Great,
still are in tumbled ruins along its edge, and the palace,
citadel, and fortress, which Josephus describes as frown-
ing there, one still can clamber over.  Save for a few
Christian ruins of which no history exists, it is as

though no one had been there since the day the Romans
left.    Even the round rocks hurled by their catapults
against the walls are lying on the ground.

The view is one of magnificent desolation, extraordinarily impressive.    Josephus exaggerates when he says
that down the precipices upon every side the ravines
were "of such vast depth that the eye could not reach
their bottoms," but I know how he felt when he wrote
it.    Far below to the eastward was the Dead Sea across
the wilderness of torn and tortured marl.    Beyond the
sea the ruins of Kerak shone upon their lofty perch,
rich in historic memories, from the ancient Moabites
to the crusaders.    To the south we could see the southern plain where Zoar lay and Sodom and Gomorrah
may have been, and to the north we lost the hills of
Moab in the rising vapor of the sea.    On the land
side, as far as the eye could reach, everything was waste
and barren—a hot, arid, lifeless desolation inhabited
by nothing save silence and solitude.    And there,
eleven miles from the nearest spring of any consequence, twenty miles from the nearest provisions, was
enacted an extraordinary human drama.

Titus had taken Jerusalem in 70 A.D.    The Jews were
hopelessly beaten.    Outlying cities, like Machærus,
where Herod had beheaded John the Baptist and
where now the Jewish Zealots made a desperate stand,
had also fallen.    Only Masada was left, and here
Eleazar and a band of irreconcilables entrenched themselves.    The Roman general, Flavius Silva, went to
besiege them.    He built a wall of rock in the Dead

Sea plain around the whole massif of Masada and shut it in. He planted eight camps of Roman legionaries in the plain to watch the wall. With incredible labor he filled in a ramp that connected the western ranges with the fortress—it still is there, a monument to the exhaustless determination and energy of Rome. Upon that ramp he brought his battering-rams, and when the outer wall was breached and the desperate besieged built still a new and inner wall of wood and earth, he set fire to that and killed the last hope of the beleaguered. Then Eleazar called his men together and when he was through speaking they went out to do a bloody deed. First they slew their wives and children; then by lot they selected ten men, who slew the garrison; then by lot the ten selected one, who slew the remaining nine, and when he had searched carefully lest any should remain alive and had set on fire the palace, he drove his sword through his own body. Nine hundred and sixty fell in that compact of suicide, and when the next day the Romans entered the fortress, two women and five children, who had hid themselves, were the only survivors in Masada.

Today, on that desolate height where in the centuries since only a few have come to disturb the scene, one feels as though the ancient tragedy had been enacted yesterday. The great wall which Silva built in the plain to shut Masada in still is there. The Roman camps are outlined yet in stone, plainly visible from the height—the walls and gates and the locations of the separate tents as distinct as though they had just been occupied.  If any Roman soldier could come back after these nineteen centuries he could go at once to the place where his tent stood and enter into the circle of stone which his hands piled.  The headquarters camp, largest of all, where Silva pitched his standard, still is where Josephus described it, and the great ramp, unbelievable unless one has seen it, still bridges the chasm to the fortress gates.

As we were negotiating our difficult descent down the sheer declivities on our return, I quoted from Vergil, "Perchance even these things it will be pleasant sometime to remember," to which my friend, looking into the broiling pit of the Dead Sea plain, retorted that he wished Vergil had been equally true in saying, "The descent to hell is easy."

It was indeed an infernal abyss to which we laboriously returned, a burning, fiery furnace of pitiless heat. If it seemed so to us, casual and comfortable travelers, what must it have been to those Roman legionaries who camped here and brought their engines of war against this impregnable rock, and to the Jews also, who in this terrific wilderness made their desperate stand for freedom and, failing it, embraced death like a bride!

## VII

Intensely interesting as are such individual sites, memorials of history's most dramatic moments, there is one place in Palestine more important still for the historian.  So far as I can discover, it is unique—the ancient Beisan—the only place in the world where men, leaving behind them the records of their successive civilizations, have lived continuously from the stone age to the present time.  Originally a bare hill of rock strategically placed just where the great plain of Esdraelon joins the Jordan valley, it was the natural guardian of the main highway across the bridge of Palestine.  Seventy feet of débris were lying over it when the archeologists began their work.  Beneath more modern accumulations they ran upon the ruins of the crusaders, an unfinished castle begun under Adam, Lord of Béthune in France, who called himself Lord of Bessan, too.  Beneath the crusaders' masonry lay the fallen fort, mosque, and dwellings of the Arabs who swept into the land the year Mohammed died, 632 A.D.  Beneath these Arab ruins the excavators found the city which Jesus knew as Scythopolis.  It bore that name for nearly a thousand years from the third century B.C.  Here they found part of the floor and some of the columns of one of the fairest churches of its time, built in 400 A.D., and, beneath that, some mosaics and bronzes from an earlier church, reared a century before and ruined in the persecution of the Christians under Julian the Apostate.

Beneath that they stood where Jesus may well have walked, for Scythopolis was less than twenty miles from Nazareth and in his day was a splendid town, exceeding Jerusalem in population.  There they unearthed the ruins of a Greco-Roman temple sacred to Bacchus, with huge Corinthian pillars six feet

through, and then burrowed down through Roman and
Greek remains into plain and unexpected relics of the
Scythians.   These wild folk swept in on Palestine
about 627 B.C.   Herodotus tells us of them and
Jeremiah and Zephaniah were stirred to prophecy by
their arrival.   Here they left their remains for a far-
off race of archeologists to ponder over.   Below them
lay the most important finds of all, the remains of
Egyptian domination.   One still can see the super-
imposed ruins of Egyptian altars marked "Ramses II"
and "Seti I," and the great Egyptian fortress, whose
charred walls yet were standing six feet high when
the excavators found them, goes back a century before
the Hebrews came.

Within sight of these very walls ten miles away
Gideon defeated the Midianites; [1] upon these walls
the bodies of Saul and Jonathan were hung by their
Philistine enemies; [2] from these walls the men of
Jabesh-Gilead in a midnight raid took down the bodies
for honorable burial; [3] and these walls, called in the
old days Beth-shean, were burned—probably by David
—as the charred bricks and melted metals of the ruins
unmistakably revealed.   What more will be disclosed
as the hill is leveled, who can tell?   But trial shafts
down to the rock already have brought up flint instruments that carry the story far back to the cavemen.

We came to this amazing place from Megiddo, where
Dr. Fisher, who superintended the excavations at

[1] Judges Ch. 7.                    [3] Ibid.
[2] I Samuel 31:8-13.

Beisan, was at work upon an even more exciting task. Without his interpretative explanations we should have understood but little of what our eyes saw. With it, Beisan became a marvelous summary of Palestine's history and a perfect illustration of Jeremiah's word, "The city shall be builded upon its own mound." [1] As one sees it now, all that "pomp of yesterday" is ruin and débris. The civilizations that are represented here one by one have passed off the stage and fallen largely on forgetfulness. Here a Corinthian column, prone in the dust, speaks of Greece, or frayed and broken altar steps recall a shrine of Egypt, or a fragment of stone roadway suggests the chariots of Rome, but that is all. Here, where empires triumphed, nothing more is left.

[1] Jeremiah 30:18.

CHAPTER III

# THE IMPRESSIVENESS OF SINAI

## I

To follow the trail of Moses and the fleeing Israelites from Egypt into the peninsula of Sinai, and at the sacred mountain to see the setting in which the Hebrew-Christian religion had its rise, had long been an ambition and a hope. No imagination of the experience, however, was half so impressive as the experience itself. Starting one evening from Suez by steamer, we landed next morning at Tor on the Gulf of Suez, the chief quarantine station for Moslems on the Mecca pilgrimage. Thence by camels we journeyed three days to the Monastery of Saint Catherine on the flank of the traditional Mount Sinai and, after three days more as guests of the Greek priests there, rode our camels for eight days to Suez, traveling in reverse, as well as we could figure it, the route by which Moses had led the Hebrews into Sinai from Egypt. Those two weeks in the wilderness remain an invaluable, ineffaceable memory.

The initial surprise came on shipboard the first morning, when we rose for an early glimpse of the peninsula of Sinai at dawn. The Sinaitic wilderness seen from the sea is not a sandy, level desert, but is chiefly distinguished by a huge, ragged mass of towering mountains filling the whole horizon to the east. This range of wildly tumbled gneiss and granite rises in its highest peak, Jebel Catherine, over 8600 feet above the sea, and repeatedly soars over 7000 feet in heights like Umm Shomer and Jebel Musa. The mountains are the more impressive because they rise so suddenly out of the flat plain—a gravel-strewn waste, blazing hot—which separates them from the sea. This plain of Kaa is over fifteen miles in width, but in the morning light the mountains look so near that one would think them some five miles away. This was our first lesson about Sinai: Moses and his fugitives, when they fled from Egypt, took to the mountains, and their new faith had its rise, as so many religious inspirations have, amid great altitudes and wide horizons.

Let the reader, if he would share our experience of Sinai's impressiveness, join in imagination our little caravan as it paced out from the compound of the Greek priests at Tor and started off across the hot plain toward the ranges. We were five travelers, with thirty-five camels and thirty-four Arabs to carry tents, provisions, water—everything to make two weeks in the wilderness a possibility to Westerners. Some day I fear folk no longer will go into Sinai by caravan. One enterprising American already has driven his automobile in from Tor and the Greek priests at the monastery on Sinai ruefully reported eleven cars as

having come from Suez in a year. They had made in
nine hours the trip which cost Moses and his fugitives
three months. In the end one foresees well-surfaced
roads up the ancient wadies and tourist parties spin-
ning gayly to and from the sacred mountain. We,
however, thankful that we had not been born too late,
went in by camel, and traveling by camel has not
changed at all in countless centuries.

Swift dromedaries are not to be had in Sinai—only
the slow-pacing pack animal making his two and a
half to three miles an hour. The lazy tread of the
patient beasts is strange at first; then worse than
strange—a torturing experience which twists every
muscle askew; but at last, when one has accommodated
his sea-legs to this ship of the desert, it becomes a
congenial, swinging gait, the recollection of which
makes one eager to try again. Nevertheless, one does
not blame the Arabs for saying that when God had
all the other animals complete he made camels from
the scraps.

The first day took us across the hot coastal plain;
on the second we went abruptly from the sand and
gravel waste into Wady Hebran and began our climb
toward Sinai. If possible, the wadies in April are more
stifling than the seacoast—desolate, waterless, shadow-
less, with no relief from the sun's full blaze. All that
second morning our dragoman consoled us with news
of a famous rock in whose cool shelter we should eat
our lunch. Already the peninsula of Sinai was throwing light upon the Book—"the shade of a great rock in

a weary land." [1]    I vividly recall our disappointment
when, reaching it, we found the grateful cool of the
huge bowlder preoccupied by Bedouin tribesmen
traveling the other way.

Late that evening we mounted the first pass and
looked down into the enclosed and altogether lovely
plain of Wady Selaf, where our tents were being
pitched. It seemed green and beautiful. It allured
the eye and was full of comfortable promise. I could
have written poetry about it. But the truth is that
all it had to offer was a flat floor of sand and gravel
between bare granite hills, a sprinkling of three-foot
broom bushes like the one under which Elijah rested
in this very wilderness and wished to die,[2] and, over
the rest of the ground, a thin coating of sparse and
faded weeds with saltwort to add a bit of greenery.
It was a poverty-stricken offering for a landscape to
make to Western eyes. Yet so barren and unrelieved
had been the desolation of the day's ride that it looked
verdant and beautiful. After all, beauty and com-
fort alike are relative. No sybarite with every modern
luxury at his command can know such exquisite felicity
as is provided by the genial softness of desert sand on
the shady side of a three-foot bush after eight hours
on a camel.

One who has known the experience will not forget
that deliciousness of evening in the desert when the
day's ride is done. The grunting camels kneel to surrender their heavy loads. The tents are pitched. The

[1] Isaiah 32:2.                    [2] I Kings 19:4.

odor of dinner drifts from the cook's domain and, as
the sun goes down, the evening's swift cool, exquisitely
refreshing, follows the blazing heat of the day.    Fifty
degrees of difference are sometimes known between
noon and midnight in the desert, so that Jacob was
speaking from experience when he said, "In the day
the drought consumed me, and the frost by night." [1]
When the camp is pitched and the camels are at their
slender grazing, the Arabs, belonging to the four
tribes of the Towara, separate into four groups, and
soon four camp fires are burning on the desert, surrounded by swarthy faces animated with eager conversation.    Then, as the darkness deepens, the moon
comes out and the traveler find himself in that most
beautiful, awe-inspiring, tranquilizing place the sons
of men can know—the desert on a moonlight night
under the stars.

## II

The first impression of the traditional Mount Sinai,
which we reached on the third day, is awesome.  We
came down over the Nakb Hawa, a pass so steep that
pack animals must be sent around another way, to
find ourselves in the mountain-girt plain of er-Raha,
five thousand feet above the sea.  A flat-floored desert
of packed sand and gravel, with a thin growth of
herbage, it stretches a mile and a half up to the base
of Sinai.  Scores of thousands easily could camp there.
All around are abrupt and jagged walls of reddish-

[1] Genesis 31:40.

brown granite rising as high as a thousand feet above the plain, and every lateral wady similarly is walled, so that every way one looks one is surrounded and enclosed by rocky bulwarks, with a peculiar sense of seclusion and protection. As the plain draws near Sinai it gradually slopes down like the floor of an amphitheater and then the twin bastions of Ras Sufsafeh, "mountain of the willow," rise abrupt, portentous, thrusting their huge mass of solid granite straight up from the plain. The solemnity and grandeur of this towering block of rock would be impressive under any circumstances; as a perfect setting for the story of Moses and the Law it is an awesome and fascinating sight.

Like most other travelers who have left records of their impressions we felt at once and each day felt the more that whether or not this is the true Sinai it furnishes the most perfect imaginable scene for the Biblical account. Perhaps Jebel Serbal, a few miles away, the one considerable rival, is the true site. There are arguments on both sides and no positive proof is likely to be found. If, however, one wishes to picture the great drama of the Law on a stage set with perfect adaptation to the scene, this immense massif of solid granite, rising sheer out of the vast, flat plain, is the place to do it. At Jebel Serbal there is no height, no valley, no plain that lends itself with any verisimilitude to the occasion.

I walked out one day alone to tramp over this desert floor where the children of Israel are supposed to have camped, and to explore the base of Sufsafeh, the massive rock from which, so tradition holds, the Law was proclaimed. The setting fits the Biblical story perfectly. Everything ever said about Sinai dovetails with easy precision into this unique, dramatic landscape.

In the delta land of Egypt, Moses and his fellow-Hebrews had lived in a flat country; Goshen, where they dwelt, is a low-lying, level floor. Then, forced to flee after his precipitate act of violence against an Egyptian taskmaster, Moses came, let us say, to this wild and isolated spot. It was a natural place for him to seek. These mountains of Sinai had been mining centers of the pharaohs for hundreds of years before Moses' day. The wadies of Maghara and Mukatteb, famous for their turquoise mines, which we passed on our return, a little to the north, are rich still in the inscriptions of these ancient miners. The earliest goes back to Pharaoh Semerkhet of the First Dynasty, thirty-three hundred years before Christ. Thirty-nine pharaohs have left their names and the records of their mining expeditions. "Behold me, how I tarried there after I had left Egypt," one foreman carved at Serabit; "my face sweated, my blood grew hot, I ordered the workmen working daily, and said unto them, There is still turquoise in the mine and the vein will be found in time. And it was so; the vein was found at last and the mine yielded well."

To this frontier land, this rough and desiccated wilderness to which the miners went out in January and from which they returned in May, Moses fled and, avoiding the mining settlements, attached himself to a Midianite family.

That he helped Jethro's daughters draw water from the well and so ingratiated himself into the family's good-will and won a wife thereby,[1] is to one who has been here as easily picturable as is a bus ride on Fifth Avenue to a New Yorker. There are excellent wells about Sinai still. Until the season when we came no rain had fallen for four years and yet the wells were plenteous and the little gardens irrigated by the Greek priests, oases of green in the dun brown of the wadies, were to be seen all round the mountain. There must be for this some deep-lying geologic reason not likely to suffer radical change in the passage of the centuries. It is easy, therefore, to imagine Moses pasturing here his father-in-law's sheep as the Bible says. Indeed, I saw a miniature Moses tending a large flock over the very plain where Moses may have led his sheep that day when he came to the "western side of the prairie," and had a life-transforming experience at "the sacred hill of Horeb."[2]   I was disappointed, however; this modern miniature asked for bakshish.

How full of dread impressiveness this mountain must have been to the escaped slave tribes from Egypt! It was extraordinarily impressive even to my eyes that a few weeks before had seen the Matterhorn, but to the Hebrews from the flat delta of Egypt it must have been a stunning sight. A friend of mine, visiting Sinai in winter, once saw a thunderstorm break on

[1] Exodus 2:16-22.          [2] Exodus 3:1 M.

these gigantic crags.  For two hours he stood in the plain, thrilled and fascinated.  Tremendous thunder crashed over the mountain.  Lightning volleyed about the crags.  The mists, forming thick on the sides, steamed up, blown by the gusty, rising air until the whole mountain seemed asmoke in conflagration.  Let the Bible itself describe the scene:  "The mountain of Sinai was all wrapped in smoke, as the Eternal descended in fire upon it; the smoke rose like steam from a kiln, till the people all trembled terribly." [1] Even minor details of the recorded scene easily fit the setting.  Sinai is indeed a mountain that can be "touched."  You can walk down the level plain and lay your hand upon its abruptly rising granite mass. "You must mark off the mountain all round and tell the people to be careful never to ascend it nor even to touch the edge of it," [2] is a command that can be literally obeyed.  Moreover, if Moses appeared in the cleft of Sufsafeh with the tables of the Law, all the tribesmen in the plain, no matter how numerous, could clearly have seen him.  It is a fascinating place in which to let one's imagination play—perhaps too fascinating.  Of course, it may be that Jebel Serbal is Mount Sinai after all.

### III

One hopes not, however, when once he has ascended the present Sinai and confirmed on the top the impressions of the plain.  One of the most rememberable

[1] Exodus 19:18 M.          [2] Exodus 19:12 M.

days of my life I spent on that upmost crest. It was
a glorious day, with clear sunshine, a few white clouds,
a cool wind from the sea, and on every side a view of
indescribable solemnity and grandeur. Sinai is one
enormous block of granite over two miles long and
nearly one and a half miles broad, rearing itself mas-
sively up nearly 3000 feet above the surrounding valleys. Slashed, as it is, with deeply cut gullies and
bastioned with peaks and towers of rock, it is in itself,
apart from any memorable associations, one of the
most sightly mountains I have ever seen. At the southern end of the huge mass, farthest away from the plain,
rises the topmost peak, Jebel Musa, the Mount of
Moses; at the northern end stand the battlements of
Sufsafeh towering straight up from the plain. Between
these two the summit of Sinai is a wildly broken,
scarred plateau 7000 feet above the sea, scooped
out in the center into a charming basin walled in by
weirdly weathered granite and watered by a deep well.

Here, as everywhere in lands of long and sacred
association, one must forget tawdry shrines and ridic-
ulous identifications of site, from the rock cleft where
God hid Moses so that he might not see the divine
face [1] to the cave from which Elijah came when he
heard the "still small voice." [2] It is the view that counts
and the memories that cluster here. The crest of Sinai
stands so clear and high that it commands a wide outlook, although the view from Mount Catherine across
the valley is wider still. On days with clear horizons

[1] Exodus 33:21-23.          [2] I Kings 19:11-13.

the Gulf of 'Akabah is visible over thirty miles away. The spectator is surrounded by a fantastic scene of mountain range beyond mountain range—an arid, scarified landscape indescribably grim and rough. The surrounding heights, like Sinai itself, are granite massifs barren of visible vegetation, multicolored with dark purples, reds, browns, scarlets, and greens as the lights change on their various blends of rock, and all of them so sawn into by ravines, cut asunder by yawning wadies, scarped and pinnacled in an endless variety of forms, that a more wild and picturesque bit of mountain scenery would be difficult to imagine. As another traveler has judged, it can be matched in grandeur, but in grandeur plus desolation it is unique.

Was it to this uplifted plateau that Moses retired to seek guidance for his liberated people? Was it on this shaggy scene of granite mountains that he looked as he wrought out the Law? Was it from this stern retreat that he came down to do one of history's impossible tasks—give a slave people freshly liberated a new religion, a new moral code, and a new national tradition, so that for over three thousand years since they have been one of the major forces in the world?

## IV

To the Western visitor the charm of Sinai is heightened by the Monastery of Saint Catherine. During the early Christian centuries anchorites by thousands gathered here and at Jebel Serbal to live in caves among the mountains, but terrible massacres were perpetrated on them by the Arabs until Emperor Justinian in 530 A.D. built a fort for their protection. The monastery grew up around that fort, and after all the intervening centuries distinct traces of Justinian's régime still remain in the monastery's servants. They are the direct descendants of those hundred Roman and hundred Egyptian slaves with their wives and children that Justinian gave to the monks. From the thousands of hermits that once were gathered here, the number has dwindled to a score of monks, but still they try to keep up the old traditions, sustaining the long and ponderous rituals of the church, and showing with pride and apparent faith the relics of the site. The very spot where the burning bush grew,[1] the very well where Moses aided Jethro's daughters,[2] the very rootage from which came Aaron's rod that budded,[3] the horrid skull and hand of Saint Catherine, decked with jewels and shrined in a casket, to say nothing of the sepulcher where the bones of monks dead for ages past are exposed to public view—such mementos of what Dr. Robinson called "mistaken piety," "credulous superstition" and "pious fraud," the solemn monks still show to the visitor.

Their library, however, is a genuine and authentic treasure. Here in this isolated spot manuscripts have been preserved that long ago in a more populous place would have been destroyed by fire or pillage. This

---

[1] Exodus 3:2.
[3] Numbers 17: 8.
[2] Exodus 2:15-17.

little room is one of the sacred shrines of the learned world and has been the goal of more than one pilgrimage of scholars. Here was found the second oldest Greek manuscript of the Bible which is known to exist, the Codex Sinaiticus, dating from about 400 A.D., and here today is the Codex Syrsin, a palimpsest, our most ancient Syriac rendering of the four Gospels, which translates an older Greek text than any that we now possess.

Altogether the monastery is an unforgetable place. It is a charming prospect as one first approaches its battlemented walls framed in cypress trees. It is a symposium of interesting traditions while one is there, from its ancient sites to the faked mosque and minaret that once saved the place from a Moslem raid. It is a picturesque memory as one recalls it nestling on the flank of Sinai 5000 feet above the sea.

## V

When the time came to go, however, we were eager for our camels and our Arabs and for the "wide awful desert" [1] of the Exodus. As I look back upon those final eight days in the wilderness, one impression is outstanding. Every day of the return trip to Suez we came more completely into the conviction that, in the Biblical story of the Exodus and in the old tradition that the fugitives came south to the group of mountains where Jebel Musa stands, we were dealing

[1] Deuteronomy 1:19 M.

with history. The verisimilitude is too convincing to be doubted.

The man who first told the story of the Exodus, as we have it in our Bible, was actually on this ground. This is the country the escaping Israelites passed through; these are the conditions they met and the difficulties they overcame. The correspondences are too intimate and constant to be caused by accident.

No one would dream that he exactly could retrace the march of Israel as the thirty-third chapter of Numbers gives it, but the plausibility of the attempt when one is on the ground is captivating. The greatest difficulty lies at the journey's beginning and its end. Pithom and Ramses were the store-cities on which as slaves the Israelites were toiling. Pithom was excavated in 1883. The memorials of Ramses II, supposed to be the pharaoh of the oppression, were plentifully found there, including colossal statues of him. Moreover, there were no indications that any city had been there until Ramses II founded it; the Hebrews were literally building the city. The Exodus, however, started not from Pithom but from the other treasure-town, which bore the pharaoh's name, and Professor Petrie thinks that he has identified the site of that eight miles west of Pithom in the Wady Tumilat. Where the camping stations were between Ramses and the crossing of the sea is quite unknown, but the best conjecture traces the Israelites up where the Gulf of Suez used to stretch its shallow waters northward toward the Bitter Lakes and, it may be, beyond. The land is dry where once a thin sea lay, and the strong east wind which blew all night [1] and left easy passage for the fugitives is not difficult to understand. Only a few years ago Major General Tulloch saw the shallow waters of Lake Menzala, a short distance north of the spot where the Hebrews are supposed to have crossed, driven back seven miles by a strong wind, leaving the lake bottom dry.

"There can be no dispute," wrote Dean Stanley in 1856, "as to the general track of the Israelites after the passage." Well, there can be, for there is, but the consensus of opinion among those who have made the trip is quite extraordinary. "They went three days in the wilderness, and found no water," [2] and we did also. That same unspeakable, blazing waste of arid sand and gravel stretches still from the wells of Moses, near Suez, three days' journey to the bitter waters of Marah,[3] where the Hebrews camped. Those waters, too, are there,—called Hawarah by the Arabs,—brackish springs in soil impregnated with natron, from which men will drink not at all and camels only grudgingly. From there the Hebrews went to Elim, with its twelve springs and seventy palm trees,[4] and it still is there —the Wady Gharandel, with a series of spring holes and how many palm trees I did not count—a whipped and beaten oasis in a dreadful desert but, for all that, a refreshing resting place. They encamped then, we are told, by the Red Sea.[5] We did too. The only natural route for them to follow down the Wady

[1] Exodus 14:21.
[2] Exodus 15:22.
[3] Exodus 15:23.
[4] Exodus 15:27.
[5] Numbers 33:10.

Taiyibeh would lead them there, and it was a fair camping ground on the sand, with the glorious blue waters of the gulf stretching to the red hills of Africa, on one side, and the foothills of the Sinaitic range, upon the other.

They next stopped in the desert of Sin.[1] We think we stopped there, too, for that narrow strip of desert from the mouth of Wady Taiyibeh south would be the natural route of the fugitives and the debouchure of Wady Maghara, where we camped, would be a fitting site for the end of one more day's march. Where Alush and Dophkah were—the next stations, named without identifying mark—no one pretends to know. But almost everyone picks up the trail once more in the Wady Feiran. That seems inevitable. The wilderness of Sinai is not a trackless waste on which one can go anywhere; its routes are marked by mountains, wadies, and well-bounded desert stretches, so that when once the direction of the Israelites is determined by that three days' wilderness without water, it is not incredible that they should be followed the remainder of the trip. And the Wady Feiran is their almost sure approach from the sea toward Sinai. At first it is a barren, blistering place—an ideal spot for Moses' conflict with the complaining, thirsty people [2]—and then it strikes suddenly into the loveliest oasis of the peninsula, "the Pearl of Sinai," with two miles of luxuriant palm trees and water in such plenty that it flows in noisy streams. Was it not the defense of their fertile

[1] Numbers 33:11.          [2] Exodus 17:1-7.

treasure from the invading Hebrews that brought the Amalekites to Rephidim to fight their celebrated battle? [1]   Most travelers say yes.   At any rate, the scene is perfect and the motive for the battle adequate.

Indeed, some ask why we should suppose that the Israelites went farther than the oasis, leaving the most luxuriant spot in the land for the stern setting of Jebel Musa.   Why not picture them as living here and let Jebel Serbal, near at hand, be Sinai?   So Christians in the early centuries thought too, and this oasis once was thickly populated with a Christian settlement, and Serbal, as well as Musa, was called Sinai.   Put the battle of Rephidim a few miles down the wady, the defenders of this view say, and let the journey which took the people to Sinai be the trek the day after the battle, when they came to the oasis of Feiran.   All this is not impossible, except that no such setting as this luxuriant oasis lies behind the story of Sinai where they "encamped in the wilderness," [2] nor in Mount Serbal is there any fitness for the carefully described occasion.   To be sure, the trip to Jebel Musa from the oasis would be very long if tried in a single day, but the idea that it was so tried is foreign to the narrative. They left the oasis, I suspect, where they would be the object of jealous hatred by all the Bedouin of the desert, and took the broad road of the Wady es Sheikh into "the wilderness of Sinai." [3]

[1] Exodus 17:8-16.                    [3] Ibid.
[2] Exodus 19:2.

## VI

One striking difficulty in the Biblical narrative—the numbers of the fugitives—must occur to every traveler. That six hundred thousand men [1] with women and children added, which would make a grand total of some three million folk, ever lived in this desert has seemed to every visitor here an appalling strain upon credulity. For one thing, so many people never could have come from Goshen, a little district of sixty to eighty square miles, where about five thousand people might live as shepherds. An exodus of three million folk would have depopulated the whole countryside of the Egyptian delta. For another thing, so many people could not live in the Sinaitic peninsula, which today supports in a poor and whipped existence five to six thousand Towara Arabs. For another thing, no such number, much less any increased descendants, ever could have settled in Palestine, which at its latest census in 1922 had a grand total of less than eight hundred thousand folk, Moslems, Christians, and Jews combined. No one can see the conditions without understanding that something is seriously the matter with the Biblical figures. Read the eighteenth chapter of Exodus and try to imagine Moses acting as sole judge and arbiter in the disputes of six hundred thousand men and their families!

In the endeavor to solve this problem many suggestions have been made. Some have imagined that bet-

[1] Exodus 12:37.

ter conditions in water and pasturage existed in the olden time. But that will not hold. This same hot, waterless, foodless desert that we see today is presupposed in the Biblical narrative, and one of the last investigators reports his judgment that conditions are, if anything, better than they used to be.

Some have ascribed the enormous numbers to exaggeration in telling a heroic tale. Such stretching of statistics is familiar to students of the Scripture, as when in the early narrative of II Samuel David paid fifty shekels of silver for Araunah's threshing-floor but in I Chronicles, written centuries afterward, he paid six hundred shekels of gold.[1] So, too, the earlier record gives David's military forces as thirty thousand, "all the chosen men of Israel," but the chronicler, centuries afterward, numbered David's "men of war, that could order the battle array," as over three hundred thousand.[2] While, however, it is possible that exaggeration is the secret, it is strange that the records should show such correspondence with the land everywhere else and then should slip so incredibly as to put three million people where a few thousand might possibly survive.

Some have fallen back upon supernaturalism and have held that the vast host was miraculously sustained, but the Biblical narrative itself prevents that explanation. Only three special providences are mentioned, and they could not solve the problem.

[1] II Samuel 24:24; I Chronicles 21:25.
[2] II Samuel 6:1; cf. I Chronicles 12:23-38.

The wind blew quails in,[1] and that still happens regularly every year. Each September the quails blow in by multitudes from Cyprus over Gaza down the Wady el 'Arish. The inhabitants of Gaza suspend their ordinary occupations and catch quails in nets as they fall wearied from their long flight, and the markets of Jerusalem are glutted with them. The flight lasts, as the Bible says, one month.[2] A friend of mine went once to Marseilles on a ship from Jaffa that carried seventeen thousand brace of these captured quails. But amazing as this sudden provision of fresh food must have been to the hungry Hebrews, it does not meet the difficulty of the numbers.

Again, the sending of manna seemed to them miraculous,[3] but for as long centuries as we have any record the Greek priests on Mount Sinai have gathered manna and are gathering it yet. It is, they claim, the gum that falls from the tamarisk bushes, and must be picked up, as the record says, before sunrise, because it melts and disappears. The Towara Arabs in extremities still eat it. But such manna could not solve the problem of sustaining three million folk; one understands as he sees it the contemptuous plaint of the people: "Nothing at all save this manna." [4] Even if the identification of manna with tamarisk gum is disbelieved and the miracle of heavenly food made as marvelous as one can picture it, it does not touch the real problem of the wilderness, which is not so much food as water.

[1] Numbers 11:31.
[2] Numbers 11:18-21.
[3] Exodus 16:4-35.
[4] Numbers 11:6.

Twice Moses is described as finding water in a marvelous way.[1] I recall how wonderful that used to seem when as a boy I heard it read, but in the desert it fits the landscape perfectly. My friend, a geologist, who spent many months in the peninsula, assures me that Arabs who know the ways of the wilderness still draw water from apparently dry cliffs, and I myself have seen an Arab dig in the sand where I would have supposed no water to be and gather a gallon of it in a limpid pool. Beside the sea, in particular, the Arabs dig in the sand and find fresh water—the seepage of the Sinaitic range running toward the shore. That Moses repeatedly found water to eke out the sparse supply in that thirsty land I have no doubt, but it still is incredible that three million folk ever drank their way through this appalling wilderness.

Perhaps, then, the theory advanced by Dr. Petrie is correct. He says that the Hebrew word *elef* has two meanings, "a thousand," and "a family," and that all our trouble comes from translating it "a thousand" here. He insists that the tribe of Manasseh, for example, did not have "thirty and two thousand and two hundred" people, as our translation says,[2] but had thirty-two families, making two hundred people altogether. He presents an appealing argument and the upshot is that, if you follow him, you get a total of about fifty-five hundred who made the Exodus. At least that fits the possibilities.

[1] Exodus 17:5-6; Numbers 20:7-11.
[2] Numbers 2:21.

## VII

It was an intriguing experience thus to ride through the wilderness, camping where it seemed probable that the Hebrews camped, trying to put oneself into the place of the fugitives and on the spot to see the Exodus as it actually was. One sympathized with the complaints of those suffering ex-slaves. Two things they wanted and told Moses so with repeated grumbling: water and vegetables. These still are the desire of all desert-travelers. Water—one never knows how priceless it is until at noonday one finds a little basin in the sand, walled with a few rocks and shaded by a palm tree, and discovers in it water for the caravan to drink and perhaps enough more to pour coolly over fevered heads and hands. Vegetables—"the cucumbers, and the melons, and the leeks, and the onions, and the garlic," [1]—for these the Hebrews clamored with wistful memories of Egypt, and while a Westerner might change the list he understands the need.

Vivid as it all was, however, and profoundly impressive as Sinai itself remains in memory, I was thankful when I came away that religiously we stand no longer at the mountain of the Law. A marvelous achievement Moses wrought there. To be sure, the scholars may be right in saying that the popular impression as to what was actually done on Sinai needs revision. The casual reader forgets that the Bible gives us two rendi-

[1] Numbers 11:5.

tions of the ten commandments.  One seems primitive and is very different from our familiar decalogue.

Thou shalt worship no other god.
Thou shalt make thee no molten gods.
The feast of unleavened bread shalt thou keep.
All that openeth the womb is mine.
Six days thou shalt work, but on the seventh day thou shalt rest.
Thou shalt observe the feast of weeks.
Three times in the year shall all thy males appear before the Lord Jehovah, the God of Israel.
Thou shalt not offer the blood of my sacrifice with leavened bread.
The first of the first-fruits of thy ground thou shall bring unto the house of Jehovah thy God.
Thou shalt not boil a kid in its mother's milk.

It is apparently of this list of commands in the thirty-fourth chapter of Exodus that "Jehovah said unto Moses, Write thou these words," and it is of this list that the narrative adds, "He wrote upon the tables the words of the covenant, the ten commandments." [1]

There is cause, therefore, for the long-standing query of the scholars as to whether the loftier laws of the twentieth chapter of Exodus, our decalogue, were not a later development under prophetic influence, afterward added, as all later laws were added, to the Mosaic code.

Nevertheless, however scholars may decide the matter, the beginning of the most fruitful religious

[1] Exodus 34:27-28.

development in history harks back to Sinai. There a great soul struck bravely out on a venture whose consequences he could not see. Yet glorious as it was, it was a primitive beginning. Belief in a mountain-god whose back can be seen of human eyes,[1] a god of war who sends his chosen tribesmen on ruthless raids to slaughter even children without mercy, is a long way behind us—or at least it ought to be.

As the bee flies it is about three hundred miles from Sinai to Sychar, but religiously it is farther still. From Sinai to Sychar—who could have guessed amid the thunderstorm upon that granite mountain that the issue of the movement there begun would be heard in quiet at a wellside where a Teacher talked with a woman about God.[2] On that memorable day I spent on Sinai's top I looked toward Sychar and in imagination reviewed the unique, astounding course of revelation which lay between. Amid the memories of Sinai's thunderous deity I heard the voice at Sychar: "God is a Spirit: and they that worship him must worship in spirit and truth."[3]

[1] Exodus 33:21-23.
[2] John 4:5-26.

[3] John 4:24.

## CHAPTER IV

## THE HEBREW INVASION

### I

WE left Moses and his fellow-fugitives at Sinai. We could not wander with them through the wilderness, make with them their vain attack on Palestine from the south, or swing around the Dead Sea's southern end past Edom to strike in from the eastern desert on the Promised Land. But we went out across Jordan to meet them in Moab and in imagination we joined their forces as they swept in on Palestine. From the vicinity of Heshbon, which the Hebrews razed and concerning which they sang their taunt:

> Come to Heshbon and rebuild it!
> Repair the capital of Sihon,
>     if you can! [1]

we followed the line of their advance and for two notable days tented with the Arabs on the very steppes where Joshua and his forces camped before they crossed the Jordan and fell on Jericho.

Never was a landscape better fitted to stimulate the imagination in picturing a historical event. From far off on the plateau of Moab, near the village of Suwei-

[1] Numbers 21:27 M.

73

lah, we could see, as the invading Hebrews saw, the
Mount of Olives towering up across the Jordan's gorge
over forty miles away.  The Promised Land lay before
them in plain view, a tempting invitation to invasion
long before they reached it.

In the Book of Numbers one reads repeatedly about
"the steppes of Moab beside the Jordan opposite
Jericho." [1]  There, having crushed the Moabites and
Amorites who had blocked their way from the desert
to the river, the Hebrews pitched their camp.  They
looked, I doubt not, to contemporary eyes like another
swarm of fierce and hungry invaders from the wilderness, and their manner of life could not have been
utterly unlike that of the Adwan Arabs in whose camp
on the same steppes we passed two memorable days.

These Arabs yet are a blend of Cain and Abel, half
agriculturists and half herdsmen.  They never have
entirely lost the ways of the desert from which, like the
Hebrews of old, they overflowed into more fertile
land.  They summer at Heshbon on the heights; they
winter on the lower steppes near Jordan; but always
they live in their long, black tents and rely on their
flocks rather than their fields.

To be entertained in their camp is to be carried back
millenniums and made to live with the ancient
patriarchs.  We went with a friend who, as a young
girl in Jerusalem, had been made an honorary member of the tribe in reward for some service rendered
by her father, and, although our coming was unex-

[1] Numbers 33:48-50 M and 35:1 M, etc.

pected, we were welcomed with the perfect hospitality which is the Arab's crowning virtue. The aged sheik's eldest son, himself the tribe's active head, met us on his splendid steed; and from the time he put his horse at the disposal of the women, to carry them across a flooded stream into the camp, to the time he rode out in state to bid us Godspeed, firing his pistols as he came, he was the ideal Arab host.

The camp was pitched beside a rushing four-foot brook that brawled down from the uplands to the Jordan. The great black-brown tents—a hundred feet long or more, made of camel's-hair cloth and so strong that the goats played freely on their tops—were pitched helter-skelter across the plain. In the morning the flocks went off to graze and in the evening came back to camp again. Slaves tended them—chattel slaves bought and paid for, or sometimes (so poverty-stricken is the Arabs' life) taken into bondage at their own request to save them from starvation. The tribe cultivates a few acres on the lower steppes, and a heavy wind the night before we came had beaten down the grain. We inquired of the sheik's son, as he rode back from inspecting it, how bad the damage was. "It is the will of God," he answered in true Arab fashion, "and God is merciful."

The picture of our entertainment is given with extraordinary fidelity in the eighteenth chapter of Genesis. Little has changed except that firearms are added to the weapons which all carry, and coffee and tobacco have come in. One compartment of the sheik's

great tent was cleared for our reception; the best rugs
and cushions were thrown upon the ground for us to
sit upon; the coffee was brewed with elaborate ritual
from the grinding of the bean to the serving of the
drink, and a rhythmic chantey was sung throughout the
process. They say that you can tell by the way they
sing it how welcome you are. The lamb was brought
from the flock and slain at the tent door; the eldest wife
cooked it in the open kettle and superintended the other
women making bread and delicacies for our evening
meal; and the meal came at last—meat, rice, and
vegetables compounded in one great dish and borne by
a bevy of slaves. Into the common dish we thrust our
hands and ate until our hunger was appeased and then,
in order of seniority, the sheik called the head men of
the tribe to eat until, at last, the remnants were turned
over to the slaves to finish. After dinner the sheik, to
the accompaniment of his *rebabeh,* a homemade lute,
sang Arab songs—love songs, foray songs, and, last of
all, a ballad on the Druses who a few miles north were
fighting off the French. Then the whole tribe danced
for us and the night ended with the mad, tumultuous
sword dance, led by a woman with a gleaming blade,
and fitted to stir up the fighting spirit of the men to
such a raid as long centuries before had been launched
from this very spot on Jericho.

## II

The view from the camp made the first stages of
Joshua's invasion clear. Perched where the heights of

Moab meet the rising ground from the Jordan bottom
three miles away, we could see the whole plain of
Jericho and the highlands back of it.  The probable
site of Gilgal, Joshua's first camp in Palestine, now
marked by a tree and called Jiljulieh by the Arabs, lay
on the flat marl about midway between the Jordan and
Jericho.  Jericho itself is an oasis, as it always has been.
The town was built there on the flatlands, so easy of
access and difficult of defense, because of the great
fountain now called 'Ain Sultan, which still pours out
its copious waters beside the ruins of the ancient city.
It is a green place still, as seen from Moab—a verdant
patch upon the brown background of the barren plain
and the wilderness of Judea rising over it.  Of course
the invaders began with Jericho, searched it out with
spies, had to conquer it before they could go farther.
And of course when they did conquer it they did not
turn toward the Judean plateau where Jerusalem stood.
There was no obvious valley to invite approach across
the wilderness.  But even from Moab one can see the
wadies, wide-open and alluring, which lead up toward
Ai, Bethel, Shiloh, Shechem, and the high places of
Ephraim, which soon became the center of the new
Hebrew life.  One could have planned Joshua's cam-
paign from that Bedouin camp in Moab and could have
seen the map of it laid out before him.

We tried to recapitulate in our imagination their
experience as we, like them, crossed the fords of Jordan toward Jericho.  What happened to make that
passage of the river so memorable?  If one goes
upstream a few miles from the fords, he finds the **river**

flowing in a serpentine channel between clay cliffs,
undercutting the banks, and carving out new waterways.
Only a few years ago the people at the fords were
amazed to see Jordan so dry that one could walk across
it, and for several hours it so continued before the
stream returned.  A clay cliff up the river had caved
in, filling the channel and forcing the accumulating
stream to reopen an old course which it formerly had
followed but long since abandoned.  One wonders if
some such thing happened at that ancient crossing of
the river.  The Western world long has made a super-
natural marvel of it, but the Biblical account, read on
the spot, suggests something much more easily imaginable: "The waters that flow down stopped and were
dammed up at a distance, at Adâmah (a town beside
Zartan)." [1]

## III

One effect of picturing the Hebrew conquest on the
very terrain where it occurred is to strip it of the glamour which centuries of Christian allegorizing have cast
over it.  For the invasion of Palestine has been allego-
rized and poetized in the thought and terminology of
the church until the original event has become difficult
to recognize.  Palestine has ceased being Palestine and
has become the Promised Land, and the story of the
conquest has ceased to be a bloody and pitiless tale of
sacked cities and massacred inhabitants and has
become a beautiful fulfilment of divine foretellings.

[1] Joshua 3:16 M.

But on the ground the bare, stark facts stare out at you.

This invasion of Palestine was ruthless business. Read the reiterated record in the Scripture and see: "They massacred all in the city, men and women, old and young alike, oxen, sheep, and asses, giving no quarter." [1] "All the folk of Ai fell that day, both men and women, twelve thousand in all; Joshua never withdrew the hand that held his javelin until he had massacred all the folk of Ai." [2] In the tenth chapter of Joshua alone one reads seven times, repeated in varying form, the dire refrain: "He sacked the place and massacred all within it, leaving not a single soul alive." And the summary of the dreadful business is pitiless enough: "Thus Joshua captured the whole country, the highlands, the Negeb, the lowlands, and the slopes, with all their kings; he left not a soul alive, but massacred every living creature, as the Eternal, the God of Israel, had commanded." [3]

So runs the unabashed record, and the only excuse which can be made for the morals of these tribesmen is that they were true to the ethics of their time and race. Indeed, a famous traveler among the Bedouin during the past century has described them as devoted to three chief things: eloquence, hospitality, and plundering. A raid upon another tribe is not yet considered theft but is regarded as we regard football, where each side tries by craft and strength to seize

[1] Joshua 6:21 M.
[2] Joshua 8:25-26 M.
[3] Joshua 10:40 M.

the pigskin. The Hebrews, with all their ruthless massacres, were playing the game according to the rules of the day.

As for the religion of it, I do not see how any one who on the ground thinks the matter through can be tempted to identify the god who was supposed to order, superintend, and bless all this with the God revealed in the greatest of the Hebrew prophets and, above all, in Christ. They are not of one spirit. The Hebrews, with their tribal god who stood for them against all others and backed them up in any assault and battery upon another folk, shared the current theology of all ancient nations. On the temple walls of Ramses III, in the plain of Thebes, we saw the gigantic figure of Amon-Re, the supreme god of Egypt, handing the king his sword and dispatching him to war; and again we saw the god receiving the returning conquerer as he slew numberless captives before him. Such was the theology of the early Hebrews. Even here upon the plateau of Moab a few years ago a great stone was found—it stands now in the Louvre at Paris—on which Mesha, king of Moab, celebrated a bloody victory over Israel and praised Chemosh, his god, for giving it. How like some passages in the Old Testament this Moabite record sounds:

Omri, king of Israel—he oppressed Moab many days, because Chemosh was angry with his land. And his son succeeded him, and he also said I will oppress Moab. In my day he spoke according to [this] word, but I saw [my desire] upon him and upon his house, and Israel utterly perished for-

ꞇver. Now Omri had possessed all the land of Medeba ...
but Chemosh restored it in my day. . . . I fought against the city
[Ataroth] and took it, and I slew all the people of the city, a
sight [pleasing] to Chemosh and to Moab. . . . And Chemosh
said to me: "Go take Nebo against Israel"; and I went by
night and fought against it from break of dawn till noon, and
I took it and slew all, seven thousand men, boys (?), and
women, and girls, for I had devoted it to Ashtar-Chemosh.

What Chemosh was to Moab, Jehovah was to Israel,
and the marvel is that with such a commonplace and
ordinary start—an idea of deity hard to distinguish from
that held by other nations and used by them to sanction
their raids and massacres—the Hebrews should have
produced so unique a consequence. Who could have
guessed that in this land, so seized, would be revealed
at last the loftiest idea of God that man has grasped?

## IV

Again and again we went down to the plain of
Jericho, for it is a fascinating spot. Here many of the
hidden waterways that drain the uplands of Judea
debouch into the plain so that while the highland
wilderness is bare and arid and the Jordan plain is
sterile marl, the land about Jericho itself is rich and
fertile. In the early literature of the Hebrews it is
called the city of palm trees,[1] and while today those
"most excellent and frequent gardens" in this "divine"
region, which Josephus praised, are sadly fallen into
disrepair, one can easily imagine how Herod the Great

[1] Judges 1:16 and 3:13; Deuteronomy 34:3.

made this place glorious for his winter residence and can see why its revenue from dates and balsam was so great that Mark Antony gave it as a prize to Cleopatra. Upon this alluring spot the Hebrew conquest fell like a thunderbolt.

The site of the ancient city which the Hebrews took is unmistakable. One of the surest means of identifying any site in Palestine is a fountain, and here the fountain is one of the most copious in the land. In all their journeys from the days in Egypt the Hebrews never had seen so plentiful a rush of water as is here.

Close to the great pools of this spring, a mile away from the modern mud-brick village, the ruined walls of the old city lie. They first were excavated less than twenty years ago. As one stands on them now he has first of all to readjust his imagination from the startling dramatics of Martin's exaggerated picture to the realities of the actual site. The city of Jericho, according to our standards, was very small—no larger in the compass of its walls than the Colosseum at Rome. As the excavators dug down through the mound they found the town that Hiel built in Ahab's time [1] and that Sennacherib probably destroyed about 700 B.C. Below that they found what seemed to be the ruins of the Canaanitish city which Joshua took long centuries before. The old walls and houses were made of sundried brick. You can see them still, and walk about upon the ruined bulwarks over which the Hebrews rushed to take the city. One even can observe the

[1] Kings 16:34.

charred lime which, so some archeologists say, marks
the burning of the city about the time the Hebrews
came.

All this makes very vivid that ancient scene of sack
and pillage.[1]  I stood upon the ruins, in an embrasure
which might have been the home of Rahab,[2] and
looked down across the plain where in full view at
Gilgal two miles away the camp of Joshua was pitched.
One easily could imagine the famous march six days
repeated at the story of which our childhood wondered.
With trumpets blaring the lusty tribesmen came up
from Gilgal, armed with rough stone or bronze
weapons, and circled the walls of the town under the
eyes of the amazed inhabitants, only to return to Gilgal.
One could imagine also the final assault when on
the seventh day the besieged, long since grown contemptuous, went swiftly down before the charge of the
Hebrews.

Jericho never has been able to withstand attack,
partly because it is built on the plain beside the fountain, with no natural altitude or declivity to make
defense easy, and partly because its climate is debilitat-
ing and its inhabitants to this day are a degenerate lot.
Whether it be Joshua seizing it from the Canaanites,
or the northern kingdom taking it from Judah, or the
Syrians capturing it in the days of the Maccabees, or
Aristobulus conquering his brother there, or Pompey,
Herod, or Vespasian, each seizing it in Roman times,
always Jericho has fallen without serious defense.

[1] Joshua Ch. 6.                    [2] Joshua Ch. 2 and 6:17, 22-25.

"That her walls fell down at the sound of Joshua's trumpets," writes Professor George Adam Smith, "is no exaggeration, but the soberest summary of all her history."

One incident which, if studied on the spot, is fitted to make the conditions of the Hebrew conquest vivid, is the story of the Gibeonites who came to Joshua at Gilgal. "They took provisions in old sacks on their asses, and old mended wine-skins, with old patched shoes on their feet and old clothes on their bodies; the bread they took was all dry and crumbling" [1]— and so provided they won a promise of safety from Joshua on the pretext that they came from a distance. As a matter of fact, if one will go up the old valley of Achor and follow on by the Wady Farah over the Judean ridge, one will come to Gibeon less than twenty miles away. The Arabs still call it el-Jib and it was well worth the donkey-ride which brought me there one morning to visualize the old town around which Joshua's early conquest swirled. Few travelers go there—it is out of the way, on a rough trail—but it is full of interest.

On the way to it from Jerusalem we traversed for a time the ruin of the Roman road over which Paul was led a prisoner to Cæsarea [2] and finally, skirting the flank of Neby Samwil, we climbed the fine hilltop where ancient Gibeon stood. Beside the great pool whose relic still is visible, the two opposing teams of twelve men each from the armies of Ish-bosheth and David met for

---

[1] Joshua 9:4-5 M.          [2] Acts 23:31-33.

a conference which ended in a fight.[1]   On this hill, by
David's orders, seven descendants of Saul were hanged
to appease the anger of Jehovah and end a three-year
famine.[2]   To Gibeon came Solomon to sacrifice before
he built the temple on Zion, because it was "the chief
shrine"; and here he had the dream in which he asked
God for wisdom.[3]

Long before these events, however, it was a chief
city of the Canaanites, and to this day I know no place
in Palestine so well fitted to illustrate the device by
which in time of siege these ancient citadels supplied
themselves with water.   One still can go down through
the rough rock opening, close to the walls, into the subterranean pool where five springs pour their overflow;
one still can see the stairs by which in time of siege the
drawers of water used to reach the pool from within the
city.   Let the outer opening be blocked and covered
and it would be besiegers, not besieged, who would
want water.

Nevertheless, though thus provided and though
"Gibeon was a large town, like a royal city, larger than
Ai, and all its men were stout fighters," [4] it was from
this fortress that the fakers went to Gilgal clothed
and provisioned like far travelers to make their peace
with Joshua.   It was around these walls in consequence that the armies of five Canaanitish kings gathered to wreak vengeance on their faithless neighbor.[5]
And it was by the Wady Suweinit, up from the plain

[1] II Samuel 2:12-17.
[2] II Samuel 21:1-9.
[3] I Kings 3:4-15 M.
[4] Joshua 10:2 M.
[5] Joshua 10:5.

to the ridge, that Joshua forced a midnight march to drive the five kings and their armies down the valley of Ajalon in disastrous rout.

So, with a few smashing blows these ex-slaves from Egypt ensconced themselves on the uplands of Palestine, but for at least two centuries thereafter their situation was precarious. Later historians telescoped the process of conquest and made it seem a brief, triumphant march from one end of the land to the other, but some of the earlier records still are left which make clear its long duration and its hazardous uncertainty. From Jerusalem on the south to Beth-shean, Taanach, and Megiddo on the northern frontiers, the Hebrews could not drive out the Canaanites from many a strategic town,[1] and in the fertile lowlands of Samaria and Esdraelon the old inhabitants still kept their hold "because they had chariots of iron."[2] Even while the Canaanites were slowly being strangled by their far more virile and aggressive foes, a new enemy came upon the scene—the Philistines, before whom the Hebrews nearly went to pieces and in desperately fighting whom they built their nation.

## VI

How keenly in our childhood we hated the Philistines! With the eager partisanship of youth we sided with Samuel, Saul, and David against these murderous foes, and sympathized with the doughty Hebrews in

---

[1] Judges 1:21, 27.          [2] Judges 1:19.

their fight against Philistia as we did with the Swiss under William Tell against the Hapsburgs, or with the Scots under Wallace against King Edward I. Even when Samson burned their corn by tying torches to foxes' tails,[1] or carried off their city gates,[2] or slew a thousand of them with an ass's jawbone,[3] or ripped the underpinning from their temple and killed more in his death than in his life,[4] we felt the glow of righteous vengeance on oppressive tyrants. As a matter of fact, the Philistines were a great people, probably the last inheritors of the Minoan civilization of Crete, and some scholars even believe that to them we owe the origin of our alphabet.

So powerful were they, so impressive in their influence, that theirs is the name we call the country by, for Palestine is the Greek for Philistia. They swept down on the coasts of Egypt, a part of that vast migration of peoples which brought the Dorians to Greece and the Hebrews to Palestine and made the few centuries after 1400 B.C. so restless and significant. We saw pictured on the walls of Ramses III's temple at Thebes his victories over these invaders, after which, driven back from Egypt, they settled on the coastal plain below the Judean ridge. It was inevitable that these two virile folk, the Hebrews and Philistines, should clash; and when they did the victory was prevailingly upon one side—the Philistines conquered Israel.

[1] Judges 15:4-5.
[2] Judges 16:3.
[3] Judges 15:15.
[4] Judges 16:23-30.

We went down to the coastal plain of a purpose to see what was left of the Philistines. Five strong cities once were theirs: Gaza, Ashdod, Ashkelon, Gath, and Ekron. Gaza, near the seacoast, still is there, one of the largest towns in Palestine, where fifteen wells of water make a livable spot in the barren sand. A cemetery with three thousand British graves bears witness to its importance in the Great War. Across the centuries its history runs clear, for it lies on the inevitable route of all invaders. From Napoleon Bonaparte, who captured it in 1799, to the Philistines who had seized it some three thousand years before, it has been one of the most fought-for cities in the world. But there is nothing left to make one think of the Philistines. One can only recall the mingled folk-lore and history of that ancient time. Here was the scene of Samson's exploit when he carried off the city gates and of his final tragedy when he pulled down Dagon's temple on the worshipers. Here the Philistines lived on after the Hebrews had driven them from the ridge, guilty of an extensive and cruel slave trade for which Amos cursed the city.[1] Here as late as the seventh century B.C. the Philistines still persisted and Zephaniah the prophet was foretelling woes for them.[2] Here Dagon's successor, the god Marna, was worshiped so long that human sacrifices were offered to him as late as the fourth century A.D.

Ashdod also exists. As everywhere on this coastal plain, highroad of numberless invasions as it has been,

[1] Amos 1:6.        [2] Zephaniah 2:4.

one hears at Ashdod the echo of endless wars. The longest siege recorded in history occurred here when, according to Herodotus, Psammitichus besieged the city for twenty-nine years. Here, too, memories of New Testament days come in, for Ashdod in the Greek language was Azotus, and Philip the evangelist preached here.[1] As for the Philistines, however, they are gone and all the memorials of them perished utterly. Only a picturesque village of mud-brick houses, with five thousand people in it, marks the ancient site. But, as of old, the threshing-floors were piled with grain from the fertile fields while we were there, and the busy harvesters easily could be transmuted by imagination into old Philistines. Here, one day long ago, the sacred Ark of the Hebrews, captured in battle, was brought in triumph to Dagon's temple,[2] while up at Shiloh on the ridge old Eli died when he learned of its loss.[3] History lends verisimilitude to that story. A temple to Dagon stood here until the Maccabees destroyed it in the second century before our Lord.[4]

As for the other three cities of the Philistine pentapolis there is little to be said. Ashkelon's site we know. It is the only one of the five directly on the coast, and if one will take a long horseback ride across the sand—so hot that you can cook an egg in it at noon—one still can see the ruins which mark the place beside the shallow, useless harbor. But the memories that cluster

---

[1] Acts 8:40.
[2] I Samuel 5:1-2.
[3] I Samuel 4:18.
[4] I Maccabees 10:84.

round these relics are not Philistine. Here Richard the
Lion-Hearted performed exploits; here Herod the Great
was born—but any Philistine memorials have vanished. As for Gath and Ekron, we do not even know
where they were, although Gath was once the leader
of the five. Perhaps Tell es Safi is the site of Gath;
and 'Akir—or, it may be, Dhikerin—of Ekron, but
nothing that interprets the Philistines to us has been
found in any one of them. Only one memorial we have
of Ekron: the devil's cognomen, Beelzebub. Baal-
zebub was once Ekron's god, the god of flies, and there
an oracle persisted for centuries so famous that even
a sick king of Israel sent down to it to learn his fate.[1]
Saving for that evil contribution, the memory of Ekron
is a blank.

So have vanished the Philistines. Their very name,
as a people, perished after the Assyrians swooped down
upon them and wrecked their nation. We might not
have known about them save as dim figures without
clear meaning had it not been that once they conquered
Israel. Once they broke unforgetably from obscurity
and wrought a mighty consequence for history: they
forced the chaotic, scattered Hebrews to unite to fight
them, and they gave David his opportunity.

## VII

Vividly to feel the crisis on the very spot where it
had one of its most acute effects, let us go to Shiloh.

[1] II Kings 1:2.

This is one place in Palestine associated with events before Christ's coming to which one should make reverent pilgrimage. The Hebrews had many shrines in those early days—at Gilgal, at Mount Ebal, at Shechem—but Shiloh overtopped them all. Here the sacred Ark was kept; here Eli ministered; here Samuel was trained for his prophethood, and here the religious life of the scattered Hebrew tribes had a common center.

What the Ark meant to the ancient Hebrew it is not easy for a modern mind to feel. Even in Old Testament times the idea which it represented became outgrown and Jeremiah foretold more spiritual days for his people when the Ark "shall never enter their minds, they shall not remember it, they shall never miss it, and it shall never be re-made." [1]    That it does thus represent a primitive stage of religious thought is clear. In Japan I saw a similar ark, the sacramental residence of a Shinto god, carried from its temple on the shoulders of a dancing, shouting crowd of devotees. They were taking their god on his annual pilgrimage through the streets of Kyoto that he might observe how his people fared. One could not see that holy chest, treated as a divine residence, without thinking of the Hebrew parallel even to the dancing with which it was at last carried up to David's shrine on Zion.[2]

Primitive though it was, however, the Ark represented a notable matter in the history of our religion. When first the Hebrews met Jehovah on Sinai, a god

[1] Jeremiah 3:16 M.          [2] II Samuel 6:12-15.

unknown to their fathers by that name,[1] he was a divinity who dwelt upon a mountain, and their desertion of that sacred site for their wanderings and conquests raised the serious question: would this deity go with them?  Up to this time in all Semitic religion we have no record of a god who left his local shrine.  The gods were immovable; men made pilgrimage to their holy places to worship them—such was the basis of Semitic faith.

Where did Moses find the revolutionary idea that the god of Sinai could come to Palestine?  Was it, as some think, from the Egyptians and their floating shrines on the Nile?  At any rate, that radical departure from an old tradition was made at Sinai and the Ark of shittim wood became the visible symbol of Jehovah's presence with his wandering people.  We may even call it a first step toward the idea of God's omnipresence.  This sacred palladium was kept at Shiloh until the fatal day when the desperate Hebrews, hard pressed by the Philistines, took it into battle that Jehovah's presence might overcome their enemies.[2]

There is no doubt about Shiloh's site; it is precisely described in Scripture,[3] and even the modern name, Seilun, is only another form of Shilonite.  One goes to it now by automobile and feels the profanation as he does so.  By the north road from Jerusalem, past many a site made memorable by Saul and Samuel, we rode in an hour to the byway that takes us across the plain to

[1] Exodus 6:3.
[2] I Samuel 4:1-11.
[3] Judges 21:19.

Shiloh. The day we came, the Danish archeologists, who sank their first trial shaft in 1922, were in the thick of their excavations. As the long lines of Arab women carried up the dirt and laid bare the ruins, our eyes were among the first to see the uncovering of the ancient town. Already we could walk among Byzantine and Roman walls; and trial shafts, driven deeper, have brought up assurance that the houses of the ancient Israelites lie underneath. The eager, excited, Danish scholar, who scrambled that day over the ruins and spent his energy alike in hard climbing and laborious English, even thinks that in some picturesque ruins of a Christian holy place near by he may be on the site of the old tabernacle where the Ark was kept. At any rate, the position is perfect. Somewhere near this spot the aged Eli waited all that fatal day for the sacred Ark that had gone down to battle. A long valley falls away in front and makes a perfect staging for his anxious vigil as he watched for the first sight of the distant messenger. Few places in Palestine can fit the Biblical narrative with more precision.

We kept vigil with him there that day and thought of all that happened to the Ark among the victorious Philistines.[1] We saw it carried in triumph to Ashdod and placed as a trophy in Dagon's temple. Then, blamed for the plague that simultaneously struck the town, it was sent to Gath and thence to Ekron, doubtless carrying the germs of pestilence with it; so from Ekron to Beth-Shemesh, still carrying the plague, the

---

[1] I Samuel Chs. 5, 6, and 7:1-2.

Ark was sent by a frightened and superstitious people, until at last it found a resting place for twenty years at Kiriath-jearim, before David carried it to Zion. So hard put to it were the Hebrews in their struggle with the Philistines that even their most sacred palladium was captured and only by force of superstitious fear ever was regained.

Meanwhile, Shiloh, never recovering from its irreparable loss, fell into decay. Centuries afterward it was in ruins and Jeremiah, impatient with folk who said that God could not desert his temple on Zion, cried: "Go to my sacred shrine at Shilo, where at first I fixed my presence; look at what I did to it, on account of the wickedness of Israel my people! So now with you." [1]

## VIII

When I first went to Palestine, Michmash was one place that especially I meant to see. If one reads the story of what happened there [2] one can understand why the visitor should wish to see it. The vivid description of the battle gives so detailed a setting that it ought to be possible still to recognize the site and to follow the fortunes of the conflict. And so it is. We walked out to Michmash—it is a few miles north of Jerusalem—one day in March, and as we worked our way down into the wady, the story of Jonathan's famous exploit received a staging ever more convincing and exact. Still the opposing crags tower up against

[1] Jeremiah 7:12 M.    [2] I Samuel Ch. 14.

each other across the wady as the record says, and one's imagination can ring up the curtain and see the battle fought upon this ancient stage. The very names, Michmash and Geba, are preserved in little Arab villages.

The six hundred Hebrews under Saul and Jonathan on one side of the narrow wady, the Philistines on the other, can be confidently located. The determination of Jonathan and his armor-bearer to cross and dare a single-handed combat; the Philistine garrison, at first contemptuous, then astounded at this signal bravery, then giving way before Jonathan's fierce onslaught, then thrown into confusion by the uprising of the Hebrew slaves in their own camp until at last the whole Philistine mob is routed as Saul throws in his men, and is driven past Beth-aven down the wady into the plain— all this can be reseen today upon the spot. Even the incident of Jonathan's eating honey on the field [1] was made the more vivid to us by the sight of two Arabs who had found a hive of wild bees and were carrying their capture home. And the discovery of modern cartridges and aerial bombs reminded us that the British routed the Turks on this very spot where Jonathan had routed the Philistines.

The Hebrew victory at Michmash, however, was short-lived. What could these ex-tribesmen from the desert, far below the Philistines in their culture and so reduced in accouterment that "there was neither sword nor spear found in the hand of any of the people that

[1] I Samuel 14:27.

were with Saul and Jonathan," [1] do against the great Philistines? All along the rocky ridge to the north of Jerusalem, to which the Hebrews desperately clung, one feels the shadow of that life-and-death struggle which made the days of Samuel and Saul romantic and tragic too. Ramah, where Saul lived, still is there, now called er-Ram; Gibeah, where Saul lived and later kept his little court, still towers up high as though to guard the wadies that run up from Philistia. When I used to read that Samuel went on circuit judging Israel, from Ramah through Bethel, Gilgal, Mizpah, and back to Ramah again,[2] I pictured a long journey. As a matter of fact, he never was more than fifteen miles from home. To some such area on the uplands the central portion of the Hebrew tribesmen clung, and there they fought a desperate battle for their very lives. Then the great crash came. Their first king, who stood a shoulder higher than any of the people, and whom, despite all their Bedouin precedents, they had made king as a last hope against the Philistines, was beaten on Gilboa, his three sons were slain, and he himself fell upon his sword.

It looked like the end. It might well have been the end had it not been for David, that amazing shepherd lad from Bethlehem whom Saul had hated with such bitter jealousy. He was before all else a vigorous, relentless patriot, and he hated the Philistines. Even when he heard of Saul's defeat and death, though he had suffered cruelly from Saul's bitterness, he cried:

[1] I Samuel 13:22.　　　　[2] I Samuel 7:16-17.

Tell it not in Gath,
proclaim it not in Ashkelon's streets,
lest the daughters of the Philistines rejoice,
lest the daughters of the uncircumcised exult.[1]

[1] II Samuel 1:20 M.

CHAPTER V

## THE CITY OF DAVID

### I

THE first impression which Jerusalem makes upon
the visitor depends largely on the visitor's previous
familarity with Oriental towns.  If he comes fresh from
Western scenes and customs and here for the first time
looks upon the East, he will find many strange sights,
sounds, and smells to which to adjust himself.  Some
will shock him; his appreciation of Jerusalem will
stumble at the start over details distressing to his senses
and his mind.  The uncleanliness, the negligence of
sanitation, the acceptance of filth and vermin as a matter
of course; the appalling poverty, blindness, and disease;
the shiftless, sodden figures that bestrew the streets; the
shameless begging, aided by all the pity-producing
artifices that can be devised; the bizarre marks of racial
and religious distinction, such as the straggling, uncut
forelocks of the Polish Jews or the knotted back hair
of the Greek priests—scores of such things will smite
his nose and eyes.  If he is incapable of overpassing
these strangenesses he may as well return where he can
feel the congenial familiarity of Broadway or the home-
likeness of Main Street Anywhere.

If, however, he has learned to look with generous eyes on all sorts and conditions of men, he soon will see light upon Jerusalem. The conditions as to sanitation are infinitely better under British rule than they have ever been before, and they are constantly improving. Anyway, the idea that cleanliness is next to godliness is Western; in a country like Palestine, where, even in Jerusalem, there is barely enough water to drink, it is a bit absurd; and admirable personalities can develop under conditions where such an idea is as yet an unnaturalized alien. As for happiness, there is probably as much per capita in Jerusalem or even in these poverty-stricken, mud-brick Arab villages, with all their squalor, as there is in the city of New York.

In the end even the traveler who at first is shocked discovers the real Jerusalem. Its narrow, winding, climbing streets; its thronged bazaars packed along the traffic ways or crowded under colonnades built by crusaders to house pilgrims; its endless riot of color in costumes that represent many faiths and races; its fascinating salmagundi of strange faces, strange animals, strange clothes, and strange accents—all these fill the eye until the Strand or Fifth Avenue seems by contrast very dull, drab, standardized, and monotonous.

Over all, of course, and saturating everything with their suggestiveness, are the memories that cluster on these ancient hills. From the Mosque of Omar, where one sees the very rock on which Solomon's altar stood, to the Church of the Holy Sepulcher, where for sixteen centuries Christians have supposed that our Lord died and rose again, one walks as nowhere else on earth amid profoundly sacred reminiscences. Nevertheless, although one enjoy the modern city and visit all the venerated sites, he has not felt the full charm of Jerusalem until he sees it first of all as the city of David.

## II

I went out to Bethlehem one day of a purpose to neglect the later, larger memories of Christ's nativity and to think only of David. I found what I wanted. I saw him. He was a sturdy, Arab shepherd boy, "ruddy, a lad with fine eyes and of a handsome appearance," [1] as the Scripture says, and he was leading a great flock over the hills near Bethlehem. So David, many a morning, led his sheep from this picturesquely perched village on its lofty hill. In his time Jerusalem, six miles north, was still in the hands of the Jebusites—"Neither did the men of Judah evict the Jebusites who inhabited Jerusalem." [2] I wonder if in his boyhood, as he played his lute or practised with the sling, which shepherds use until this day, David dreamed that some day he might capture the city for Israel and become a powerful sheik.

It is twelve miles down-hill from Bethlehem to the Vale of Elah, where David fought Goliath—a good morning's walk for a lad laden with presents for his brothers in the Hebrew camp. Of course, as all students of the Bible know, it is an open question whether it was David who did fight Goliath. One passage says dis-

[1] I Samuel 16:12 M.          [2] Judges 1:21 M.

tinctly that he did and describes minutely how he did it.[1]   Another passage says just as distinctly that it was "Elhanan the son of Jaare-oregim the Beth-lehemite" that "slew Goliath the Gittite, the staff of whose spear was like a weaver's beam." [2]   And another passage, written centuries later, endeavors to resolve the difficulty by saying that it was Lahmi, the brother of Goliath, whom Elhanan slew.[3]  Whatever the scholars may decide, however, the imagination of the centuries is clear: we still see that fight between the Philistine giant and the Hebrew shepherd boy.   Moreover, whatever the facts may be, the truth is there—it is a veracious picture of David's life work crushing the Philistines.

The Vale of Elah, now the Wady es Sunt, broke upon us as startling in its realism as though the great fight had happened the day before and the armies just had struck camp and disappeared.   From what others had said I had expected confirmation of the Bible story in the landscape, but nothing quite so realistic.   It was as though in some familiar play the actors just had left the stage, and one who knew the drama well recognized the scene at once on entering.

Modern names suggesting sites associated with the fight are near at hand—Shuweikeh for Shocoh, Zakariya for Azekah, between which the Philistines camped—and a few old terebinths still recall the reason for *Elah*,

---

[1] I Samuel Ch. 17.
[2] II Samuel 21:19.  Note that the King James' Version endeavors to solve the difficulty by adding the words, indicated by italics, "the brother of."
[3] I Chronicles 20:5.

"oak," the valley's ancient name. The hostile camps on the sloping hillsides opposite each other, boastful Goliath challenging the Hebrew champion between them, the youthful David with his sling pitted against this human dinosaur in his heavy armor, and the sudden smashing victory—all fitted with ease into the scenery. Even the brook bed is there where David gathered his five smooth missiles, and we found still plenty of round stones the size of hen's eggs exactly fitted for a shepherd's sling. A native Arab added the last touch to our illusion about the recent fight. We asked him the name of the thorn bushes which covered the floor of the valley, and with entire solemnity he answered that he did not know the name but that they had grown from the tent pegs of the Philistines when Goliath fought there with David. As we rode up through the Shephelah hills to the ridge and passed a company of gaily dressed Arab women returning from a festival, I almost expected them to break into the ancient song:

> Saul hath slain his thousands,
> And David his ten thousands.[1]

### III

Few continued stories in Scripture are more lighted up by a knowledge of the land than the wanderings of David as he fled from the jealousy of Saul. The caves at Adullam, where he gathered his band of malcontents,[2] are there today in the Shephelah hills below the

---

[1] I Samuel 18:7.            [2] I Samuel 22:1-2.

Judean ridge, still called 'Aid el-Ma.   Thence across
Jordan one can follow him to Moab and then back
again to hide in the forest of Hereth,[1] east of Adullam.
Keilah—Kila now—which he rescued from the Philistines,[2] is a few miles away, and thence his tracks lead
to the desert of Ziph,[3] southeast of Hebron, where one
finds the old names still.   Maon, where Saul pressed
David close,[4] is Main today; Carmel, where Nabal
sheared his sheep when David planned to kill him,[5] is
el-Kurmul; and when at last Saul's anger drove the
fugitive to alliance with the Philistines, whom he hated,
and to hiding in their cities,[6] one who knows Philistia
can follow his trail in large part and guess the
rest of it.   When David was through with that
experience he knew intimately not only the land
he was to rule but the territory of his chief enemy
as well.

It was at En-gedi that I felt most vividly the meaning
of those fugitive years in David's life.   Down through
the wilderness of En-gedi, which lies between Bethlehem and the Dead Sea, Saul hunted David.[7]   We came
at it from the side of the sea, surprised at first to
recall that always in ancient literature En-gedi is
described as beautiful.   From the Song of Songs, where
the ardent lover calls his sweetheart a "cluster of henna-
flowers in the vineyards of En-gedi,"[8] to the picture of
palm groves there which Josephus draws, or the fair

[1] I Samuel  22:3-5            [5] I Samuel  25:2-13.
[2] I Samuel  23:1-5.           [6] I Samuel  27:1-7.
[3] I Samuel  23:14-18.         [7] I Samuel  24:1-2.
[4] I Samuel  23:24-26.         [8] Song of Solomon 1:14.

impressions given by Jerome and Eusebius, one would gather that En-gedi was a gracious, far-famed oasis. It takes imagination today, however, to see exuberant beauty there. One comes down the western shore of the Dead Sea and a few hours from the northern end beaches his boat where once the famous gardens grew. A few acres are watered by copious springs, and in comparison with the saline, sterile environs of the seacoast they do blossom verdantly. A few sidr trees, some apples of Sodom,—the modern osher,—little groups of acacia, a sprinkling of broom bushes, a few thin patches of grain, some parched and withered vegetables, and a half dozen ponds with reed and cane—such is the sight which presents itself. There was even a threshing-floor and we saw the grain dumped on it from the laden donkeys. But it looked like pitiful subsistence for the half-starved Arabs who count this spot their choice possession—the one watered, fruitful place which they can call their own.

Climb the mountain that ranges up from the coastal plain and you come into full view of that wild and arid "wilderness of En-gedi" where Saul with three thousand men hunted David "upon the rocks of the wild goats." [1] There, on the crest of the crag, is a lovely spring hole fed by two fountains and shaded by a spreading sidr tree. As we sat there, fatigued by the hard, hot climb, listening to the sound of running waters as the spring's over-flow rushed down the mountain to bring fertility below, David came in upon us. He was a handsome, strapping,

[1] I Samuel 24:1-2.

youthful Arab, armed to the teeth, who that day had crossed the wilderness from Bethlehem through the torrid wadies among whose caverns Saul had pressed his man-hunt. Our Arab told us that all day long he had seen no spring, nor knew of any, although it was through his own territory he was traveling. There was only this clear spring hole on the crest of En-gedi, toward which all day his thirst had turned. This spring has flowed for unknown centuries. A ruined crusader mill, once turned by its rushing waters, still stands a few rods off. As far back as En-gedi was beautiful, which is as far as the records go, this spring must have flowed. One may be sure, I should suppose, that David went there to drink. To identify the cave where he could have slain Saul and would not [1] is impossible; this wilderness is full of caverns, which even during the last century were the haunts of bandits. But the spring is there, and I never shall think of David the fugitive again without reseeing that picturesque and sturdy Arab youth who came in from the wilderness and laid aside his arms to drink and bathe with us in the fountain of En-gedi.

## IV

It was in Hebron that David first was king. The visitor goes there now, some twenty miles south of Jerusalem, thinking chiefly of the older days of the patriarchs. There Abraham bought from the Hittite the cave of Machpelah to bury his family in, and the

---

[1] I Samuel 24:1-7.

story of the bargain still remains the most charming description of Oriental bartering that ever has been written.[1] The traditional cave of Machpelah today is a Moslem shrine covered with a mosque whose huge foundation stones carry the memory back to the building of Herod the Great. Only since the British occupation has the ordinary non-Moslem visitor been allowed within it. The Prince of Wales and a few privileged ambassadors had been admitted, but no others. Now, however, one who carries a letter from the Grand Mufti in Jerusalem will find a hospitable welcome. Locked in the subterranean caves, the reputed tombs of Abraham, Isaac, Jacob, and their wives Sarah, Rebekah, Leah, still constitute one of Islam's most sacred shrines, and in the mosque above, around cenotaphs covered with rich tapestries, endless pilgrims pray.

But no one enters the cave of Machpelah itself. The last known entrance was by awestruck crusaders, who walled up their place of invasion and clamped it with iron bands still to be seen. To be sure, a colonel in the British service, at a critical moment in the last war when Hebron just had been evacuated by the Turks, was sent to seek some responsible persons with whom the conquerors could deal, and, searching through the mosque, he reports coming upon a secret door, going down an inclined plane, and entering the great cave below the sanctuary. When, however, he came back later, having discovered the importance of what had befallen him, he could find no door at all where he

[1] Genesis 23:3-20.

thought one ought to be. In any case, the only communication with the sacred cave which the visitor knows now is the carefully capped opening beside which sit scribes who for a consideration write prayers to Father Abraham and drop them down into his presence. For five piasters my prayer for a safe journey and a happy return was sped into his sepulcher and then I was hurried away to see Mohammed's footprint in the solid rock.

It was David, however, who most of all drew me to Hebron. When Saul fell at Gilboa, far in the north, David left the wilderness, was made king in Hebron and reigned there seven and a half years [1] before he overthrew Saul's lingering dynasty, consolidated his kingdom, seized Jerusalem, and put his capital there. The memorials of David here are very slight, but they at least are genuine. "Writ in water" is a metaphor for transiency in all our Western world, but in Palestine it could stand for permanence. The surest memorials in the Holy Land are writ in water, from the Sea of Galilee or the fords of Jordan to the well at Sychar. Here, too, in Hebron, David's memory is kept by two places where water flows, and it is characteristic of his stern career that both memories are of bloody deeds. Just outside the city is still the well of Sirah, from which, to David's deep regret, Saul's old general Abner was called back to be stabbed by Joab at the city's gate. [2] And beside the great pool of Hebron, still one of the noblest in the

[1] II Samuel 2:11; I Kings 2:11; I Chronicles 29:27.
[2] II Samuel 3:26-27.

land, David executed the murderers of his rival, Saul's
son Ish-bosheth.[1]

Such was the rugged training, made very vivid when
one follows it in this rugged country, by which the
shepherd lad from Bethlehem, now become sheik at
Hebron, was prepared for his amazing place in history.

At last the hour struck, and with the Philistines fairly
at his mercy he started north from Hebron with thirty
thousand men to take Jerusalem and make it the city
of David.

## V

If one would get at the real Jerusalem as it was at
first, one must leave the present city altogether. Let
him go out Saint Stephen's gate and, turning from the
road into the valley of the Kidron, walk down the deep
wady, in ancient times much deeper still, from which
the eastern walls of the temple area rise sheer. Soon
he will have left the walls altogether and will be skirting the bottom of the hill Ophel until he reaches one
of the most interesting places in the world, the so-called
Virgin's Fountain, which in the Bible is known as
Gihon. I suppose that of all the travelers who come to
Jerusalem only a few ever come here, and that of these
not many are stirred by what they see. Yet this fountain is the origin of Jerusalem. Without this fountain
no city ever would have been here, and around the fountain and because of it the most impressive portion of
mankind's spiritual drama has been played upon these
hills.

[1] II Samuel 4:8-12.

The water still is flowing copiously, a plentiful, unfailing though intermittent spring, the only considerable fountain close to Jerusalem.  Still the Arab women in an almost constant stream come with their empty receptacles and return picturesquely carrying them high perched upon their heads.  The old home-made clay jars unfortunately have almost vanished and the omnipresent Standard Oil tins take their place.  The Jebusite city which David came to seize was built upon the steep hill above this fountain.  From within the city a shaft ran down into the pool—its relics still are there—so that even when the walls were close beleaguered the besieged could taunt their enemies from their lofty citadel. "You will never get in here," cried the Jebusites to David; "blind men and cripples could drive you off!" [1]

The importance of this fountain to Jerusalem was conspicuously manifest three centuries later, in the days of Hezekiah, when Sennacherib, king of Assyria, swooped down upon the city.  Always the main problem of Jerusalem's besiegers has been water.  The city stands upon a rude and desiccated ridge with the very desert creeping close up on one side and without river, brook, or copious fountain on the other.  To this fact may be attributed the elaborate preparation of aqueducts and cisterns within the city, whose huge vestiges impress the traveler yet, and to this fact may also be ascribed the brevity and ill success of many a siege.

When, then, Sennacherib was on his way, ransacking Judah, as he tells us in his inscriptions, until he took

[1] II Samuel 5:6 M.

forty-six of Hezekiah's walled towns and shut the king himself "like a caged bird in Jerusalem, his capital city," the king and people, though terrified at this greatest peril that ever had befallen Zion, nevertheless thought in time about water and how the lack of it would cripple the Assyrians. Why leave Gihon for Sennacherib to drink? Hezekiah, therefore, dug one of the most interesting emergency tunnels known to history. He carried the fountain of Gihon 1750 feet through the solid rock of Ophel; he brought it out upon the other side into the broad pool of Siloam within the city's walls, and he covered the outer entrance to the spring so that the Assyrians could not find it.

You may read the record in the Bible [1] but it is even more interesting to climb through the tunnel itself and see with your own eyes. We started from the inner end at the pool of Siloam and waded through to Gihon. Every step of the tunnel bears evidence that it was indeed dug in an emergency. The work is rough and uneven, the walls rudely shaped, and the tunnel itself of unequal width and height. At times there was ample space above our heads; at times we crouched with our faces almost in the water. Again and again in digging it the workmen ran off their course and left behind, as evidence, rough culs-de-sac from which they had to retreat and start again. The straight line from Gihon to Siloam through the rock would have been 1090 feet. They took 1750 feet for their tunnel, bending far round in their course, perhaps of a purpose to avoid some holy

[1] II Kings 20:20 and II Chronicles 32:1-4.

spot, perhaps because, without compass, they missed their way. That the boring was done from both ends is evident; one can see plainly still the rough, uneven juncture where the workmen brought their two shafts together, not troubling to disguise the unequal levels of their walls and ceiling. Perhaps that very day Senna-cherib was coming up over Scopus to thunder at their gates.

In our party was my friend, Mr. Jacob Spafford, born and reared in Jerusalem, who forty-five years before had been one of a group of adventurous boys that among the first of modern folk explored the tunnel. It was a similar group of boys that discovered the famous inscription of the original builders. I saw it later in the Imperial Museum at Constantinople. It is by far the most notable inscription of the Jews yet found in Palestine. Far on in the tunnel itself we saw the cut in the rock wall from which it had been taken. This is a translation of it:

The boring through [is completed]. And this is the story of the boring through: while yet [they plied] the drill, each toward his fellow, and while yet there were three cubits to be bored through, there was heard the voice of one calling unto another, for there was a crevice in the rock on the right hand. And on the day of the boring through the stone-cutters struck, each to meet his fellow, drill upon drill; and the waters flowed from the source to the pool for a thousand and two hundred cubits, and a hundred cubits was the height of the rock above the heads of the stone-cutters.

Through this ancient tunnel we crowded our way, knee-deep in water, and came at last to Gihon. There, three hundred years before the tunnel's boring, David had pressed his siege around that spring.  In the old rendering of the Hebrew text, now seriously—and, I doubt not, rightly—questioned, it was through this pool of Gihon and up the inner shaft into the city that David's men climbed and so seized the citadel.[1]  At any rate, he captured the stronghold and made it Davidsburg.

Let one come up from the pool beneath Ophel to the crest of Ophel itself and he will find little to remind him of so significant a history.  One must understand this spot, not by sight but by insight.  A few poor Arab houses now are here and the ground is tumbled by the spades of excavators looking in vain for the lost tombs of the kings of Israel.  One, however, can rebuild in imagination the old Jebusite city whose future was to be so incredibly important to the world.  It was a tiny town, approximately 4250 feet around its outer walls, but its hill rose steep on three sides, and on the north ran up into a sharp ridge defended by a tower.  The archeologists have helped us all they could to make the story vivid.  They have but lately uncovered some ancient bases of the city's wall and they say that very probably the lower strata are from the fortifications of the Jebusites.

Here David lived and reigned.  From here he delivered his final, smashing blows on the Philistines.  From this perch he looked out across the world and, seeing Egypt and Assyria feeble, pushed his borders out until from Damascus, which held his garrisons, to the border

[1] II Samuel 5:8.

of Egypt he was king.  Here he brutally sinned,[1] and here he reared a tabernacle for Jehovah and brought up the holy Ark from Kiriath-jearim to put within it. When his own son Absalom rebelled against him it was from Ophel that he went down into the Kidron valley, climbed the ascent of the Mount of Olives on the other side, and struck off in flight across the wilderness of Judea, while Shimei, of the old clan of Saul, followed cursing him, "Begone, begone, you bloody rascal!" [2] And when, once more, the old warrior was in the ascendent and Absalom was defeated and killed,[3] up through the wilderness toward Olivet, where long afterward a greater than he came to Zion, he returned to Ophel to grow old and die.

When, at last, around his death-bed a palace conspiracy was afoot to crown Adonijah instead of Solomon, David was successfully beforehand.  He sent his bodyguard with Solomon down to the sacred fountain Gihon; there Solomon was crowned and then brought up into the city to sit upon the throne.[4]  One recalls it as one stands amid the Arab women coming still with their water jars to Gihon—this pool witnessed Solomon's coronation.

## VI

I do not see how one can stand on Ophel revisualizing the reign of that amazing shepherd king, around whose name such endless legends since have gathered, without

[1] II Samuel Ch. 11.
[2] II Samuel 16:5-7 M.
[3] II Samuel 18:6-15.
[4] I Kings 1:5-40.

trying to estimate his character. If one start with any humane, modern standard, there is excuse enough for Shimei's judgment on him, a "bloody rascal." The record of his pitiless procedures stands plain in Scripture: "When David conquered a country he left neither men nor women alive";[1] "David never left a man or woman alive . . . 'in case,' he thought, 'they may betray us' ";[2] "When he defeated Moab, he arranged the natives in lines, making them lie down on the ground; two lines of them were put to death, and one line spared alive." [3] I went out one day to 'Amman, the ancient city of the Ammonites, and recalled the time long gone when David's forces under Joab besieged that town and by David's order Uriah, one of his most faithful servants, was sent up under the walls that he might be slain, and his wife, Bath-sheba, become David's. There are black records against this ruthless, passionate, bloody man.

There was in David, however, another side, a dashing chivalry, a spontaneous generosity so engaging that he has charmed the interest and admiration of many centuries. Saul hated him, pursued him, sought his life, yet twice when he could have slain Saul with a stroke he would not take vengeance.[4] With Saul's son, according to Eastern standards, he should have been at feud, but, instead, he plighted with Jonathan one of history's most famous friendships.[5] Saul's family strove to continue the old dynasty and Ish-bosheth was David's

[1] I Samuel 27:9 M.      [3] II Samuel 8:2 M.
[2] I Samuel 27:11 M.     [4] I Samuel 24:1-7 and 26:7-12.
[5] I Samuel 18:1-4 and 20:16-17, 41-42, etc.

rival for the kingship; yet when Ish-bosheth's servants slew him and brought the severed head to Hebron, David's wrath was murderous: "By the life of the Eternal, who has rescued me from every strait!—when a man told me, 'Saul is dead!' supposing he had brought good news, I seized him and killed him at Ziklag; that was the reward I gave him for his good news! And now, when scoundrels have murdered an honest man in bed within his own house, how much more shall I requite you murderers and wipe you off the earth?" [1] Even when Shimei cursed him he refused vengeance: "Let him alone! let him curse away! The Eternal has told him to!" [2] Of all faithless, abominable sons, David's son Absalom might well be thought the chief, yet when he fell, seeking his father's life and throne, David's heart broke in unforgetable lamentation: "O my son Absalom, my son, my son Absalom! would I had died for thee, O Absalom, my son, my son!" [3] To know how he bound men to him in deathless devotion, read the story of three men who, hearing him express a wish for a drink from Bethlehem's well, broke through the Philistine ranks at night and walked twenty-four miles to Bethlehem and back to bring it to him. [4] Strange combination David was of virtues and vices— loyal and lecherous, magnanimous and murderous—but his vices were the common traits of his bloody time; in his virtues he often anticipated the future.

He was a true prototype of Saint Louis of France, a

---

[1] II Samuel 4:9-11 M.
[2] II Samuel 16:11 M.
[3] II Samuel 18:33.
[4] II Samuel 23:13-17.

pious, loyal, generous, blood-thirsty crusader who left
his record all up and down the coast of Palestine as he
strove to stem the Saracens.   According to his generation's standards, Saint Louis was a saint indeed, lovable
and valiant, but that did not keep him from slaughter-
ous deeds, whether in war or out of it.   He counted
slaying Moslems one of the chief works of God's children.   Even casual heretics were fair targets for any
handy weapon.   "A layman, when he hears the Christian law mis-said," exclaimed Saint Louis, "should not
defend the Christian law, unless it be with his sword,
and with that he should pierce the mis-sayer in the mid-
riff, so far as the sword will enter."

That kind of saint David was also, and one who has
lived through the murderous spectacle of all Christendom at war may plausibly wonder whether we have
yet outgrown his vices or achieved his virtues.   He, like
many a modern man, had a strangely jumbled ethical
judgment.   He still is credited, even in our Bible, with
two kinds of song:

> Jehovah is my shepherd; I shall not want [1]

and

> I chase my foes and kill them,
> I never turn till they are killed,
> I kill them, felling them till they cannot rise;
> they fall down at my feet. [2]

## VII

One  thing  which  David  did  before  he  died  was

[1] Psalm 23:1.          [2] II Samuel 22:38-39 M.

fraught with such consequence as the wildest dreamer
could not have guessed: he bought the threshing-floor
of Araunah. It still is there and every visitor to Jerusalem goes out to see it. Nearly three thousand years
have passed since David bought it, and this old wind-
swept rock where Araunah the Jebusite once separated
wheat from chaff is today one of the most sacred spots
on earth to three religions. More marvelous than all
the marvels that are shown the visitor by credulous or
venal guides who point out here the place where
Gabriel's hand dented a rock, or there the hole where
the souls of the dead gather weekly to worship Allah,
is this central marvel of the ancient threshing-floor
become the world's most holy shrine.

"Go up and erect an altar to the Eternal at the threshing-floor of Araunah the Jebusite," [1] said Gad, the prophet, to King David when a pestilence was destroying
the people. The order represents exactly the lie of the
land: David went up—up from his city on the hill of
Ophel, along the sharp ridge to the eminence where
no city yet had been but where, near a great flat rock
with a natural cave beneath it for a granary, Araunah
threshed his wheat. Today one must sweep away in
his imagination the huge walls of the temple area that
Herod the Great built, and see the rough rock of the
hill reaching its apex in Araunah's windy height.

Of course, that rock today is enclosed in a building,
and since that was inevitable one must be thankful that
it is so gloriously beautiful a temple as the Mosque of

[1] II Samuel 24:18 M.

Omar. Of all public places in Jerusalem it seems to me most worshipful. Chaste and lovely, its mosaics mellowed by time, its stained glass glorious, its proportions filling the eye with satisfaction, its atmosphere subdued and reverential, its memories unparalleled—it is a natural place for prayer. No wonder the ignorant crusaders took it to be Solomon's temple and carried back the plans of it to be rehearsed with variations in more than one Western church. Not least among our reasons for gratitude is the fact that when, at the close of the seventh century A.D., Abd el-Melek built it, he left uncovered and unspoiled in the center, surrounded only by a balustrade, the great rock of Araunah's threshing-floor and the sacred cave beneath.

Let us stand there now and in review recall the amazing story of this unique spot. Here David built an altar and made of it a sacred high place. Here, after him, Solomon built his famous temple to the westward and on this rock in front of it reared his altar of burnt-sacrifice. You can see yet the channels graven to draw off the blood through artificial orifices into the cave beneath. Not a stone of Solomon's temple has been left that can be recognized—only this ancient, sacred rock on which the altar rested, and the cavern into which the blood of the sacrifices flowed. Nearly four centuries his temple stood, increasingly the center of the admiring love of Judah, and then was utterly wiped out when in 586 B.C. Nebuchadnezzar demolished the city. Here, two generations afterward, the returning exiles reared the second temple, so poor in comparison with the first that the aged, who could recall the earlier building, wept when they saw the new one being reared.[1]

Until 20 B.C. this temple of the exiles lasted and then Herod the Great, whose building operations one sees all over Palestine and as far off as Athens, crowned his energetic love of gorgeous edifices with a new temple in Jerusalem. He enlarged the temple area, built up the great, new platform with splendid walls still standing, and when all was ready, one thousand specially trained priests in eighteen months put up the temple proper. Not a stone of it remains that can be recognized except one in the Imperial Museum at Constantinople: a sign warning all Gentiles on pain of death not to enter the temple's inner court. I read it with curious awe. It is the only piece of writing in the world which we may be sure that Jesus read. For in this temple of Herod Jesus and the doctors talked when he was twelve years old;[2] from its courts he drove the money-changers when he was a man;[3] and beside this rock he stood where our feet stand, and watched the evening sacrifice upon the altar.

The prophecy in Matthew's Gospel, however, that not one stone should be left upon another[4] was soon fulfilled. When, after Titus' destruction of the temple in 70 A.D., a fresh Jewish rebellion brought Hadrian down upon the city in tremendous rage in 134, the town was razed, the name Jerusalem outlawed and Ælia

[1] Ezra 3:12; Haggai 2:3.
[2] Luke 2:41-50.
[3] Mark 11:15.
[4] Matthew 24:1-2.

Capitolina substituted. All Jews were forbidden to come near the site, and on the spot where for centuries Jehovah had been worshiped rose a Roman temple to Jupiter.

The earliest Christian pilgrims whose records we possess saw that pagan temple here; and then the darkness falls and we know little of the site for centuries. When Helena, mother of Constantine the Great, came here to find the holy relics, her interest was not to discover where the Jewish temple stood, but where Christ had died and risen again. Her name is associated with the Church of the Holy Sepulcher, not with the Dome of the Rock. That there were buildings of Justinian's upon the temple area is clear, but just what they were we cannot tell. Early in the fourth century the Jews were allowed once a year to weep here for their ruined city and when the Moslems came under Caliph Omar they found the holy place covered with rubbish which the Christians had thrown here to spite these Jews.

It was the Moslems who redeemed the site, made it their most sacred shrine next to Mecca, created a tradition that Mohammed himself had prayed here, and built over the ancient cavern their beautiful mosque. And if it is the Moslems who redeemed the site, it is the Christians who were guilty of one of its worst profanations. Let another writer, who knows Palestine as well as any man alive, say what he thinks of the crusades: "that extraordinary series of piratical invasions, commonly called the Crusades, by which Palestine was harried for about a hundred years, and the undying tradition of which will retard indefinitely the final triumph of Christianity over the Arab race." As for what these first crusaders did in this temple area we are left to no second-hand account. An eye-witness has described it, and those who think ancient David bloody, who are horrified at what Nebuchadnezzar and Hadrian, the pagans, did here, should read his words: "In Solomon's Porch and in the temple our men rode in the vile blood of the Saracens up to the knees of their horses." So fell Jerusalem from Moslem into Christian hands in 1099, and, after the slaughter, so we are told, with sobs of joy the crusaders went down to the Church of the Holy Sepulcher and prayed.

It took but a few years to put the city back into Moslem hands and send the crusaders fleeing out of Palestine. Then succeeded the long, barren centuries of Saracen and Turkish rule, until Allenby came into the city and the new day began. But even today no Christian may enter the sacred place on a Friday, when the Moslems worship here. Still no orthodox Jew comes into it for fear he may walk above the sacred hiding place where he thinks the Ark is waiting, or tread, it may be, on the Holy of Holies itself. Still, after all these centuries, it is a holy shrine to the Moslem, a wistful memory to the Christian, and a desperate hope to the Jew. Did ever another threshing-floor have such a history?

I stood long in silence by this ancient rock and the place gave my imagination wings. I saw the one who walked these pavements nearly two thousand years ago, who called the temple here his Father's house, and from Olivet yonder looked down upon it while he prayed in agony the night before he died. Still his Gospel of good-will judges the world. Moslem or Christian or Jew must stand or fall as he practises good-will or lacks it. That standard which he set as the crux of the Eternal Judgment sifts men and nations yet and will sift them to the end. And as I looked, his figure faded into another which long before had labored here. I saw Araunah the Jebusite still separating the chaff from the wheat.

## CHAPTER VI

## FROM GILGAL TO GALILEE

### I

GILGAL was the first holy place at which the Hebrews worshiped when they had crossed Jordan;[1] Galilee was the home of Jesus. In space they are some sixty miles apart, but in the quality of religion which they represent they are infinitely distant from each other. Yet the religion which flowered out in Galilee can be traced back stage by stage to that primitive Bedouin faith which, entering Palestine for conquest, made the rude circle of stones at Gilgal its holy shrine.

That is what *Gilgal* means: a "circle of stones." It was the Palestinian Stonehenge. There Joshua worshiped, Saul was crowned king,[2] Samuel hewed Agag in pieces before the Lord.[3] There, four centuries after the conquest, Israelites still were sacrificing bullocks; and Amos and Hosea, with their loftier views of God and his worship, were protesting against the paganism of the shrine.[4] As late as the seventh century A.D., a traveler, Arculf, tells us that a church on the ancient site still enclosed the sacred stones. Only the bare name

---

[1] Joshua 4:19-24.          [3] I Samuel 15:33.
[2] I Samuel 11:15.
[4] Amos 4:4-5 and 5:5; Hosea 4:15; 9:15; and 12:11.

Jiljulieh now remains to mark the place, and of the other Gilgals in Palestine, three or four of which are mentioned in the Bible, nothing from antiquity is left. But the memories of what they stood for are strewed all over Palestine, so that I do not see how one can travel there without being reminded continually of the primitive beginnings of our faith, the far-off, unlikely origins from which the religion grew that in the Hebrew prophets and at last in Jesus had so consummate a fulfilment.

## II

For a vivid visualization of those early, crude beginnings one need not trust his imagination. One group of people, the Samaritans, have carried over into our day some of the most ancient religious customs in the world. If one would see the sacrifice of animals still performed with meticulous desire to fulfil the Law of Moses in its uttermost detail, one can do so by spending Passover with the Samaritans on Mount Gerizim. The night I spent there, as a guest of the high priest, was one of the most interesting and illuminating experiences of my pilgrimage. It carried the mind back across millenniums to the Israelites of Joshua's time and David's at their worship.

Come north with us, therefore, from Jerusalem, an hour's ride by automobile, to the base of Gerizim. There we must alight and either walk up the steep path to the summit or, if we are so minded, ride up on donkeyback. The crest is a noble, elevated plateau 2800

feet and more above the sea, with one of those comprehensive views over the length and breadth of Palestine
which make it always so dramatic and picturesque a
land.   Here at Passover time we shall find the whole
Samaritan community living in tents.   They move up
from their homes in Nablus, at the mountain's foot,
and for a week they celebrate out of doors the ancient
rite of the Passover.

Walk among these tents and consider the incredibly
strange things that this scene represents.   The Samaritans themselves have had a long, checkered history.
When the Assyrians ruined the northern kingdom in
the eighth century B.C., they settled Cuthites, Avvites,
Sepharvites and Hamathites—pagan folk from their own
domains—in the place of the exiled Israelites.   These
strangers brought their own gods with them, but,
straightway falling upon evil times, they blamed the
trouble, according to the religion of their generation,
on "the god of the land," whose proper worship they
did not know.   So a priest of Jehovah was sent to
instruct them in the Jewish ritual, that they might
appease his wrath.   "They feared Jehovah," says the
record, "and served their own gods." [1]  These folk inter-
married with the Israelitish remnants, and from this
mongrel race, with their hybrid religion, rose the Samaritans.   With the enthusiasm of converts they became the
most reactionary of all the tribes that worshiped
Jehovah.   They possess still some of the oldest manuscripts of the Mosaic Law in existence, and they claim

[1] II Kings 17:24-33.

that Moses alone is the true prophet of God and that all after him, beginning with Eli and Samuel, have been perverters of the people. With the return of the Judean exiles to Jerusalem, when the Samaritans were mercilessly snubbed by the Jews [1] and bitter hostility arose between them, the exclusiveness and conservatism of the Samaritans were accentuated.

Gerizim alone has been for centuries their holy mountain. Here they think Abraham would have offered Isaac; [2] here they are sure was Jacob's Bethel; [3] here, they read, Joshua pledged the invaders to Jehovah's service; and in their edition of the commandments another is added—to worship in Gerizim. When the woman of Samaria at the well of Sychar pointed to Mount Gerizim, saying to Jesus, "Our fathers worshiped in this mountain," [4] she was true to a tradition which went far back in history.

How the Jews hated the Samaritans the New Testament records. There were no dealings between the two, [5] says the Fourth Gospel, and when the Jews wished to speak spitefully of the Master they called him a Samaritan. [6] At last, however, common disaster fell upon these ancient foes. The Romans crashed down on Gerizim as they did on Zion, and on this mountaintop Vespasian massacred 11,600 devotees.

In these tents, on their ancient holy mountain, with the site of their former temple close at hand, the shriveled remnants of this ancient cult gather yearly to keep

[1] Ezra 4:1-3.
[2] Genesis 22:1-14.
[3] Genesis 28:10-22.
[4] John 4:20.
[5] John 4:9.
[6] John 8:48.

the Passover.    There are less than 150 of them now,
but faithfully they celebrate, by the old rite of animal
sacrifice, the flight from Egypt.  I had difficulty in believ-
ing all that my eyes saw: the British governor of
Jerusalem sitting on Mount Gerizim by moonlight while,
a few feet away, the Samaritan high priest in his cele-
brant robes performed the blood-sacrifice of seven lambs
according to the Mosaic ritual handed down from his
ancestor Aaron.

The ritual began at sunset.   About thirty miles away
the Mediterranean Sea shone clear on the horizon, and
as the sun went down, riding the water like a golden
galleon, forty-odd white-robed men, each with his prayer
rug before him, began their long preparatory prayers
before the Passover sacrifice.   A rough stone enclosure,
some fifty-four by twenty-one feet in size, was the scene
of the ritual.   Here with many genuflections, falling on
their knees and touching their foreheads to the ground,
and with much ceremonial stroking of the beard when
the Law of God was mentioned, these forty men chanted
their prayers.   Yet glorious as the setting was on that
historic mountain, with the full moon taking up the
task which the sun had just resigned, and impressive as
was the sense of immemorial antiquity flooding the rite
that was being celebrated, little solemnity attended the
scene.

The Samaritans themselves were in earnest, but scores
of Zionists from everywhere and Moslem youths from
Nablus were up to see the show.   They crowded the
stone walls around, fell off and clambered up again with

much chatter of tongue and crash of rock, while huck-
sters cried their edibles and drinks, and in general the
atmosphere of a country fair pervaded the scene. Even
a tent full of constabulary with British officers was in
the offing, lest a previous year's violent disorders should
be repeated. Nevertheless, one could not escape the
impressive fact that he was in the presence of the last
blood-sacrifice left from the Jewish religion for modern
eyes to see.

How very crude and carnal it all seemed—the loud
bawling of the prayers, the smoking trench altar built,
according to Mosaic orders,[1] of earth and uncut stone,
the three slaughterers with glistening knives waiting for
their cue, the seven lambs wandering about the enclosure
in innocent unawareness of their fate. Then the moment
for action came when the worshipers, with stimulated
exultation accentuating the word "slay" with the full
volume of their voices, read in the ritual, "Then shall
all the convocation of the assembly of Israel slay it."
Like lightning each of the slayers cut one lamb's throat
and leaped to another until the seven lay in their last
convulsions on the ground beside the altar. To be
quite candid, the ritual was of the sort which we seclude
in butcher shops. It left the white robes of the priests
red with blood and, save as a reminiscence of antiquity,
had nothing to recommend it to modern liking or
respect. The wool of the lambs was plucked, the car-
casses were trussed up and carefully cleaned according
to ancient usage, until at last the seven lambs on seven

[1] Exodus 20:24-25.

poles were carried off to be thrust into the earth oven where, for hours, a roaring fire had been blazing in expectation of their coming.

While the sacrificed lambs were cooking, the community might do as it would till midnight. As guests of the high priest we sat in his tent and through a skilled interpreter talked with the venerable old man about his religion. His complacency, his sense of superiority, his certainty that these few Samaritans alone among men knew the truth about God and practised it, were fascinating. The millions around him, he said, were forgetting the divine Law; only his little group of despised people were keeping it. He nestled comfortably into that conviction. From every point of view, he said, the Samaritan religion alone was perfect. Could Jews or Christians divide their edition of the ten commandments into two tables so that the same number of words and letters would be on each? Never! The Samaritans, however, could with their edition. That seemed to him positively to prove the perfection of his faith. He had visited, so he told us, London, Paris, Constantinople, and always had tried with open mind to welcome new truth, but he had come back to Gerizim certain that no religion was so flawless as the Samaritan. All others were simply more or less pleasing superstructures, he declared; only the Samaritans had solid foundations in the Mosaic Law. So the old man, venerable of aspect, amiable in spirit, talked on into the night, as archaic as the blood-sacrifice he had just administered.

The Passover was eaten at midnight.  As the hour drew near, the community gathered restlessly around the smoking pit from which the cooked lambs were being drawn.  Swiftly dismembered and distributed into seven large pans, the sacrificial animals were carried down into the enclosure about the trench altar.  Then the eating hastily began—a hurried, eager swallowing of the meat to represent the anxious, hasty meal in Egypt on that night long past when the people fled from Pharaoh.  The groups of men, women, and children crouched around the pans, thrust in their fingers, snatched their morsels.  It was a rapid, noisy meal with two regulations observed for ceremonial completeness; no non-Samaritan might touch a mouthful and no remnants of the lambs might be left unburnt.  We saw it finished—the sacrifice completed, the shreds consumed, each tent marked with holy blood sprinkled from hyssop, each baby's lips touched with a morsel from the sacred meal—and then we retired to our uneasy slumber on the floor of the high priest's tent.

We rose the next morning to see sunrise from the upper crest of Gerizim, where once the Samaritan temple stood.  The great rock of sacrifice where the altar rested still is there.  To the north Mount Hermon's snowy summit grew pink with the dawn; to the south the mountains of Judah one by one came out from the twilight; to the west the Mediterranean waited for the light; and eastward the sun came grandly up over the plateau of Moab.  None of these things, however, moved us so deeply as a sight in the valley far below.

There, in plain view, was Jacob's well. There the Master and the woman of Samaria had discussed the competing claims of Gerizim and Jerusalem, and the Master had overpassed them both. Yet so persistent are religious convictions, right or wrong, that a dwindling, degenerate community still is contending for Gerizim against the world. They are our contemporary ancestors in religion. In bloody sacrifices such as this our Jewish-Christian heritage began. Into mental molds represented by such rituals of shed and sprinkled blood some of our earliest Christian theology was run. On that ancient mountain we had seen one of the early origins of our faith.

## IV

One keeps seeing these origins everywhere, alike in Palestine and in the desert. The Arabs of the desert are true Semites still. In mental outlook, as in blood, they are descendants of that ancient stock from which the Palestinian races—Amorites, Canaanites and Israelites—were born. Assyrians, Babylonians, and probably Egyptians were Semites, too, so that the Hebrews themselves and all the people whose cultures influentially impinged upon them, saving the Philistines, were of Semitic stock.

Numberless new and powerful forces have played upon the scattered branches of this ancient race, but one spot has been isolated from modernity—the desert. That cradle of the Semitic people still retains its ancient life and thought. Only a few years ago a sheik's bride from the Adwan Arabs visited the American Colony in Jerusalem. She had never seen a flight of stairs. She was terrified at the prospect of ascending them. At last she crawled up on hands and knees and was miserable with fear until she was taken down again. So unaffected by the events of centuries has the desert been! There, today, with amazing perseverance, old Semitic ways of thinking still persist, and even a casual traveler, if he have eyes and ears, can gain a fresh impression of attitudes and ideas which lie at the source of our Hebrew-Christian faith.

Much nonsense has been talked about the desert as the place where monotheism developed originally and where it naturally belongs. As a matter of fact, monotheism developed among the city-dwelling Greeks before it was known in the desert. It took Mohammed to make the Arabs monotheistic, and even yet their practical, working religion is largely fear of evil spirits and reliance on the power of special saints and holy places. The gods of the Arab today, as of old, are localized, and he goes on pilgrimages to their shrines.

We saw sacred trees, for example, from Sinai to Esdraelon. One often reads about them in the Bible— "the sacred oak of Shechem," [1] or "the oaks of Mamre," [2] and after all these centuries the Arabs, whether of the desert or the village, think this terebinth, or that acacia, or yonder shittah is the dwelling-place of superhuman powers. One sees the branches hung with bits of cloth as votive gifts to propitiate the spirits, and

---

[1] Genesis 35:4 M.          [2] Genesis 13:18 and 18:1.

watches the gestures of reverence—such as stroking the face—or the whispered word of prayer, as the people pass.   Once on the plain of Esdraelon we nearly lunched in the shadow of one and just in time moved out to less holy ground for our repast.

One reads in the Bible repeated passages about the "high places" where the people worshiped.[1]   They still are here, the ancient ones in ruins for the archeologists to excavate, but modern ones still in use where some Arab saint supposedly is buried and where local Moslems come to pray.   In the early days of the Hebrews every village had its high place, and from Petra, south of the Dead Sea, in ancient Edom, to Megiddo, on the edge of Esdraelon, they still are visible.   Petra is best preserved, with its great rock altar, but even at less obvious places, like Gibeon, we could discern the old libation cups, carved in the solid rock, on what was probably the great high place where Solomon offered a thousand burnt offerings and had his famous dream.[2]

As for sacred stones, such as the circle at Gilgal, Semitic worship was organized around them.   At the high place of Gezer, when it was uncovered a few years ago, the row of huge monoliths still was standing where of olden time the Hebrews worshiped.   One of the most persistent elements in the religion of the people, against which the prophets long fought in vain, was the sacredness of these symbolic stones, anointed by the

[1] II Kings 17:9-11 and 23:8; Ezekiel 6:6, etc.
[2] I Kings 3:4-15.

early worshipers with blood or stroked with oil. Down to the time of Hosea, Jehovah was so worshiped in Israel, and the reform under Josiah [1] had to destroy these sacred emblems of Deity [2] on the high places of Judah.

As for such an aberration as the golden calf, under the form of which the rebellious people worshiped Deity at Sinai [3] and, at Dan and Bethel, even symbolized Jehovah,[4] that probably came from Egypt. The sacred cow can be seen in image or inscription yet in many an Egyptian temple. While, however, I knew this and knew also that clay images of sacred cows were still being exhumed in Palestine, it was exciting to see a golden calf. They found one this past year near Gaza. Workmen chanced upon an Egyptian tomb, dating some fourteen centuries before Christ, and in it was a calf, the image of the dead man's god, whose perfectly preserved hoofs and badly battered, gold-leaf body we saw in Jerusalem. One who would truly picture these Hebrews, therefore, as they swept in on Palestine, must imagine primitive folk from whom no observer could have guessed such a development as actually has come. Not until centuries after were they monotheists. They believed in Jehovah as an army at war might believe in their general. Other gods were real but theirs was the strongest. So the Hebrews, as they attacked Palestine, swore allegiance to their deity among many gods, and cried:

[1] II Kings 23:1-25.
[2] Genesis 28:22; Hosea 3:4; Deuteronomy 7:4-5.
[3] Exodus 32:1-6.          [4] I Kings 12:28-29.

Jehovah is a man of war:
Jehovah is his name.

. . . . . . . . . . . . . . . .
Who is like unto thee, O Jehovah, among the gods? [1]

Moreover, when they seized the Promised Land they
worshiped Jehovah in all the primitive ways the desert
knew and in many new ways assimilated from the Canaanites. With their local high places, their sacred trees,
fountains, and rocks, their circles and rows of holy
monoliths, their bloody sacrifices, they were the children of their age. At the beginning one cannot distinguish them from Moabites or Edomites. Why should
so unique a consequence have come from them? That
is the marvel of their history.

## V

To be sure, they did bring from the desert with them,
like all their race, a fierce religiousness. One who lives
in the desert for only a little while can see why. Those
immense, intolerable bad lands, with their heat by day,
their cold by night, their thirst and their starvation, are
so imperious in what they do to men and allow so little
that men can do for themselves, that they beget a profound sense of dependence on superhuman powers. The
Arab ascribes everything to God. One is so utterly at
the mercy of powers not his own that, as between what
God does and what man can do, man's effort is nothing
and God's is everything. It either rains or it does not;
either the cool wind comes from the sea or one swelters

[1] Exodus 15:3,11.

in the heat; either the slender forage for the camels grows or it withers. What can man do? Our Western civilization is vividly conscious of man's mastery over nature; the desert-dweller is even more vividly conscious of his utter dependence on fate. The desert is the best place on earth in which to be a Calvinist. There free will is at the ebb and predestination fits the very landscape. So natural is fatalism to the desert that Mohammed's gospel ran through Arabia like the wind, and *Islam,* which means "submission," was the name of it.

The Arab, therefore, today as always, lives and moves and has his being among superhuman powers of which he stands in fear or on which he relies. Nothing is too difficult for him to believe; miracles are every-day occurrences. A group of my friends, on serenade, stopped under a sacred tree to make preparations for their music but, discovering where they were, moved off to another place to practise. Before an hour had passed the simple event had become a miracle; one Arab was telling another that under the sacred tree they had tried in vain, with all their might, to coax a single tone from their instruments, while elsewhere they could play with ease. A recent traveler to Sinai in winter passed through a slight snowstorm, which to some fellahin from Egypt who were with him was utterly unprecedented. "What is it, master?" they cried, and one of them gave answer: "The Lord is sending us rice from heaven." The traveler is probably right in thinking that the story so interpreted will be retold for years, perhaps for cen-

turies.   Passing a sacred tomb, we ourselves heard the
camel-boys talking about the miracles performed there.
The last one particularly impressed them:  a thief, trying to steal from an Arab worshiper, found his arm
stiffened and palsied so that he could not carry his
booty away.

One lives here in the atmosphere of the Arabian
Nights.  The world of normal regularity and scientific
law grows dim and the mind is transported back to
prescientific days, when anything could happen and
everything that did happen was immediately ascribed
to God.  I showed an Arab sheik an ingenious clasp
on a hand-bag.  His exclamation was entirely characteristic:   "How wonderful is God!"

One feels afresh how far from the real issue our
Western literalism is when it takes from an ancient
Semitic literature wonder-tales about the sun and moon
standing still, or creation-stories about the making of
the world in six days, or narratives of marvel and magic
of any kind, and tries to pound and press them into
scientific fact.  Science is the one thing of all others that
such stories most certainly are not.  Indeed, science, as
we understand it, is the one thing of which the Arab
yet cannot see the first principles.

Ask the Arab his explanation of anything and you
are met, not with science, but with a charming, dramatic
story or a symbolic comparison.  "What is electricity?"
one Arab recently asked another.  "Suppose," was the
reply, "that you had an elongated dog, so long that

from his tail you could not see his head; yet if you stepped on his tail he would squeal at his head. Well, electricity is a long dog; it can stretch from Beirut to Damascus and yet when you press it in Beirut it is in Damascus that it squeals."

Is that science? Yet he would be a hardy soul who would say it was untrue. It is a most vivid and telling way of stating truth and now, as always, it is the method of the Semitic people. They never have had scientific or philosophic minds; they always have been dramatists and poets.

"The belief in miracle is always difficult: nowhere is it so difficult as on the traditional site," wrote Dr. John Kelman after a visit to Palestine. I should suppose that that would be the almost universal experience of travelers. It is hardest of all to believe that the desert suddenly yawned and swallowed up the men of Korah's household [1] when you are in the desert itself. It is easier at home to think that Christ walked on the Sea of Galilee [2] than when you yourself are on the sea. But the deeper difficulty in taking seriously a miracle-narrative involving the rupture of natural law lies, not alone in the physical setting of the land, but in the mental setting of the people. They think in terms of miracle yet. They see things that we see and when they narrate them afterward the events have become miraculous. One comes away sure that miracles are relative, that the difficulty with many of these old narratives is not so much in the basic event around which they started

[1] Numbers 16:30-33.          [2] Mark 6:47-50.

as in the immense difference between the Oriental and the modern Occidental mind.

At any rate, when one endeavors to picture the invading Hebrews, one sees that they must have been at an early stage of development, not only in their religion but in their world-view. Seven centuries after they raided Palestine, Herodotus, the Greek, seriously reported the story that in Egypt "the sun had four times risen out of his usual quarter, and that he had twice risen where he now sets, and twice set where he now rises." We need not, then, expect the Hebrews, massacring the citizens of Jericho with stone hatchets, to know anything more of astronomy, human history, or natural law than they knew about monotheism or humane morals.

## VI

Indeed, the endeavor to see clearly the manner of worship in which these religious progenitors of ours believed carries us farther down than we yet have gone. Come out from Jerusalem by the Jaffa gate on donkeyback some morning and ride through the valley of Hinnom. It is difficult to believe that we are here on the original site of the New Testament's hell, but such is the case. The word for hell in New Testament Greek is *Gehenna*—a transcription of the Hebrew "valley of Hinnom."

The idea of a future hell of fiery torment for the wicked goes a long way back in human thought. Dr. Breasted took me into a treasure chamber of the great museum in Cairo and on the coffin lid from an old Egyptian tomb pointed out the most ancient picture of hell in the world. It comes from at least four thousand years before Christ. One still can see the fiery red river and lake whose grim symbolism has come down across the millenniums to us.

When, however, the Hebrews took over this idea of a future perdition and between the Old and New Testaments developed it, they lit on one of their own valleys, running down the southwestern side of their own chief city, as the dreadful place whose name should signify hell. Nor is the reason difficult to understand; in the valley of Hinnom their fathers had practised human sacrifice.

I recall vividly the pleasant morning when we rode down amid the gardens and olive trees that now make the valley a gracious spot. It did not look infernal. It was inviting and fertile. But in imagination one could see the dire events that had cursed forever the valley's name. As late as the seventh century B.C. Jeremiah still could cry, "They have erected shrines to Topheth, in the valley belonging to Ben-Hinnom, for burning alive their sons and daughters—a thing that I never ordered, a thing that never entered my mind." [1] Repeatedly the record of that dreadful piece of primitive religion recurs in the Bible. [2] As we traveled down the valley on that April morning, picture after picture rose in memory: Jephthah slaying his daughter as a burnt-

[1] Jeremiah 7:31 M.
[2] II Kings 23:10; II Chronicles 33:6, etc.

offering to Jehovah;[1] Samuel hewing Agag in pieces
before the Lord;[2] the king of Moab sacrificing his
eldest son to gain the favor of his god Chemosh;[3] Ahaz
and Manasseh, kings of Judah, burning their sons alive
in sacrifice.[4]    Many thrilling sights the archeologist
uncovers for modern eyes to see, but some sad sights
too, and none sadder than the bones of babies buried
in ceremonial urns beside altars on which in all probability they, the first-born, had been sacrificed, or the
skeletons of sons and daughters slain and buried as an
offering under the cities' foundation stones.[5]

Here, then, in the valley of Hinnom, the later prophets saw the picture of hell.   Here, it is said, for centuries after the terrible business of human sacrifice was
over, the city's rubbish was perpetually aflame.   It took
a long time, however, a desperate struggle, and a unique
revelation of God and goodness to attain the height
of spiritual insight from which Hinnom seemed infernal.
I never appreciated that long, hard, upward climb from
Gilgal so much until I went to Palestine, for there one
walks still under sacred trees, over high places, beside
holy stones; there one sees the very spots where first-
born children once were burned to make God kind;
there one even stands on the site of the great temple
on Zion and remembers that once, as today in India,
prostitutes as well as priests were part of the sacred
staff.[6]

---

[1] Judges 11:30-40 M.
[2] I Samuel 15:33.
[3] II Kings 3:26-27.
[4] II Kings 16:2-3 and 21:1, 6.
[5] E.g. I Kings 16:34.
[6] II Kings 23:7 M; Hosea 4:14 M.

## VII

This is the gist of the whole matter: one could hardly pick a more unlikely folk than those Hebrews at Gilgal from whom to expect the supreme religious contribution of all history. When their later prophets looked back upon their early days and with deep humility confessed that there was no reason in themselves why God should have chosen them for their peculiar eminence, they saw the situation truly.

Even in religion seers from other nations were well abreast or far ahead of Israel in lighting on ideas that afterward Israel uniquely illuminated. The Greeks, in the person of Xenophanes, were asserting a pure monotheism about the time the Great Isaiah of the Exile was asserting it. As for the Egyptians, Ikhnaton struck out boldly for solar monotheism a century before Moses was born, and the ancient Book of the Dead anticipates even the Master's parable, when it sums up the requirements of the divine judgment: "I gave bread to the hungry, water to the thirsty, clothing to the naked, and a ferry to him who was without a boat." Yet neither Greece nor Egypt taught the world the loftiest truth about God and goodness. Nothing stranger or more incredible could be imagined in advance than that their successful competitors should be the Hebrews from Gilgal.

Neither the people themselves nor the environments that played most forcefully upon them contained any hint of such a consequence. One feels that fact keenly as he travels in their land. The ancient religious background of the Semitic race is thoroughly saturated with polytheism and, despite the vision of occasional sporadic seers, from the Euphrates to the Nile the Semites kept on being polytheists. Of their race only the Hebrews rose, centuries before Christ, into a tremendous doctrine of ethical monotheism.

Moreover, the Semitic people are intensely conservative. Yet the Hebrews achieved one of history's most radical revolutions against precedent and tradition, and by the eighth century B.C. their seers already had headed away from many gods, human sacrifices, bloody altars, blasting superstitions, toward the magnificent position of Micah: "What doth Jehovah require of thee, but to do justly, and to love kindness, and to walk humbly with thy God?" [1]

Moreover, the Hebrew people gave no promise in other realms of any special light or leading. When Thales in Greece, for the first time in history, was foretelling the date of a solar eclipse, that of 585 B.C., the Hebrews were explaining creation by childlike stories. When in the third century B.C. the Greeks, who had already seen that the earth is a sphere, by the use of variant shadows actually estimated its circumference, no Jewish writer had given any indication that the old Semitic cosmology of a flat earth and a bowl-like heaven had been overpassed. As in science, so in art; nothing original or inventive came from the ancient Hebrews. On religious principle they painted no pictures and

[1] Micah 6:8.

carved no statues; even Solomon's temple was built with the aid of workmen imported from Tyre, and Hezekiah's tunnel was as crooked and as full of false leads as only unskilled laborers could make it. Yet these people, without special excellence in other realms, rose to such heights of spiritual insight as have made them the ethical and religious teachers of a large part of humankind and have made the Scriptures that came from them and flowered out from the teaching of their Messiah far and away the noblest product of the spirit which we possess in history. That is the real miracle of Palestine. Quite apart from any special theological explanation, one of mankind's most astounding exploits was achieved here: a people in whom was no visible promise of such eminence did actually pass from Gilgal to Galilee.

# CHAPTER VII

## JOURNEYS TO THE PROPHETS' HOMES

### I

ONCE in Florence, Italy, a friend of mine enjoyed a unique and unforgetable experience. He was permitted to take from its treasured seclusion the original telescope of Galileo, and on a clear night he saw, through the very lens which Galileo used, the heavenly sights which Galileo, first of all mankind, had witnessed. The experience was awe-inspiring. He was seeing the moons of Jupiter and the rings of Saturn through the very telescope by means of which they first had been disclosed.

Some such experience in another realm awaits the patient and thoughtful traveler in Palestine. It was through the lens of this land that some of the sublimest spiritual disclosures of history were made. Here truths immeasurably influential on mankind were either seen first or seen best. Many of them have become commonplaces now—we are familiar with them from our infancy—but they take on fresh marvel and clothe themselves with new significance when we go back to Palestine itself and see them through the medium by which, in the first place, they were discovered.

This is particularly true in the understanding of the Hebrew prophets.  In that unique development from Gilgal to Galilee they were, so far as human instrumentalities are concerned, the chief performers.  It was they who brought monotheism out of polytheism, asserted righteous character to be the central attribute of the one God, purged his worship of superstition, and exalted personal and social goodness as the only acceptable service which man might render him.  They are the glory of Israel.  Without them the Hebrews would have been no better than the Moabites; with them the Hebrews have ranked with Greece and Rome as builders of the Western world.  And while it is their writings, not the ruined sites of their old towns, that best reveal and interpret them, no pilgrimage to their homes can fail to vivify and illumine the understanding of them.

## II

The prophetic movement in Israel runs far back into the nation's early days. . We catch dim glimpses of it in bands of Hebrew dervishes dancing and shouting to the accompaniment of "a psaltery, and a timbrel, and a pipe, and a harp," [1] even inducing trance states by their frenzy, so that once, when Saul fell under their influence, he lay naked all one day and night.[2]  These prophetic bands had headquarters at Ramah, Naioth, Bethel, Jericho, and Gilgal, and one reads of them—

---

[1] I Samuel 10:5.          [2] I Samuel 19:24.

fierce patriots and partisans of Jehovah—in the days of Samuel and Elisha.

They were a strange background and origin for the great prophetic figures that rose after them.  I thought I saw the modern left-overs of their spirit in the whirling dervishes in Cairo crying the name of God with such rhythmic iterations of sound and movement that they fell unconscious doing it.  One is even more reminded of the old prophetic bands when one sees the dancing troupes at a Moslem festival in Palestine, like Neby Musa, come up from the back country or the edges of the desert to Jerusalem.  They are fierce conservatives, terrific devotees of Allah against all his competitors, and they stir alike themselves and their hearers by their tireless, rhythmic dancing and their reiterated chants.  I never shall forget standing at Saint Stephen's gate and watching them whirl and stamp their way in toward the Mosque of Omar, singing repeatedly their defiance of the Zionists, who have come, they think, to seize their land: "O Zionists, what are you doing here?  What part have you with us?  If you stay here it will be for your burial!"  So of old the Hebrew prophetic bands danced and sang against the Philistines, against the Canaanites, against all that was new, strange, foreign, and hostile to Jehovah's supremacy, until at last the individual prophetic figures arose and launched one of the most influential reformations in man's history.

Elijah was the earliest titanic personality to emerge, and while he left no writing we know what he stood for and still can trace the setting of his activity in the landscape.   No one is sure where the brook Cherith [1] was, famous in Elijah's life history, except that it was on the east of Jordan.   But the traditional Cherith is the Wady el Kelt, which debouches from the western wilderness near Jericho.   Like many another piously identified site, it has been made as accessible as possible, even though moving it from the east to the west of Jordan was necessary.   Similarly, in Egypt, the site where Moses was taken from the bulrushes used to be uncomfortably far up the river from Cairo but recently has been moved down within easy reach of the tourist. False though the identification of the brook Cherith is, however, it does as well as any, since we do not know the true one, and we spent a Sunday there amid its weird desolation.   Out of some such wild and isolated spot, watered by a copious spring, it may be, as is the Wady el Kelt, and provisioned by "ravens,"—a miracle, say some; a folk-tale, say others; the totemistic name of a tribe of Arabs, say the rest,—Elijah used fearlessly to come to confront the king and queen with their sins or to defy the priests of Baal.   It was easier to imagine him after we had spent the day there in the wilderness —a rugged, gaunt, ascetic, austere man, emerging fearless of the face of mortal clay, moved by two passions only: a fierce passion for Jehovah against the Baals, and a stormy indignation against injustice and oppression.

It is about the plain of Esdraelon that one feels most vividly the presence of this portentous man.   Come to ancient Jezreel, where Ahab and Jezebel established one

[1] I  Kings  17:1-7.

of their royal residences, where Naboth was murdered that his vineyard might become the king's,[1] where Elijah faced Ahab down with towering wrath against the outrage, and where, at last, the dogs ate up the flesh of Jezebel as he had said.[2]   The general location, as so often happens, is plainly writ in water.   Here the fountain of Jezreel, now known as 'Ain Jalud, flows copiously still.   In its natural estate it poured out fifteen feet broad and two feet deep from the foot of Mount Gilboa, and today the Zionists, by channeling other springs into it, establishing a modern reservoir, and putting in a pumping station, have at once spoiled its beauty and increased its usefulness.   The poor, bedraggled Arab village of Zerin, less than two miles from the spring's first outpouring, probably represents in location the ancient site of Jezreel.

It is the water, however, which is the true remembrancer of this site's storied past.   This was the stream where Gideon tested out his men, rejecting those who knelt down to drink and choosing the three hundred who caught up water in their hands.   This stream reflected the gleam of Gideon's lamps that night when the covering pitchers suddenly were broken and the Midianites were thrown into a panic by the Hebrews' battle cry: "The sword of Jehovah and of Gideon." [3] This fountain was the rendezvous of the Israelites before the battle in which, on the rugged mountains just above, Saul and his sons fell.[4]   Here, too, grew Naboth's vine-

[1] I Kings 21:1-16.
[2] II Kings 9:30-37.
[3] Judges 7:20.
[4] I Samuel 29:1 and 31:1-6.

yard, watered by this copious spring, so that one can understand his stout refusal to accommodate even royalty by selling it: "Jehovah forbid it me, that I should give the inheritance of my fathers unto thee." [1]

Today the most interesting modern spot in the vicinity is a Zionist colony, the largest communistic group in Palestine. The members have come mostly from Russia and are thoroughly imbued with the socialistic doctrines which for years have been the refuge of the oppressed in that unhappy land. There were, at the time of our visit, four hundred and fifty workers, men and women, in the colony, and a hundred children. They hold all things in common; no private property is allowed; and while the charge of free love is unfounded they do bring up their children in communal nurseries and schools and not in families. Moreover, the nurseries and schools are admirable, with trained nurses and assistants in attendance, and with scientific methods quite amazing in the poor board shacks and temporary huts in which the colony has started. It is a brave, industrious, venturesome group of pioneers who here have struck in their roots beside these ancient waters, and it awakened strange meditations to see them harvesting grain with modern reapers on the very spot where once their ancestor thrashed the Midianites.

Even more stimulating to the imagination is the crude picture of Karl Marx which hangs at the head of their dining room. He, as it were, is the patron saint of these modern Jews from Russia. For the most part they have

[1] I Kings 21:3.

no other saint. They permit a synagogue service for the old people in the colony—"We do not interfere with them," said a young man, as though that attitude were very tolerant—but the youth and strength of the community are without any conscious religion whatever, save devotion to their social ideals. Karl Marx crowns their assembly hall and looks down upon them when they eat. He means to them a friend of the worker, a passionate protagonist of social justice, a hater of Czarist oppression and the cruelty of modern industrialism. Whatever we may think of his economic theories, his presence there is impressively suggestive. Karl Marx looking down on the site of Naboth's vineyard—how strange a coincidence! For he seems to be brooding still over the ancient, unsolved problem of social injustice which Elijah met there.

The height of Carmel, on which traditionally Elijah's great conflict with the priests of Baal took place,[1] lies some sixteen miles from Jezreel, and one cannot be on the spot without feeling, as in few places in Palestine, the impressive verisimilitude of the scene. Carmel was called the "holy headland" as far back as the inscriptions of Thutmose III, in the fifteenth century before Christ. Here, of old, was a sacred high place and to this day the Druses make pilgrimages and worship on the height. I vividly recall the day I climbed up the side slopes of Carmel from Esdraelon to a point of vantage from which the scene of Elijah's eventful tour de force was visible. There was Jezreel, from which the

[1] I Kings 18:19-40.

prophets and the priests of Baal, with throngs of people, came up to the ordeal on the holy hill. Yonder was the height on which the ancient altar of Jehovah had been cast down, which Elijah rebuilt.[1] In the valley was the brook Kishon with its many tributaries from the hills, to which Elijah brought the priests of Baal to slay them. Above the scene of sacrifice itself was the spur from which the servant of Elijah could see the Mediterranean and watch the cloud come up "as small as a man's hand."[2] And down toward Jezreel again, across the Kishon's course, which, when in flood, still swamps our modern motor cars, I saw Ahab fleeing in his chariot lest the rain should overtake him, while Elijah girded himself and traveled the sixteen miles faster than the lumbering chariot wheels could go.[3] The scene is one of those vivid landscapes into which the narrative of the Bible fits perfectly, and to have been there makes more luminously real the titanic figure of Elijah.

### III

Amos and Hosea were the first Hebrew prophets whose writings have come down to us, and, while we do not know where Hosea lived, the site of Amos' home at Tekoa and the principal scene of his ministry at Bethel can still be visited. Let the visitor take his imagination with him, however, for he will see two rock-strewn, barren heights on which, if Amos move again,

[1] I Kings 18:30.
[2] I Kings 18:44.
[3] I Kings 18:45-46.

it will be because the traveler has been gifted with the power of conjury. Nevertheless, the trip to Tekoa was a rememberable experience. We went by automobile to Bethlehem and then took donkeys some five miles to the abrupt and rugged height from which the wilderness drops down to the Dead Sea far below. There stood Tekoa and on these steeps Amos once was "a herdsman, and a dresser of **sycamore-trees.**" [1]

The barren hillcrest has an impressive view on one side to Bethlehem and Frank Mountain and, on the other, over the tumbled peaks and precipitous wadies of the wilderness to the Dead Sea and Moab rising out of it. The spot today is uninhabited. The summit itself, a great, bare crag, is strewn with a tumult of stones which reveal yet the occasional line of a wall or suggest the foundations of a house. That an old Christian town once stood here is evident; the remains of a church are recognizable and a finely preserved baptistery still lies on the ground. Cisterns are everywhere—seventy of them, said the native Arab who was with us—dug in the rock to keep the slender store of water on that arid height. All around is wilderness. We left the olive trees of Bethlehem behind us and then saw no trees more, not even one sycamore to recall the industry of Amos, until we went back again. Our donkeys trod for that five miles on rock, acres of rock, slipping often on the smooth, flat surfaces, so that I understood Amos' figure of impossibility: "Shall horses race over crags?" [2]

Barren as the site is, it is a fit remembrancer of Amos.

[1] Amos 7:14.                    [2] Amos 6:12 M.

Passage after passage in his brief collection of sermons, grew luminous as we sat upon the summit of this devastated hill and looked out over the scene which was his world. It was over these crags and peaks of the wilderness, upon whose summits he looked down, that he saw Jehovah tread "upon the high places of the earth." [1] It was over this mountainous wilderness that the great winds blew which, with their dryness or their rain, made or unmade the year's prosperity, so that he called Jehovah him "that formeth the mountains, and createth the wind." [2] Up through this wilderness came the wild beasts that harried the flocks, frightened the villagers, and gave the prophet some of his most vivid figures: "As the shepherd rescueth out of the mouth of the lion two legs, or a piece of an ear, so shall the children of Israel be rescued"; [3] "As if a man did flee from a lion, and a bear met him." [4] From this isolated hillcrest at night the full circle of the sky shone clear and here he learned to know God as him "that maketh the Pleiades and Orion." [5] Here, too, amid hard work, simple fare, and wide, stern landscapes, was developed that resounding appeal for social righteousness which makes Amos yet one of the great figures in the spiritual history of man.

Even more than Tekoa, Bethel, the chief center of Amos' ministry, requires the imaginative eye. For Tekoa was probably always bare and simple, but Bethel was royal and luxurious. No one would think it now.

---

[1] Amos 4:13.
[2] Ibid.
[3] Amos 3:12.
[4] Amos 5:19.
[5] Amos 5:8.

It lies almost as far north of Jerusalem—ten miles—
as Tekoa is south of it, and on the site of it the mean
and tawdry village of Beitin houses some four hundred
Arabs. Four springs are here, the secret of the location's
long and varied history, and a large rock-hewn reservoir still is visible.   Besides this nothing strikes the eye
except rocks—huge and tangled masses of curiously
weathered rocks, rising at times like weird stairs up the
hillsides so that some have thought they still could see
the ladder, reaching up to heaven, of which Jacob
dreamed here.[1]   That the old traditions of the place
should be associated with a sacred rock which Jacob here
anointed and made an altar seems entirely natural.
Some think they still can discern, near the town, the
remnants of an old stone circle, a sacred Gilgal.   Certainly Jacob, or anybody else, might well have slept here
with a stone for a pillow; save on a stone there is little
room for a man's head anywhere.   As for the literal
probability of the performance, my doubts were set at
rest when, at Tekoa, one of our Arabs stretched himself
on a rock, chose a large stone for a pillow, and went
so soundly to sleep that it was with difficulty we awakened him.

In the high days of the northern kingdom under Jeroboam this site of Bethel was a royal residence.[2]   Here
stood the golden calf at whose shrine, instead of at
Jerusalem, the northerners worshiped Jehovah.   Here
was the priesthood and the established cult with all its
perquisites and powers; and hither came Amos from

[1] Genesis 28:10-22.          [2] Amos 7:13.

Tekoa, daring king and priest alike with his thunderous denunciation of their paganism and idolatry. He took his life in his hands but he feared God so much that he feared no one else at all. Even these bare rocks become a holy place, a proper shrine of pilgrimage, as one thinks of him, almost eight centuries before Christ, proclaiming here a message so far ahead of his time that most of the human race and a large part of Christendom have not yet caught up with it.

He fearlessly attacked the whole sacrificial system in Israel as vanity. He bitterly denounced the social evils of a selfish and dissolute time when men "sold the righteous for silver, and the needy for a pair of shoes." [1] He hurled his defiance specifically against Bethel and its worship until royal and priestly cliques combined to crush him. He exalted God as universal in his rule, as no mere tribal deity, and as asking nothing of any man anywhere among any people except righteousness. That was a tremendous and revolutionary message to come from the lips of a Tekoan herdsman and to resound on these stone hills of Bethel in the eighth century B.C.

I stood there thinking of all the superstitions of Islam and the mummeries of degenerate Christianity that curse Palestine today, and of our popular religion in the West with its cheap and credulous substitutes for goodness— its ritualism, creedalism, ecclesiasticism—and I wondered afresh at that astounding man who on this spot twenty-seven centuries ago thundered the truth as though God himself were speaking:

[1] Amos 2:6.

I hate, I despise your feasts, and I will take no delight in your solemn assemblies.  Yea, though ye offer me your burnt-offerings and meal-offerings, I will not accept them; neither will I regard the peace-offerings of your fat beasts.  Take thou away from me the noise of thy songs; for I will not hear the melody of thy viols.  But let justice roll down as waters, and righteousness as a mighty stream.[1]

## IV

Micah is another prophet whose home we know.  We went down to it one day in harvest time and the memories of that trip are among the most stimulating of our stay in Palestine.  Leaving Hebron, we turned toward the Philistine country and found ourselves running through scenes of such agricultural and pastoral plenty as we had seldom witnessed in the land.  The valley of Eshcol, through which, long ago, the spies returned to Moses with a laden litter of fruit,[2] still is identified with considerable probability, and we found it yet a fertile place with vineyards the fairest that we saw, where for the first time I understood the Biblical figure of plenty:

> A fruitful bough by a fountain;
> His branches run over the wall.[3]

Here, between Hebron and Beit Jibrin, were olive trees and pomegranates, flocks larger than I had seen before, and golden grain-fields, with the villagers hap-

[1] Amos 5:21-24.          [3] Genesis 49:22.
[2] Numbers 13:23.

pily at work carrying the treasure of an unusually
fertile year to their heaped-up threshing-floors.

Beit Jibrin itself is one of the most curiously interesting places in Palestine.  Here are those astounding subterranean dwellings which carry history back millenniums before Christ.  Here also is a series of well-
preserved tombs cut in the chalk hillsides by Sidonian
Greeks and still displaying with little impairment their
elaborate preparations for the dead and their richly
painted decoraticns.  Here from 200 A.D. is the mosaic
floor of a Roman villa, beautifully wrought and well
preserved, and from 500 A.D. come the apse of a church
and a part of its floor with this inscription in Greek
still legible:

Of Christ, the universal King, I his blameless priest Obodi-
anus of the gentle heart, have embellished with mosaics the
house, its floor and entry, by the hands of my own disciples.

Of all the memorials of this site's checkered past,
however, from the cavemen down to the Arabs of the
present mud-brick village, whom we watched busy on
their ancient threshing-floors, I looked longest at a bare
mound, Tell Sandahannah, which with certainty has
been identified by excavations as the ancient Maresha-
Gath, the home of Micah.  Nothing is to be seen here
now by the physical eye.  Only the ancient name is preserved in Khurbet Merash—ruins a half mile away.
But one who knows what once was done here by a
solitary prophet, whose voice is far from silent yet,

walks with reverence about this hill on which his home was built.

He, too, proclaimed a God of righteousness whom nothing could content save good character in man and just relations in society.   His scathing wrath against those who "covet fields, and seize them," [1] who "walk haughtily," [2] who cast women "out from their pleasant houses," [3] who "abhor justice, and pervert all equity," [4] who "judge for reward," "teach for hire," and "divine for money," [5] must have made him a disturbing character in this ancient valley.   A generation and more after Amos he prophesied here and carried on the message of his predecessor.   If the sixth chapter in the book came from his lips, he lived on into the evil reign of Manasseh and saw in Jerusalem, not twenty-five miles away, the sacrifice of first-born children burned in the valley of Hinnom.   Perhaps in this valley also he saw his fellow-villagers not only come before Jehovah, as he said, "with burnt-offerings, with calves a year old . . . . with thousands of rams . . . with ten thousands of rivers of oil," [6] but even saying, "Shall I give my first-born for my transgression, the fruit of my body for the sin of my soul?" [7]   I saw still in an old rock surface what looked to me like ancient libation cups such as I had seen on the high places, as at Gibeon.   Did Micah stand where we stood and see their horrid sacrifices which our

[1] Micah 2:2.
[2] Micah 2:3.
[3] Micah 2:9.
[4] Micah 3:9.
[5] Micah 3:11.
[6] Micah 6:6-7.
[7] Micah 6:7.

eyes hardly could image and which our nerves certainly could not endure?

If so, the more amazing was his sheer leap of spirit
to a statement of truth which no generation can out-
grow.  Over two millenniums and a half have passed
since then and yet, when President Eliot of Harvard was
asked to choose a description of true religion to be put
upon the walls of the Library of Congress at Washing-
ton, it was the words of Micah, from this ancient town
on the edge of Judah, which he selected.  They are as
marvelous a sally of insight in their way as that of
Copernicus when he grasped the truth about the physical
universe.  Still the world, Christian and non-Christian
alike, awaits the time when they shall be understood and
translated into life: "What doth the Lord require of
thee, but to do justly, and to love mercy, and to walk
humbly with thy God?" [1]

## V

While Micah was teaching in this outlying settlement
on the edge of Philistia, another prophet was walking
the streets and deeply influencing the life of the nation's
capital.  Isaiah was a man of the city.  Like Savonarola
at Florence, he built himself into the life of his town.
Jerusalem never would have meant what it has meant in
history had it not been for Isaiah.  Says George Adam
Smith, "Jerusalem may be said to be Isaiah's Jerusalem
even more than she was David's or Solomon's."

[1] Micah 6:8, King James' Version.

One who, having lived there, now picks up the prophet's sermons, feels as he could not feel before how intimately the busy life of Judah's metropolis penetrated Isaiah's mind.  All through the book the familiar physical details of the city are prominent—its conduits [1] and pools,[2] the softly flowing waters of Siloam,[3] its rock-hewn sepulchers,[4] its fortified walls,[5] its crowded housetops,[6] its temple courts,[7] and the precipitous wadies that surround it.[8]  But especially the human life of the city reechoes through the prophet's words.  Of high rank though he was, with easy access to the princes and the king, he walked these streets for three years bare-footed, with his upper garment gone, in protest against the city's sin.

He scourged the women of his time, "with outstretched necks and wanton eyes, walking and mincing as they go, and making a tinkling with their feet." [9] He scourged the religious leaders who "stagger with strong drink"; [10] the rulers who "grind the face of the poor"; [11] the landlords "that join house to house, that lay field to field, till there be no room"; [12] the pious hypocrites who pray while their "hands are full of blood"; [13] the spiritualistic mediums "that chirp and that mutter"; [14] the idolaters with their sun-worship and tree-

---

[1] Isaiah 7:3.
[2] Isaiah 22:9. 11.
[3] Isaiah 8:6.
[4] Isaiah 22:16.
[5] Isaiah 2:15.
[6] Isaiah 22:1.
[7] Isaiah 6:1.

[8] Isaiah 7:19 and 22:7.
[9] Isaiah 3:16.
[10] Isaiah 28:7.
[11] Isaiah 3:15.
[12] Isaiah 5:8.
[13] Isaiah 1:15.
[14] Isaiah 8:19.

worship, their new moons and sabbaths; [1] and in general he left a devastating record of the moral tone of his Jerusalem.

He did more than that, however. He believed in Jerusalem. In his day the Assyrians wrecked the northern kingdom, which made Judah the sole representative of Hebrew faith in Palestine. In his day also the Assyrians wrecked all Judah except Jerusalem, which emphasized the peculiar strength and sanctity of Zion. The time was ripe, therefore, to exalt the holy city as the chosen of God, his elect, inviolable dwelling, his "hearth and altar," [2] as the prophet called it. Isaiah seized the opportunity. "Jehovah hath founded Zion" [3] was his cry; in "Jehovah of hosts, who dwelleth in mount Zion" [4] he saw the future glory of the redeemed city; and despite all his scathing denunciations of sin and his predictions of consequent doom, it was he who largely created that faith in God's purpose for Jerusalem which later came to be the organizing center of his people's hope. It was he who in a sense launched the idea that today makes Zion the sacred city of three faiths.

I sat at lunch one day with an English jurist who holds a high position in Palestine. He represents the finest culture of our century, and as a Zionist Jew he is giving his life to the renaissance of Judaism in the Holy Land. He could discuss any subject other than Zionism with a lawyer's impersonal objectivity, but

[1] Isaiah 17:8, 10-11; 1:29 and 1:13-14.
[2] Isaiah 29:1 M.    [3] Isaiah 14:32.    [4] Isaiah 8:18.

when he spoke of Jerusalem his emotion rose. He loved her. He believed that Providence could not have done all that had been wrought through his people only to leave their sacred city in alien hands. His confidence in the success of Zionism rested ultimately on that flaming faith in Jerusalem and what God intended yet to do there. He was a true representative of one of the oldest, most persistent, most memorable traditions of passionate loyalty in human annals, the devotion of Jews to Jerusalem.

In a real sense Isaiah was the initiator of that tradition. He walked these streets, hating the city's sin and proclaiming, like Amos and Micah, a God of righteousness who would be content with nothing that man could offer him except to "cease to do evil; learn to do well; seek justice, relieve the oppressed, judge the fatherless, plead for the widow." [1] But he also saw a vision of a triumphant future and passionately preached it. It was he who made the victorious word Immanuel —"God with us"—a permanent symbol in the religious vocabulary of the race. It was he who dreamed of a coming messianic king who should make Zion's name glorious: "Of the increase of his government and of peace there shall be no end, upon the throne of David, and upon his kingdom." [2] It was he who concentrated the devotion of his people so powerfully in Jerusalem and taught them so ardent a faith in her future that even when, a century afterward, the city was ruined utterly and the nation was in exile five hundred miles

[1] Isaiah 1:16-17.                    [2] Isaiah 9:7.

across a blazing desert, their vows were still of loyalty
to her:

> If I forget thee, O Jerusalem,
> Let my right hand forget her skill.[1]

## VI

Perhaps the most thrilling of the prophets' homes
to one who knows the life story of the man born there
is ancient Anathoth.   It still is called 'Anata and it is
the undoubted home of Jeremiah.   One may walk to it
or ride on donkeyback, as we did, because it is only two
and a half miles from Jerusalem.   We went up past the
British cemetery where the dead of the last war lie
buried on the hillside overlooking Jerusalem, and then,
climbing over the brow of Scopus, where Titus, the
Roman general, encamped when he besieged the city,
rode down in a half hour more to the little, dirty, dis-
reputable stone village of 'Anata.   Its streets are narrow and unkempt, its inhabitants bedraggled, its houses
and courtyards unbelievably filthy, and its total aspect
poverty-stricken and repellent.

Yet, as so often happens in this strange land of
Orientalisms, lovely, as well as unlovely, we found
charming courtesy awaiting us in this unlikely spot.
In the absence of the head man of the village, a citizen
volunteered to take his place; he saluted us with the
dignity and welcomed us with the hospitality of the
true Arab; and, learning that we wished a vantage

[1] Psalm 137:5.

point upon a housetop where we could see the view that Jeremiah saw in youth, he guided us to the most favorable spot himself. The way led through a smoke-begrimed, malodorous house where still, as in ancient times, the lower portion is given to the cattle while on a stone platform above them the household sleeps.

As for the Arab who guided us, I salute his memory. He was planning to come to America within a year to join his brother, then in New York, and he had his papers ready, which he showed with pride. I expect that some day he will call upon me as he promised, a strange visitor from Jeremiah's birthplace to be sending up his name in a New York apartment house. If he comes he will be cordially welcomed, as he well deserves—he is the one man I met in Palestine who refused bakshish when it was offered to him.

Such is 'Anata to the casual view—an uninviting, unsanitary, half-ruined Moslem village; and I can understand why many a traveler might wonder why any visitor should choose to go there, or going, should see anything worth while. If, however, a man have the gift of shutting his eyes on the visible and seeing the unseen, he will look here on a strange, influential history. Anath was a goddess worshiped in Palestine long before the Hebrews came. We find her mentioned in Egyptian monuments from the fifteenth century B.C. on, and at least two towns in Palestine were named after her.[1] Anathoth is the plural of Anath, so that on this hilltop, which seemed at first so

[1] Jeremiah 1:1; Joshua 19:38.

bedraggled and unalluring, we have at least this interest to start with: multiplied shrines of the goddess Anath used to stand here, and here resounded the orgies of her worshipers and the cries of her sacrificial victims.    When the Hebrews came they put Jehovah in Anath's place, but the old name still clung.

Here in the days of Solomon came a notable family exiled from Jerusalem.    Abiathar, the high priest, had conspired against the coronation of Solomon and, when Solomon seized the throne, he and his family were sent over the hill to Coventry on his country acres in Anathoth.[1]    Some three centuries later, his heritage probably running back to this ancient priestly family, Jeremiah was born here—greatest of the Hebrew prophets, so it seems to me, and the noblest exemplar of personal religious life before our Lord.

His common reputation represents him as a weeping prophet, dolorous and pessimistic, given to lamentation.    As a matter of fact, he was a lyric poet, a religious saint, a social reformer, and a practical statesman compact in one.    He was a man of deep emotion and sympathy, capacious for vicarious grief, and at the same time a lion for courage either to attack evil or to endure contumely.    For over forty years his unflinching public ministry continued.    He saw his country go through reforms full of hope, and disastrous reactions full of disillusionment.    He saw Jerusalem fall twice before the armies of Babylon, who left it at last, as he foretold, "a heap of ruins."[2]    He was hated by his

[1] I Kings 1:7 and 2:26-27.        [2] Jeremiah 9:11 M.

own people because he was their clearest-sighted citizen and told the unpalatable truth, yet they could not escape his haunting influence.  His fellow townsmen of Anathoth conspired against his life;[1] in Jerusalem he was put in the stocks,[2] imprisoned in a muddy cistern,[3] threatened with execution;[4] yet he neither lost his faith nor trimmed his message.  At last, when all his daring insight and wise counsel had been justified by the events, he was dragged, an unwilling exile, to Egypt,[5] to die—so tradition says—a martyr by the Nile. Few lives more exciting have been lived and few lives have been lived more nobly.

Here, then, this titanic prophet was born and here also, as he tells us, on a spring morning when the almond trees were blossoming, which we saw too, he received his call to speak to Judah.  The view which nourished his youth and inspired so many of his vivid figures is the one thing little changed by the passing centuries.  Still one looks down to the Dead Sea and the Jordan valley seventeen miles away, while in between stretches the spectral confusion of hills and wadies across the wilderness.  Still one sweeps his eyes northward and westward from hillcrest to hillcrest, each one full of memories of Saul and Samuel and the brave days of the nation's early conflict.  Read Jeremiah's prophecies in this setting, where the man was reared, and you can feel the landscape and the homely customs of the country people back of all of them.

[1] Jeremiah 11:21.
[2] Jeremiah 20:1-2.
[3] Jeremiah 38:6-7.
[4] Jeremiah 26:8-11 and 38:4-5.
[5] Jeremiah 43:1-7.

More than once he speaks of these "bare heights" [1] on which familiarly he looked. Repeatedly this wilderness creeps into his figurative speech: "Have I been a desert to Israel?" [2] and the winds that blow across it blow through his book also: "no breeze to winnow and to cleanse, but a wild, tearing wind." [3] Again and again the wild animals come up from this wilderness, figures of ravenous foes: "a lion from the jungle" or "a wolf from the steppes," [4] and a ruined heritage to him was a "carcase torn by hyenas." [5] Here he watched the migratory birds, especially the storks, thousands of which we saw passing over Palestine: "The very stork of the air knows when to migrate." [6] Here he saw what any traveler sees yet: "some desert scrub, that never thrives, set in a dry place in the steppes." [7] And in hot, rainless, famished seasons he had watched on these heights "wild asses . . . upon the knolls, panting for air." [8]

The correspondences between landscape and book are startling, and the smaller, homelier touches of familiarity with the daily life of a region such as this increase the vividness of the prophet's words. The "leaky cisterns that can hold no water"; [9] the animals that have broken their yoke and snapped their harness; [10] the vines of a "right good stock" that have become "degenerate"; [11] men "taking cover within

[1] Jeremiah 3:2 M; 3:21 M; 7:29 M.
[2] Jeremiah 2:31 M.
[3] Jeremiah 4:12 M.
[4] Jeremiah 5:6 M.
[5] Jeremiah 12:9 M.
[6] Jeremiah 8:7 M.
[7] Jeremiah 17:6 M.
[8] Jeremiah 14:6 M.
[9] Jeremiah 2:13 M.
[10] Jeremiah 2:20 M.
[11] Jeremiah 2:21 M.

woods and caves, and clambering the rocks"; [1] idols "like scarecrows in a field"; [2] tents blown down, "the ropes all broken"; [3] "a lovely spreading olive-tree . . . blasted in a thunderclap" [4]—such figures in Jeremiah's book grow very vivid when one has visited Jeremiah's home.

One hopes that somewhere he knows today the unforeseeable fruitage of his work. Jesus read Jeremiah and was deeply stirred by him. When in Jerusalem the Master cleansed the temple and in the heat of his earnestness quoted the Scripture that rose spontaneously in his mind, it was from the great seventh chapter of this ancient prophet that the words came flaming to his lips.

These prophets whose homes we know established the tradition which with varying fortunes and with diverse quality extended from Elijah through Malachi. After the Exile the prophets lived in Jerusalem, the one holy city of the Jews, with a little fringe of rocky territory round it, which made up the new Judea. They were the builders of the true Judaism. They were the men through whom God at sundry times and in diverse manners spoke in times past unto the fathers. It was their insight and courage, their vision and valor which prepared the way for the Prophet who was to come.

[1] Jeremiah 4:29 M.
[2] Jeremiah 10:5 M.
[3] Jeremiah 10:20 M.
[4] Jeremiah 11:16 M.

# CHAPTER VIII

## WITH THE MASTER IN NAZARETH

### I

THERE is no place in Palestine where the traveler, if he be a Christian, runs greater danger of disillusionment than in Galilee. Here we have moved from the Old Testament into the New and the memories that chiefly cluster here are not of bloody battles nor of thunderous prophets, but of him who spake as never man spake. One who adores him may expect too much of the town he grew up in and the lake by which he preached. One may anticipate a more mystical sense of his presence than these tawdry villages, these untenanted shores of Galilee, these hills, even when starred with numberless flowers, are able to produce. Some do leave Galilee almost sorry that they came.

Such an impression, however, is bound to be dissipated if one stay long enough to love the land, and if one have come in the first place remembering that the Master lived a human life amid commonplace surroundings. For one so prepared to see him, the Son of Man will walk these hills again. His boyhood in Nazareth, the kind of house he lived in, the heights he climbed, the flowers and trees, flocks and fields he

loved, the work he toiled at as a carpenter, the wider
world he ventured into beside the lake, and the busy,
varied, human throng that first followed and then
abandoned him—such things grow vivid and luminous
in Galilee.

To gain a unified impression of this compact country,
let us begin by climbing Safed.    It rises in the midst of
the land 2770 feet above the Mediterranean upon the
one side, and 3452 feet above the lake upon the other.
It has a long and varied history, from battles between
crusader and Saracen to famous schools of Spanish
rabbis driven here by persecution, and the town upon
its crest is one of the most picturesque in Palestine.
We climb it now, however, with no thought but to
see from the summit the panorama of Galilee.    The
eye can sweep the whole compass of it, from Carmel at
the Mediterranean, around by the hills of Nazareth
and Mount Tabor, past the Jordan valley and Gilead
beyond, over the Sea of Galilee, far below, to Hermon's white dome in the north and the rising summits
of the Lebanons.    One understands why this little land
came to be called Galilee, which means "circle" or
"circuit," and one feels the awe of taking in thus, at a
glance, the scene of the Master's ministry.

Yonder in Nazareth he grew up, preached there his
famous sermon, and was angrily rejected by his fellow
townsmen.    Across this broken landscape with its gray-
rock mountains, its bare and stony moors, its broad
sweep of fair grazing lands, its scattered forests and
its fertile valleys, he made his way to the lake, where

the busiest life and the swiftest, most ardent thinking of his time and country were at work.  Here beside the sea he made his home, and Capernaum, as Matthew said, became "his own city." [1]  Here he gathered his disciples, picking Peter and Andrew, James and John, from the fishermen and Matthew from the tax-gatherers, trained here his little band, and went out with them across this broken, varied countryside that lies before us, covered in his day with many villages.  Here he met the growing opposition of the orthodox and for a time retired northward beyond the mountains to the coasts of Tyre and Sidon.  After this he returned to make a tour of the Greek cities that flourished, as their ruins still reveal, in Trans-Jordania yonder.  Then, as the crisis grew dark, he went up the Jordan, past the Waters of Merom, which lie plainly in our view, to Cæsarea Philippi, beneath the brow of Hermon, and received there from Peter the acknowledgment of his messiahship.  Thence, one day, with his wondering and fearful followers, he set his face southward over the road past Tabor to Jerusalem and crucifixion.

How swiftly the story can be told!  How easily the compact scene of its occurrence can be summed up by the eye!  Fifty miles from north to south, twenty-five to thirty-five miles from east to west—that covers Galilee.  But the smallness and swift visibility of the land only increase the marvel of that life whose Gospel here took on such universal meaning that today one sees

[1] Matthew 4:13 and 9:1.

Christ walking on the water
Not of Gennesareth, but Thames!

## II

The place to begin a more intimate acquaintance with Galilee is naturally Nazareth.  As one comes up the north road from Jerusalem, one sees it first far off across the Samaritan foothills and the valley of Esdraelon.  The buildings which now crown the highest hill above the Master's home town are clearly visible thirty-five miles away.  Having thus seen them from afar, one slips swiftly down into Esdraelon and soon, upon the other side, is climbing the steep road which runs crisscross up the hills where the plateau of Galilee rises a sheer thousand feet from the plain. There, on the edge of the plateau, nestling in a sheltered cup so that the village proper is visible only from the neighboring heights, lies Nazareth.  The reverent visitor who comes to this sacred spot with a pilgrim's spirit but unprepared to withstand the guile of guides and the pious chicanery of churches is likely to be shocked.  He is shown, as the chief if not the only sites, the purported spot where Gabriel announced the incarnation to Mary, with pillars marking the precise places where each stood; the rock-cut grotto also, supposed to be the house where Mary lived; the workshop of Joseph, which is probably an ancient cistern; and, if the visitor still show signs of equanimity, even the tomb of Joseph, the kitchen where the Virgin cooked, and a table from which the Master ate after his resurrection.

The truth is that no sound reason exists for taking seriously any of these sites. Only one spot in Nazareth associated with the Master can with confidence be identified—Mary's well. This copiously flowing spring has doubtless been here since the land was first inhabited. Because of it the village of Nazareth was built here on the neighboring hill. To its constant supply the women for centuries have come, as they do still, to fill their water-jars and exchange the gossip of the village. Here one stands on a spot which he may be sure Jesus and his mother often visited. This was probably the first spring that Jesus knew; and many a thought of his, about giving a cup of cold water,[1] or experiencing the divine Presence as living water,[2] may here have had its first suggestion. There is nothing in the fountain itself, walled up and modernized, nor in the soiled and thirsty villagers who gather here to wash and drink and talk, that allures the eye or stimulates the spirit. That, in part, is the marvel of it. In Jesus' day, as now, the fountain, the village that stood near it, and the villagers who lived there—the entire physical and human matrix in which his life was set—were probably to ordinary eyes thus dull and drab and uninspiring. "Can any good thing come out of Nazareth?"[3] Nathanael asked. You cannot explain Christ by his environment; his secret runs far back into the abysmal depths of personality.

[1] Matthew 10:42.          [3] John 1:46.
[2] John 4:10.

The fact that this spring alone in Nazareth can be identified as a site associated with the Master does not mean that the traditional sites lack interest. The present church over the so-called workshop of St. Joseph was built in 1838 but there was a church over Joseph's supposed home which pilgrims saw as early as the seventh century and which, destroyed in the eighth century, the crusaders rebuilt. The present Church of the Annunciation, covering the site of Gabriel's embassage and the Virgin's home, was completed in 1730 but there was a church on this spot, so its supporters claim, as far back as the time of Constantine. Neither of these sites, however, carries back the tradition within reaching distance of the Nazareth in which Jesus lived; even those who plead their cause admit that until the time of Constantine Nazareth was altogether Jewish. Under such conditions what chance is there that the remembrance of Mary's home and Joseph's workshop should have been preserved through three centuries and a half?

The only interest which these sites possess lies in the memories of twelve centuries and more of pilgrimage during which the ends of the earth have worshiped here. From the time of Bishop Arculf, in the seventh century, what diverse devotees here have bowed! Saint Louis, king of France, fasting and with a hair shirt next his body, here worshiped so devoutly that one companion said, "Since the day when the Son of God took flesh of the Virgin Mary in this place, never was office celebrated with so much solemnity and devotion." Here Saint Francis of Assisi poured out his soul in prayer, and here Napoleon Bonaparte paid such homage as his character allowed. Here the modern pilgrim also may make a shrine of devotion if he will, even though he knows that the house of Mary and the workshop of Joseph are lost forever.

## III

If one would reconstruct the boyhood of Jesus in this little town, so charmingly situated in its nest among the hills, he may leave the churches and go out into the present village. Between seven and eight thousand people live here now—nearly five thousand Christians, some twenty-five hundred Moslems, and a very few Jews. Many changes have taken place since Jesus' boyhood; the town has been wasted and rebuilt in the wars that have ravaged Galilee; its very site may have shifted southward on the hill. Yet, were he to come back, he would find some things not greatly altered.

So little have village houses changed that many a residence in Nazareth would remind him of the home he lived in. On the plain of Sharon or in Esdraelon, where stone is scarce, houses are made of sun-dried brick, but on the ridges, where rock is plentiful, they are generally made of stone. Come up these narrow, winding, unsanitary streets of Nazareth and you can see houses still into whose simple, ancient architecture the family of Jesus might move today and feel at home.

One large, square room suffices for the house.   The
walls of rough-dressed stone are from three to four feet
thick and the roof is of stone, domed up and covered
with clay mortar rolled hard to shed the rain.   An
outside stairway runs up to the roof, for that is a cool
place to sleep when nights are warm, a convenient dry-
ing place for fruit, and even, as I have often seen, a fair
grazing ground for goats when grass is growing.
Sometimes an "upper room" is built there, which is
something of a luxury.   The outstanding feature of the
interior is a masonry platform raised eight to ten feet
above the ground, supported on stone arches, and
reached by a narrow flight of steps.   Here the family
live when they are indoors by day, and here they sleep
at night.   Two miniature windows high up from the
ground furnish all the light and air save that which
may come through the door; and an open fireplace,
with a chimney or without one, furnishes warmth in
winter.   In winter, too, the space beneath the family's
raised platform is filled at night with household animals, sheep, goats, dogs, and chickens, and their warm
presence is counted on in lieu of fire.

In some such home the Master spent his boyhood.
He seems to have known mud-brick houses too,
through whose walls thieves could dig,[1] and he certainly knew houses whose roofs were thatched with
reeds, not built of stone.[2]   Such variations one can see
today in Palestine but, as for the interior, it seems to
have come down across the centuries changed little if

[1] Matthew  6:19.                    [2] Mark 2:4.

at all.   Until one has seen these homes one does not understand the story of the nativity at Bethlehem. Despite the tradition of our Western world, with its endless lovely settings in music, poetry, and legend, no barn or stable is mentioned anywhere in Scripture in connection with the birth of Jesus.   Matthew even calls the place where the wise men found him a "house." [1] It is we Westerners who, reading that the new-born babe was laid in a manger, have therefore imagined a stable or a barn.

The truth is clear, however, when one sees the village houses of Palestine.   There was no room for Mary on the sleeping platform of that house in Bethlehem used as an inn, so that she lay beneath it on the ground where the animals were kept and there, in the empty manger, laid the new-born babe.   That overflow of either family or visitors from the platform to the space beneath is not unusual and it need imply no rudeness. Mary when a child had doubtless often slept below the platform when unexpected visitors arrived, and at Bethlehem she gratefully accepted so warm a shelter in her hour of need.

Not the house alone, but many a custom and conversation in the family would be familiar to the returning Jesus now.   The ideas of this singularly static land persist with little change across the centuries.   The very chauffeur who drove us to Nazareth, for all the modernness of his locomotion, told us a story of his mother that might have come from the Bible.   She had

[1] Matthew 2:11.

had four daughters and like every Arab woman wanted, most of all, a son. She made pilgrimage, therefore, to Hebron, like Hannah going to Shiloh, and at the Mosque el Khalil, sacred to Abraham, the "friend of God," she made her vow that if God would grant her a man child she would name him Khalil, "friend." Her prayer was granted. Her next baby was a boy, and Khalil, a special gift of God to us as well as to her, drove us all over Palestine.

That Gabriel had told a woman like Mary that a man child was to come would not sound strange to a family in Nazareth today. "I do not know," writes Dr. Rihbany, a Syrian, born and reared a few miles to the north, "how many times I heard it stated in my native land and at our own fireside that heavenly messengers in the forms of patron saints or angels came to pious, childless wives, in dreams and visions, and cheered them with the promise of maternity." That Jesus was born under a special star might be said of a child born in Nazareth this year. "I was brought up," writes Dr. Rihbany again, "to believe that every human being had a star in heaven which held the secret of his destiny and which watched over him wherever he went." The journey to Jerusalem when Jesus was twelve years old would not be strange for a lad in Nazareth now. Still the people of the land believe in pilgrimage and practise it assiduously; still a great day in the family arrives when the young child is old enough to join his first *zyara* with the household. Still the story of Jesus' experience when he was twelve

is in its setting so true to the customs of the country
that one who went on two pilgrimages here before he
was fifteen says that the record in Scripture is like a
personal reminiscence.

Today in the fields Jesus would see husbandmen let-
ting wheat and tares grow together until both were ripe
and then plucking out the tares for burning immediately before the harvest.[1]  I watched the process with
fascinated eyes one glorious day on the plain below
Nazareth.  Still he would see women on their thresh-
olds sewing patches on garments that look as though
they would stand no patching more;[2] or chaffering in
the markets over the price of food;[3] or fearful of
demons that attack their children,[4] and narrating to
the neighbors tales of ghostly mischief; or dreading as
a quite intolerable shame the loss of a silver coin from
the headdress, which is alike a woman's dowry and her
chief display; [5] or waiting, as of old, for the bridegroom
to come home with his bride; [6] or even rubbing the
new-born children with salt and wrapping them with
swaddling clothes as mothers here have done at least
since the days of Ezekiel.[7]

Indeed, the returning Jesus would find far more
familiarity in this little village, for all the changes
in it, than our eyes can see.  Into the shops of the
carpenters I am sure he would go and discover there
few strange tools or new methods.  Here is the true

[1] Matthew 13:30.
[2] Matthew 9:16.
[3] Cf. Matthew 10:29.
[4] Mark 9:17-29.
[5] Luke 15:8-9.
[6] Matthew 25:1-13.
[7] Ezekiel 16:4.

"Joseph's workshop" and not in that empty cistern
covered by a church.  In one of these little shops—run
by members of the Master's race, with relatives in
Newark and Brooklyn—I saw the carpenters making
plows and yokes, which in Palestine have not changed
their shape for ages.  Still the one-handled plow is
seen in the fields, scratching a thin line through the
rocky soil, and as I watched the plowman with goad in
one hand and one hand on the plow I understood why,
where we would use the plural, Jesus used the singular:
"having put his hand to the plow." [1]   As for yokes,—
the Master said he made them easy for men's souls as
for their oxen,—they still are shaped as in ancient
times, and here, using their bare feet for the vise, and
roughly shaping the wood by hard toil with strange
old tools, the carpenters of Nazareth are working still
as Joseph toiled when Jesus helped him.

## IV

Of one sight familiar to the returning Jesus we may
be sure—the view from the hills above the village.  In a rapidly changing country like America,
a mature man returns to some picturesquely situated
town where he spent his boyhood to find many alterations, beneath which, however, he still can delight in
the old familiar aspect of the land.  Such changes as
in America happen within a lifetime have not happened
even yet in the landscape about Nazareth since Jesus

[1] Luke 9:62.

walked these hills. Buildings have come and gone, but still today he could feed his eyes and his mind on that sightly panorama which, as a boy, he loved—an outlook of such beauty and such historical suggestiveness as can seldom be paralleled.

One who comes to Nazareth with time and care enough to walk these hillcrests above the village is likely to be as deeply stirred by the consciousness of companioning with the Master as anywhere in Palestine. These hills he did most certainly frequent; on this far-flung view he assuredly looked long hours with quickened thoughts and ardent sympathies. From here he could see nearly sixty miles in one direction and over twenty in two directions more. The whole sweep of the plain of Esdraelon lies beneath the eye. To the westward Carmel throws its promontory out to the Mediterranean and over it one can see the sheen of the sea far to the south and again northward, at the curved beach of Acre, can watch the shining simitar of the surf cutting into the land. The long crest of the Carmel range is in clear view across the plain and the eye travels southward over it far down among the mountains of Samaria. Then, ranging eastward, the view takes in Gilboa, Little Hermon, Tabor, the Jordan valley, the hills of Gilead, and, turning northward, climbs up the mountains, among which Safed stands, and rests at last upon the far white crest of Hermon.

Often in Christendom children have been taught the stories of the Bible, not from books but from mosaics in the churches, as in Saint Mark's in Venice. An

even fairer opportunity surrounded the Master's boyhood; he could see a map of his people's history
from the hills.   Mount Tabor and the brook Kishon,
with their recollections of Barak's victory,[1] the plain
where Gideon surprised and broke the hosts of
Midian;[2] Endor[3] and Gilboa,[4] with their memories
of Saul; Shunem, where Elisha sojourned;[5] Carmel,
where Elijah triumphed;[6] Jezreel, where Naboth's vineyard was,[7] the Jordan valley with its memorable associations; the Lebanons, whence Solomon's cedars came;[8]
Hermon, from which "the dew . . . cometh down upon
the mountains of Zion";[9] and the Mediterranean, picture of that future day when "the earth shall be full
of the knowledge of Jehovah, as the waters cover the
sea"[10]—what a mosaic of the history and symbolism of
his people nature spread before the Master's boyhood!

Closer at hand, upon the hills of Galilee, one yet can
see in all their beauty what the Master saw and loved
because "Solomon in all his glory was not arrayed like
one of these."[11]   The wild flowers of Palestine one
almost hesitates to speak his mind about lest he should
seem to exaggerate.   They are superlatively beautiful.
One of our leading American botanists, hailing from
California,—so that he should know what wild flowers
are,—stated while we were there that there were more
specimens of flowers to be counted in a given area in

[1] Judges 4:12-16.
[2] Judges 7:12, 19-21.
[3] I Samuel 28:7-25.
[4] I Samuel 31:1-4.
[5] II Kings 4:8-10.
[6] I Kings 18:19-40.
[7] I Kings 21:1-16.
[8] I Kings 5:6, 8-10.
[9] Psalm 133:3.
[10] Isaiah 11:9.
[11] Matthew 6:28-29.

the Holy Land than anywhere else in the world. In springtime, when the rains are over, they bespangle the land with beauty. Wherever one goes, even in arid wilderness stretches, one hears the Master's injunction to "consider the lilies of the field, how they grow." [12] Anemone, poppy, cyclamen, phlox, ranunculus, lupine, oleander—scores of varieties in such brilliance and profusion as I never saw elsewhere fill the fields of Palestine from Moab to the Lebanons. In well-watered places where soil and rain have happily conspired, their brilliant colors, framed in gray rocks and olive-green branches, make a blend so perfectly commingled by nature that the result is beautiful to the point of tears.

All who live in Palestine, however, and all who visit here long enough to know, agree that the wild flowers are loveliest in Galilee. There is hardly a hillslope in that blossoming land in springtime on which the Master could not point to the profuse and brilliant beauty of the flowers, and one who walks beside the Sea of Galilee finds Wordsworth's picture of the daffodils of England true to the poppies and anemones of Palestine:

> Ten thousand saw I at a glance,
> Tossing their heads in sprightly dance.

For a long while I sat upon the hillcrest above Nazareth with the Master's far-flung view across the Holy Land, and at my feet his fields of flowers. Upon

---

[12] Matthew 6:28.

the brim of the hill an Arab plowman, guiding his ancient plow with one hand and wielding his goad with the other, was breaking up the ground for the spring sowing.  Two little children were playing among the fresh and fragrant furrows.  It was the Master's world, out of doors, with flowers, husbandmen, children, and God.

## V

Not nature alone, however, but a contemporary world of dashing and adventurous human life was within the Master's view from this hillcrest.  The idea that in an isolated village he lived a secluded boyhood is far from true.  There, for example, in plain view from Nazareth's hilltop, less than four miles northward, Sepphoris stands, deserving as well as any town in Palestine to be called a "city set on a hill." [1] Around that town, when Jesus was about eleven years old, Judas the Galilean, whose revolt was still remembered after Jesus died,[2] started a desperate rebellion against Rome.  He gathered a powerful company of reckless patriots, armed them with weapons seized from the king's armory in Sepphoris, and raised a standard around which rallied the furious nationalism of the Jews.  On that day when Judas was slain and his army scattered by the Romans under Varus, when burning Sepphoris sent up its smoke to heaven and its inhabitants were sold into slavery, where can one imagine Jesus except among the crowd of Nazareth's

[1] Matthew 5:14.             [2] Acts 5:37.

inhabitants who from this hillcrest must have watched the scene? And when two thousand men suspected of complicity in the revolt were later crucified, can it be that Nazareth, so close to the rebellion's center, utterly escaped? The Master's first acquaintance with the Cross did not begin as in the charming picture where, a little child, with outstretched arms he casts a cruciform shadow on the ground; it probably began in the terrific spectacle of Varus' soldiers crucifying folk he knew, when he was barely twelve years old.

So, from his earliest youth, the Master was surrounded by the swift and eager movements of his time and knew well its hot and stormy passions. Palestine had not been happy for many years and the fury of the people under Roman rule had long been dangerously seething. Herod the Great, who, as another said, stole to his throne like a fox, ruled like a tiger, and died like a dog, had seized Jerusalem with a Roman army in 37 B.C., in a victory so murderous that he himself had asked the Romans whether they purposed making him king of a desert. His ruthless and ambitious power had not spared Galilee. He had seized Sepphoris too, and on a day when "God sent a snow" the citizens of Nazareth had climbed these hills to watch his legions crush their neighboring town.

Herod the Great had died when Jesus was a child, and tales of his murderous rages and savage deeds, as well as of his glorious buildings, must have been traveling like a conflagration from tongue to ear throughout the Master's boyhood. It was Herod Antipas, "that

fox," Jesus called him,[1] who ruled Galilee during the
Master's youth and manhood.[2]   His royal residence for
years was at Sepphoris, and the neighboring village
lads must often have seen the princely retinues that
came and went, and heard rumors of the intrigues and
cruelties of the court.   When Antipas first stole his
brother's wife, for denouncing which John the Baptist later lost his life, it was no distant crime that stirred
the indignation of Nazareth, but a shocking indecency
in the next village or, at most, in the new capital,
Tiberias, by the lake.

Everywhere in Palestine revolt was rife.   Judas the
Galilean had left, as a relic of his rebellion, a sworn
fraternity of Zealots fanatically determined to win
release from Rome, and one of them, Simon, later
joined the discipleship of Jesus.[3]   Could Nazareth be
so close to Sepphoris and not have its group of Zealots
too?   In Judah rebel chiefs rose in constant succession,
doing small harm to the Romans, says Josephus, but
affecting their own people like a pestilence that walk-
eth in darkness; and, as for the Galileans, they were,
he writes, "ever fond of innovations, and by nature dis-
posed to changes, and delighting in seditions."

No quiet, isolated, rustic youth, therefore, can be
imagined for the Master.   The glorious days of the
Maccabees, when the Jews were free, had many a
memorial in Galilee.   Up past the Galilean lake Jonathan Maccabeus had pushed his march to a resounding

[1] Luke 13:31-32.                [3] Luke 6:15; Acts 1:13.
[2] Matthew 14:1; Luke 3:19 and 9:7; Acts 13:1.

victory at the Waters of Merom, and at Ptolemais on
the Mediterranean, whose curving seabeach Jesus could
see from his hillcrest, the same Jonathan had been
betrayed and captured.  In the midst of such stirring
memories of the past, and surrounded by the tumult of
an angry people fretting for revolt, the Master grew
to manhood.  Such an environment might easily produce Judas the Galilean, but how could it produce the
Man of Galilee?

## VI

We are forever indebted to Professor George Adam
Smith for making vivid, as he has done, the meaning of
the highroads in the homeland of the Master.  "Galilee is covered with roads to everywhere," he says, and
while that is not true today it is clear that it used to be.
For if northern Palestine was the narrow land bridge
over which invading armies had to march in the endless
wars between the Euphrates and the Nile, it was also
the land bridge for the numberless caravans that did
the daily business of the world.  If one went from the
coasts of Tyre and Sidon to Capernaum, or from Gilead
to the port of Joppa, or from Ptolemais to the Sea of
Galilee, or from Egypt to Assyria, or from Jerusalem
to Tiberias, or from Damascus anywhere southward to
market or shrine, one passed through Galilee or across
Esdraelon just below it.

While, therefore, "wars and rumors of wars" [1] were

[1] Matthew 24:6.

familiar to the Master, a busy commercial life amid
the stern security of Roman rule was also part of his
environment.   From his hillcrest he could see merchants and pilgrims in their caravans moving back and
forth across the plain.   They emerged northward from
the mountains of Samaria or headed southward toward
Jerusalem; they swung over the pass at Megiddo from
the plain of Sharon, or they crept up from the Jordan
valley out of Gilead; they came down over the hills
from Damascus, or they brought from far countries
wares landed at the ports of Tyre and Sidon.   And
looking westward he could watch, white-winged upon
the sea, some

> Quinquereme of Nineveh from distant Ophir,
> Rowing home to haven in sunny Palestine,
> With a cargo of ivory,
> And apes and peacocks,
> Sandalwood, cedarwood, and sweet white wine.[1]

It is not strange, then, that in the most characteristic
teaching of Jesus one finds himself, not in close con-
fines, but on an open road.   Some one is always going
somewhere.   The prodigal son goes to a far country;[2]
the traveler falls among thieves;[3] the merchantman is
off with his caravan in search of fine pearls;[4] friends
on a journey arrive unexpectedly, requiring hospitality;[5] the householder leaves his servants and the noble-
man his subjects to travel widely and return again.[6]

---

[1] John Masefield: Cargoes.      [4] Matthew 13:45.
[2] Luke 15:13.      [5] Luke 11:6.
[3] Luke 10:30.      [6] Matthew 25:14,19; Luke 19:12-13.

I cannot read these parables now without seeing Jesus as a boy on his hilltop above Nazareth, watching with eager eyes the caravans weaving in and out across the plain, and dreaming of the lands they came from and the goals they sought.

## VII

One spot in Nazareth quickened my imagination about as much as the hills above it. The parish church of the Greek Catholics is built on the site of the traditional synagogue in which it is supposed that Jesus preached when his neighbors turned against him and drove him forever from the town.[1] One still can see the old foundation stones on which this little village sanctuary, thirty feet long by twenty-six feet wide, supposedly was built. While there is no certainty that we are here on an authentic site, it is not impossible. Sacred places are not lightly changed. Nazareth, with its synagogue, remained exclusively Jewish for centuries after Christ was here, and we pick up the trail again in the sixth century when the Pilgrim of Piacenza mentions the synagogue in Nazareth. This at least may be the spot where the Master's fearless sermon against the racial prejudices of his fellow townsmen and in favor of God's care for Syrian and Sidonian as well as Jew aroused the ire of Nazareth.

If so, it was here that the Master as a boy sat at the feet of some local teacher and learned the Jewish

[1] Luke 4:29.

Law.  Josephus, who was governor of Galilee thirty-
four years after Jesus' ministry there, wrote that the
Jews recognized their duty to educate their children
in the customs and commands of the forefathers "that
they may imitate them, and being nourished up in them
may neither transgress them, nor have any excuse for
ignorance of them."  Up to this village synagogue,
therefore, year after year the children of Nazareth
would come.  One wonders what kind of teacher saw
the lad from Mary's home sitting for the first time on
the floor of the synagogue in the circle of his scholars
and looking up at him with wide and eager eyes.  I
suspect he was of the school of Hillel—who, when
Jesus was a boy, was still alive—a brother in spirit
to Gamaliel, who instructed Paul, a liberal, that is,
who against the excessive strictness of the school of
Shammai endeavored to give the Law a sensible,
humane interpretation.  Did he, perhaps, observe the
kindling soul of this son of Mary?  Was it questions
which he had raised in the boy's mind that Jesus discussed with the doctors at Jerusalem when he was
twelve years old?[1]  Did this unknown rabbi and his
growing charge fall into close and stimulating friendship and walk the hills together, as well as study in
the synagogue, discussing problems of the faith and
the conflicting views of Essenes, Sadducees, and
Pharisees?

All this we cannot know, but one thing is sure—
the Master was acquainted, not simply with the Scrip-

[1] Luke 2:42, 46-47.

tures, but with the finest teaching of the rabbis too.
The Mishnah, which gathered up their wisdom, was
first written down after Jesus died, but the sayings
themselves had been current for many years. That
they may have influenced the Master in his youth is
probable; it is not probable, on the other side, that
his words would be embodied by official Jewish teachers who hated him. One notes with interest, therefore, the close kinship between the Master and the
best of the rabbis. His word about taking a beam
from one's own eye before taking the mote from the
eye of a brother [1] is paralleled by Rabbi Tarphon: "If
he (the reprover) say to him, Take the mote from
thine eyes, the other replies, Take the beam from thine
eyes." His saying, "With what measure ye mete, it shall
be measured unto you," [2] occurs word for word in the
Mishnah. His saying that "every one that looketh on
a woman to lust after her hath committed adultery
with her already in his heart" [3] is akin to the words
of Rabbi Shimeon ben Lakish: "He that committeth
adultery with his eyes is also to be called an adulterer."
His admonition about "yea" and "nay" being sufficient
without the bolstering of oaths [4] is like the saying of
Rabbi Eliezer: "Yea is an oath and nay is an oath."
And his warning against giving to be seen of men [5]
is akin to the same rabbi's saying: "He who ostenta-
tiously gives alms to the poor—for this, God will
bring him to judgment." One catches the tone of

[1] Matthew 7:3-5.
[2] Matthew 7:2.
[3] Matthew 5:28.
[4] Matthew 5:34-37.
[5] Matthew 6:2-3.

Jesus' teaching in many a fine and lofty passage from
the rabbis: "How doth it affect the Holy One, blessed
be he . . . whether a man eat food unclean or clean";
"Almsgiving and good works outweigh all the commandments in the Law"; "They who are insulted yet
insult not again, who hear themselves reproached yet
answer not again . . . of them Scripture says, They
that love him are as the going forth of the sun in his
might."

Our imagination, therefore, of the unknown teacher
of Nazareth whose instruction kindled and whose
friendship encouraged the Master's boyhood is not
unjustified. How stirred he must have been at first
by the eager responsiveness and the flaming insight
of the pupil, and at times how troubled too! "Every
man who possesses real vitality," says Professor Gilbert
Murray, "can be seen as the resultant of two forces.
He is first the child of a particular age, society, con-
vention; of what we may call in one word a tradition.
He is secondly, in one degree or another, a rebel against
that tradition. And the best traditions make the best
rebels." Of this truth the Master's life presents a perfect illustration. How anxious the teacher at Nazareth
must have been as he saw this spiritually minded youth
whom he so loved going beyond the acceptance of the
rabbis' best traditions into revolt against their insuffi-
ciency. Dangerous thoughts were afire in that boy's
mind. He was not content with the narrow nationalism of his people. He was thinking deep thoughts
about God and duty so free from the entanglements of

cult that they were likely to become universally human, capable of being taken up, thought through, and lived upon by men of any race at any time. No village teacher could have grasped that idea or wished to grasp it. I stood one day spellbound in the little synagogue sympathizing with that amiable, liberal, yet conventional man who anxiously discerned there for the first time the new wings on which his favorite pupil yet would fly.

Meanwhile, year after year, we may picture Jesus going up to the Passover in Jerusalem. Luke tells us that his parents went up every year [1] and, while the Master's first pilgrimage with them is specially recorded, there is every reason to suppose that after that he joined the annual caravan from Nazareth to worship in the temple. He, too, traveled. He, too, knew his country and its capital as well as its Scriptures and the teaching of its rabbis. While, therefore, after Joseph died he worked as a carpenter to support his mother and her growing family, he was whetting inward tools fit to match the keenest dialectics of the famous rabbis. Yet how little his fellow townsmen understood what was going on within him! How blind they were to the difference between him and them! By inevitable steps the day of revelation came, when they stood before him shocked and angry at his strange new teaching—"Is not this the carpenter, the son of Mary, and brother of James, and Joses, and Judas, and Simon? and are not his sisters here with us?" [2]

[1] Luke 2:41.                    [2] Mark 6:3.

The presence of the traditional synagogue site makes the scene of Jesus' rejection by his fellow-townsmen vivid to the visitor.  Somewhere along Jordan John the Baptist had been drawing the crowds from all Palestine and, whether at the fords near Jericho or at Abarah, north of Beisan, where Esdraelon drops to the river, Jesus had gone to be baptized.[1]  The burden of his family's support apparently was eased; his brothers were growing up; he was thirty years of age and the day of his public teaching had arrived. Already he had been in Capernaum and had aroused attention there.[2]  His family's anxiety about him doubt-less had begun—a solicitude so acute that a little later they concluded that he was beside himself.[3]  Our imaginary rabbi must also have been concerned at the fearless unconventionality of this erstwhile scholar and at his amazing deeds, but still, like a true teacher, he clung to his faith in his pupil and to the village syna-gogue one Sabbath welcomed the boy of Nazareth, now become a man with a resounding name.

What painter could reproduce the scene—the car-penter preaching to his old associates who thought they knew him well; the strained expectancy of Mary and the family; the hopefulness and yet the fear of the rabbi trying to be loyal still; the sermon, then, with an old text driven home to a new issue and with a clear attack upon the cherished racial prejudices of the Jews!  I walked up and down the little synagogue

[1] Mark 1:2-11.
[2] Luke 4:23.
[3] Mark 3:21 M.

until I thought I saw it all—the rising wrath of outraged orthodoxy, the grief of the family, the disappointment of friends, the despair of the teacher who finds
his pupil flying now beyond his utmost reach, until
the pent passion of the crowd can be no more repressed.
Out of the synagogue and down the narrow streets
of Nazareth I followed the mob that dragged the Master to the precipice which stands there yet—the Mount
of Precipitation it is called today—whence, it well may
be, the angry villagers proposed to cast our Lord.

Such was the end of Jesus' residence in Nazareth.
So far as we know he never returned to it again.    It
is today a shrine alike of beautiful and tragic memories.    Here his boyhood must have been wholesome
and radiant—

> A little Child, a Joy-of-heart, with eyes
>    Unsearchable, he grew in Nazareth,
> His daily speech so innocently wise
>    That all the town went telling: "Jesus saith." [1]

Yet here he was rejected by his friends and where first
he had seen a crucifixion his own crucifixion cruelly
began.

[1] Katharine Lee Bates: At Nazareth.

# CHAPTER IX

## THE GALILEAN MINISTRY

### I

WHETHER on their first visit to the Sea of Galilee most travelers will find delight or disillusionment predominant, I cannot guess. There is occasion for both. We saw the sea first from the top of Tabor, lying emerald-green and beautiful among its hills, ten miles away. The charm and sorcery of its distant loveliness, with none of the disillusionment of a nearer view, first captivated us and, like Whittier, we still in memory

> ... pause on the goat-crags of Tabor to see
> The gleam of thy waters, O dark Galilee!

As everywhere in Palestine, however, when one comes close to sacred places, so often barren, soiled, common, and poor, the visitor must adjust his thought to what he sees as he draws near Galilee. If Jesus mourned over the coming woes of populous and prosperous cities like Capernaum and Chorazin, how grieved would he feel now if he should come again over the hills from Nazareth to the lake that was the center of his ministry! Still it is lovely in its set-

ting.  It lies 682 feet below sea level, and the hills
rise from its shores on every side except where Jordan
enters from the north and flows out toward the south.
Some thirteen miles long and at its widest about seven
miles broad, it presents an enchanting picture.  From
the crest of the heights that fall sharply away into its
deep depression, its restless sparkle of waters, its well-
meadowed shores, and its encompassing hills afford
an arresting and rememberable view and would do so
even if no associations clustered here.

Jesus must often have paused upon these hills and
brooded over the scene beneath, but what he saw was
very different from the view today.  Here in the
Master's time ran trunk roads, with busy traffic passing
to and fro and tax-gatherers sitting at the custom-
houses to collect the tolls.  Here were cities which he
could compare with Tyre, Sidon, Nineveh, and from
which, as public attention centered on him, "a great
multitude followed him, and they thronged him." [1]
Here were noblemen's houses with many servants, [2]
wealthy landlords whose barns must be torn down and
built larger to receive the harvests; [3] not rustic sins
alone, but those which curse cities—public prostitu-
tion, [4] jealous social distinctions, [5] bitter poverty close
to self-indulgent wealth. [6]  Here on the lake were fleets
of fishing boats, and on the shores miles of nets to be
dried and mended.  Such is the picture in the background of the gospels.  Everywhere about the lake the

[1] Mark 5:24.
[2] John 4:46,51.
[3] Luke 12:18.

[4] Luke 7:37.
[5] Luke 14:8-9.
[6] Luke 16:19-20.

Master moved in the midst of populous, opulent, cosmopolitan life where a man might gain the whole world and lose his soul, and where at times the exacting throng so wearied him that he had to go apart and rest awhile.[1]

This picture, unconsciously drawn for us by those who told the story of the Master's ministry, is confirmed by Josephus. Only a short generation after Jesus died he was military governor in Galilee. He, too, continually visited beside the lake, and his picture of the land is everywhere congenial with the gospels' portraiture. How utterly incredible is the attempt to dissolve Jesus into a myth! No one, I think, who ever visited Galilee has been tempted to surrender common sense to that highly sophisticated and baseless supposition. It is not only true that the invention of him and his parables would require a genius like his own; it is also true that, not simply in large outlines which could be artificially devised but in all the small, intimate, unconscious implications of the narrative, the gospels and Galilee fit each other perfectly. If there were any doubt of that, Josephus should settle the matter. The Galilee he ruled and described a few years after Jesus died is the same Galilee the gospels unwittingly portray.

In Josephus we read that there were in Galilee two hundred and four cities and villages, the smallest of which numbered about fifteen thousand inhabitants, and while ancient estimates of population, largely

[1] Mark 6:31.

unchecked by accurate statistics, are as notoriously suspect as modern guesses at the number of people in a congregation, the statement of Galilee's governor must mean at least a populous countryside. He himself fortified nineteen places under his charge. Everywhere in Josephus' descriptions of Galilee, as in the gospels, we hear of an eager, energetic people and a land never "destitute of men of courage or of a large population." About the lake the land is "so fruitful that all sorts of trees can grow upon it . . . for the temper of the air is so well mixed that it agrees very well with different sorts"—especially walnuts, palm trees, fig trees, olives. Particularly lovely is that portion of the lakeside which is "watered from a most fertile fountain, which the people of the country call Capharnaum."

In Josephus' pages, as well as in the gospels, the lake itself is famous for its fish, some of them "different both in taste and appearance from those elsewhere." Of Galilee in general he assures us that "all of it is capable of cultivation, and it is every where fruitful," and this fertility has issued in a highly organized and prosperous economic life with monopolies like that for selling choice Galilean oil to the merchants of Cæsarea or to the Syrian Jews. Nor are the interests and attitudes of the people other than the gospels picture them. Here, too, they are eager to be rid of their infesting devils, and Josephus knows about a root of rue so powerful that "if it be only brought to sick persons, it quickly drives away those who are called demons." In his pages we even meet the Pharisees

who "valued themselves highly upon the strict observ-
ance of the law of their fathers, and made men believe
they were highly favored by God."

Today, however, this busy, wealthy life of Galilee
which moves so restlessly through the narratives of
Jesus' ministry and Josephus' administration is altogether gone. The towns have vanished that the
Master knew, except Tiberias; the trees have fallen and
the hills are bare; where gardens grew are morasses,
and the lake itself is empty of sails and the shores
idle and untenanted. Only the outlines of unaided
nature remain to indicate the setting of the Master's
ministry. The lake is lovely still. Sunrise and sunset and the full moon on its restless waters are as Jesus
saw them. These hills knew his prayerful vigils, and
the Jordan still pours down its flood from Hermon's
snows, but the civilization that once prospered here
is gone. At Bethsaida, with Bedouin tents to mark
the site, at the country of the Gerasenes, with swamps
now underneath its beetling, unpopulated headland,
at Capernaum with its tumbled ruins, at Chorazin on
its barren hill—everywhere one finds that the things
which were seen have proved temporal and only the
unseen is eternal,

> Where the quiet-colored end of evening smiles
> Miles and miles
> On the solitary pastures where our sheep
> Half-asleep
> Tinkle homeward through the twilight, stray or stop
> As they crop.

## II

Of the nine cities that made a continuous ring of population round the lake when Jesus taught here only Tiberias remains. When Jesus was twenty-one years of age in Nazareth, A.D. 16, Herod Antipas founded and began to build this town, and, when Jesus was twenty-seven, finished and occupied it as his capital. Built as it was, however, over an old Jewish cemetery, it was long considered ceremonially unclean and Herod was compelled forcibly to gather its inhabitants from among foreigners and the lower types of Jews. So far as we know, Jesus never set foot within it, and in the gospels its presence on the lake is mentioned only once.[1] One visits it today, therefore, with little consciousness of the Master's presence.

Thither, after the destruction of Jerusalem, the leading Jewish rabbis moved and, reversing its long reputation as an unclean place, made it the chief center of rabbinic teaching. The ruins of a large castle, possibly of Herod's building, still are here, which Jesus may have seen. Here, too, is an ancient synagogue, and outside the city, to the south, have been exhumed traces of buildings, inscriptions, and sarcophagi which go back to the days when the Palestinian Talmud was being written here. There can be no mistaking the site, because the famous medicinal hot springs of which Pliny and Josephus tell us still flow copiously a little to the south. It was these springs which doubt-

[1] John 6:23.

less drew to the lake from far distances many of the
sick folk of whom we hear in the Master's ministry.
Today five thousand Jews live in the town, together
with over two thousand Moslems and an inconsiderable
sprinkling of various Christians. One of those strange,
teasing juxtapositions of incongruous things in which
Palestine abounds is presented by an able and devoted
group of Presbyterians from Scotland endeavoring to
make Christ triumphant beside the lake where long
ago Christ himself was first welcomed and then
refused.

It is outside Tiberias, among the hills and along the
lake shore, or upon the waters when a squall blows up
and boatmen labor at the oars, that one most keenly
feels the Master's companionship. That there is at
times depression in the scene must be confessed. These
vacant shores, with their swift and tingling life
departed, keep conjuring up the voice that said, "Woe
unto thee." [1] Mejdel, for example, three miles from
Tiberias northward, is the ancient Magdala whence
Mary Magdalene came. One who has loved the story
of her redemption by the Master, has pictured her
beside his Cross and early at his tomb, or has imagined
her dressed in the splendor of the later legends that
grew up around her, looks dissatisfied upon the gruesome, loathly group of squalid mud-brick hovels that
occupy the site of her home town. Our ears as well
as eyes were thus distressed, for a poor Moslem widow,
lately bereaved, sat in the dust beside her husband's

[1] Matthew 11:21.

grave and, covered with dust herself, wailed her lament aloud for all the world to hear. How far a fall this town has had since Tiberias was Herod's capital and the lakeside hummed with eager life!

The site of Chorazin, now called Kerazeh, where Jesus must have taught and healed, naturally calls out the pilgrim's expectation. Coming and going, it requires a toilsome two hours' walk from the lake shore to visit it today. No more do the great roads pass by it, thronged with merchants and animated, like nerves, with stirring news of battles, imperial policies, new monopolies, fresh revolts, disasters, scandals, crimes, and politics. We could not even find a path, but followed sheep trails or tramped across open fields where every footstep was a profanation, it crushed so many flowers.

The situation of Chorazin still retains the indications of its old nobility, for it crowns the crest of a lordly hill, with wide views both inland and lakeward. Saving the outlook, however, it is a lonely, desolate site. We climbed the rough hillside to its ruins, to find close at hand the black tents of the Bedouin and shelters for their sheep built of rocks from the ancient walls. We walked long in silence among the tumbled stones where, without doubt, the Master once walked too. One building still is impressive in its wreckage —the synagogue. How old these finely sculptured stones may be, or this stately seat where once, I suppose, the head rabbi sat, no one can confidently say. The synagogue probably goes back to the high days

of the Jewish rabbis here in the early centuries after
Christ.   But it well may occupy the situation of the
older building which Jesus knew and in which he may
have taught.   Unrelieved desolation now claims the
scene.   As we turned to go, dropping bakshish into
the hand of a tatooed Bedouin woman who sat lonely
among the ruins in sight of her tattered tents, the mist,
which all the morning had hung thick among the hills,
condensed into a sudden, driving rain, and we left
the forsaken jumble of stones with the Master's words
oppressively meaningful:   "Woe unto thee, Chorazin."

### III

Were the Master suddenly to return he would no
longer find either throngs to crowd him from the beach
or boats to retreat to if they did.   Day after day the
sea is empty of sail, and when one wishes to explore
the shores upon the other side a boat must specially
be summoned from Tiberias.   We started one morning
across the lake for the country of the Gerasenes, where
Jesus healed the demoniac and where the swine
plunged headlong to the sea.[1]   Kersa is the modern
name.   The sheer cliffs still there make a picturesque
setting for the story.   As for life, however, there was
little to be seen—wild ducks, a pair of storks pausing
in their migration, a few Bedouin tents and straggling
flocks; no more.

From Kersa we tacked up the lake to the Jordan's

[1] Luke 8:26-35.

inlet, where the wind rose suddenly, as of old on Galilee, and the rush of waters from the river helped to toss a heavy sea. Here, after much labor at the oars, we landed near where Bethsaida used to be. Its very name means "the house of fishing" and while, as Josephus tells us, Philip the Tetrarch had advanced it "to the dignity of a city, both from the number of inhabitants it contained, and its opulence in other respects," it was still in Jesus' day a place where folk could walk the shore and see fishermen at their work. Neither signs of a fishing settlement, however, nor remains of a city's "opulence" are left today. The Jordan flows swiftly down toward the sea past nothing more permanent than Bedouin tents—except memories. They always will cluster here, where Jesus walked with his disciples, where he retired for quiet when he heard of John the Baptist's death, and whence, with five thousand people following him on foot, he withdrew into a desert place.[1]

The most interesting spot beside the lake is, of course, Capernaum. Its site—Tell Hum—is the more certain because the archeologists, so reluctant to unite on it, seeking so diligently elsewhere to find the Master's home city, in recent years with such increasing confidence have been swinging toward a common center in these most impressive ruins. Here have been uncovered the remains, remarkably preserved, of a beautiful old synagogue, so old that one inevitably thinks of the Roman centurion in this very town who in Jesus'

[1] Luke 9:10-17.

day had commended himself to the favor of the Jews by embellishing the city with a synagogue.[1]   This impression has been deepened by the fact that this ruined structure was built on classic models, with beautiful Corinthian capitals, rich entablatures, and even forms of living creatures sculptured in the stone. The Franciscan fathers are today rebuilding it, as far as may be, from the ruins, and so much of it is left that the future visitor will see the shape and outline and some of the profusely ornamented decorations of this ancient place of worship.   At least, it is the kind of synagogue that a wealthy Roman might have built, and even if this identification be wishful thinking and the synagogue be really from the second or third century A.D., as most archeologists suppose, it still helps to make vivid the Master's ministry in this, his favorite town beside the sea.

The situation still is beautiful.   The outlines of many foundations lying uncovered upon every side indicate a populous community.   Here lived Simon Peter and his brother Andrew; [2] here dwelt also Peter's partners, James and John, the sons of Zebedee; [3] and here were done those mighty works that drew to the Master the attention of the entire lakeside and bound to him in deathless loyalty his little group of followers. Today, among the silent ruins, with only a Franciscan monastery near at hand and even there only a monk or two visible quietly working in the garden, it

[1] Luke 7:1-5.                            [3] Luke 5:10.
[2] Mark 1:21,29.

taxes one's imagination to picture what Capernaum used to be. The silence now is broken only by the rustling branches or the lap of waves upon the beach. Then the city was one of the chief stations on the great caravan-route from Damascus to the Mediterranean ports and Egypt, and the markets, the custom-house, the tax-gatherers, the Roman garrison, the exports of famous fish from the sea and similarly famous wheat from the land, the gatherings of Jewish teachers for their conferences,[1] and the constant passage of caravans, pilgrims, and couriers with news of the whole world must have made it a thriving center of cosmopolitan life.

All sorts of people gathered here—Greeks from the prosperous cities of the Decapolis across the lake, Romans in military service or on civil embassage, merchants from the Euphrates and the Nile, Bedouin from the desert, Dives in his wealth and Lazarus in his poverty, and, as for the Jews, all kinds of them, renegades and patriots, the strictest literalists and the loosest compromisers. Among the disciples whom Jesus chose here were found strange contrasts. How could Simon the Zealot, follower of Judas the Galilean, a fanatical rebel against Rome, agree with Matthew the tax-gatherer, who sat in the custom-house of Capernaum and collected tolls for Herod Antipas? One who pictures the Master, therefore, whether in Nazareth, his first home, or in Capernaum, his second, as secluded in a rustic environment, where he might dream ideal

---

[1] Luke 5:17; cf. Matthew 9:1-8.

visions apart from stubborn facts, misconceives the
situation utterly.   At few places in Palestine could he
have been more in the tingling center of political and
commercial business than here in Capernaum, which
he himself described as "exalted unto heaven." [1]

## IV

From Capernaum the Master and his disciples went
out through all of Galilee upon their tour of healing
and teaching.   None of the visited villages especially
mentioned in the gospels can we positively identify.
Three sites are plausibly suggested for Cana, and Nain
is probably Nein, a mean and squalid settlement today,
six miles southeast of Nazareth, on the north slope
of Little Hermon.   One who from some height like
Safed looks over Galilee can imagine the charming
countryside with its many nooks and valleys sprinkled
with those two hundred towns and more of which
Josephus tells, and can picture the travels of the
Master during the high days of his popularity.   At
last, however, when the pressure of hostility against
his new Gospel became too menacing, he "went
away into the borders of Tyre and Sidon." [2]   He was
no stranger there; already "a great number of the people from . . . the sea coast of Tyre and Sidon" had
gathered around his ministry at the Sea of Galilee [3]
and, when he reached the western crest of the Galilean

[1] Matthew 11:23.                    [3] Luke 6:17.
[2] Mark 7:24.

plateau and looked out across the glorious coastal plain where the ancient cities of Phœnicia lay, he was still within the circle of his friends.

We went to Tyre and Sidon one memorable day, skirting the seashore northward from Haifa. Here the Mediterranean is at its loveliest. The coastal plain is more fertile than any other spot I saw in Palestine, and the foothills of the Lebanons rise up splendidly beyond it. Tyre itself, over thirty miles north of Haifa, is one of those many places where only enough is left to form a nucleus for the traveler's imagination. We made our way from the mainland through the accumulated sand that choked the causeway built by Alexander the Great; thence we walked through the poor and shrunken town and stood on the jetty of its choked-up harbor, to see a few fishing smacks where once rode the navies of the world. Then we returned to the mainland beach, to sit in meditation on Ezekiel's prophecy about Tyre, so improbable at the time and yet so obviously come true: "She shall be a place for the spreading of nets in the midst of the sea." [1]

A fascinating procession of historic scenes can be conjured up as one sits on the beach and watches the shriveled remnants of this famous city. Embassies from David to Hiram, King of Tyre, about the "cedar trees, and carpenters, and masons" [2] for the royal palace in Jerusalem came here. Along these shores fishermen gathered murex shells to make the Tyrian dye which brought the city wealth, and when the shells grew scarce ships scoured the sea for them and launched

[1] Ezekiel 26:5.     [2] II Samuel 5:11.

thereby a naval empire the like of which the world had never seen. From this now-shrunken port ships trafficked up the Nile, along the shores of the Black Sea, among Tyrian colonies on the North African coast, and in Sicily, Sardinia, and southern France. Spain was a market for them. The merchants from these shores worked tin mines in British Cornwall and built depots in the Scilly Isles and the Isle of Wight. From this port the traditional Dido sailed to found Carthage. Here came the Assyrian and Babylonian conquerors from the Euphrates with their ruinous sieges and bloody massacres. Here were shipped the cedars for the second temple, which the returning exiles built on Zion.[1] Here Alexander the Great besieged the town by sea and land for seven months and when it fell slew eight thousand of its inhabitants, crucified two thousand more upon the shore, and sold thirty thousand into slavery. Paul spent seven days here,[2] and later a Christian church took the place of the great pagan temple. Here Origen, the famous Christian teacher of the third century, died. At last, in the conflicts of the crusades, the Saracens so wrecked the town that it never rose again. No wonder that Kipling used Tyre with Nineveh as a symbol of the vanished "pomp of yesterday."

To these coasts the Master came; saw here in Tyre, it may be, the prodigal in a far country wasting his substance with riotous living;[3] perhaps visited Zarephath near Sidon, now plausibly identified with Sarafend,

---

[1] Ezra 3:7.
[2] Acts 21:3-4.
[3] Luke 15:13.

where Elijah ministered to the widow;[1] saw probably some such glorious scene as greets the eye today in Sidon's plain, where orange and lemon trees, palm, banana, fig, apricot, and olive trees grow in rich profusion; visited the proud cities where were all the things after which the Gentiles seek;[2] and watched "the rulers of the Gentiles lord it over them."[3]   As for memorials of his visit, no monument celebrates his unnoticed coming.   His name is not among the age-long records of great conquerors who, from the ancient Hittites to the modern French, have engraved the stories of their conquests on the northern cliffs where the Dog River meets the sea.   But on the hills above Sidon we saw one thing to remind us that he had been here—an orphanage where abandoned Armenian children were being cared for by the Near East Relief.   It was a finer monument than Sennacherib, Nebuchadnezzar, or Alexander had left upon these shores.   It was evidence that sometime Jesus of Nazareth had passed this way.   I stood upon that noble hillcrest among the children and, looking down upon the cities where so many a victor's greed had had its way, recalled afresh that

> . . . . . . . . . . . . . . conquering
> May prove as lordly and complete a thing
> In lifting upward as in crushing low.[4]

[1] I Kings 17:8-16.            [3] Matthew 20:25.
[2] Matthew 6:32.
[4] Elizabeth Barrett Browning: Sonnets from the Portuguese XVI.

## V

From Tyre and Sidon the Master returned to his
ministry by the Sea of Galilee, but when hostility to
him grew so virulent and menacing that a crisis plainly
was at hand, he went up the river with his disciples
a day's journey from Bethsaida to Cæsarea Philippi.
One of the few disappointments of our trip lay in the
fact that we could not go there too.  By those springs
of Jordan, where Peter acclaimed Jesus as Messiah, the
French were endeavoring to crush the Druses, and
instead of visiting the site with memories of the Prince
of Peace, we stood upon the hills far off and listened
to the firing that echoed, volley after volley, from
below.

Syria under French rule is a sad sight; no more
disastrous travesty of a mandate from the League of
Nations can easily be imagined.  Especially in Cæsarea
Philippi, where our Lord explained to his disciples the
necessity of his Cross, it was tragic to see "Christians"
still trying to extend "Christendom" by fire and sword.

This ancient site bears now the name Banias, reminiscent of the god Pan's sanctuary which here stood beside
the springs of Jordan.  Once again flowing water made
and still maintains a rememberable site.  Here one of
the chief fountains of Jordan pours copiously from the
flank of Hermon and, cradled in a luxuriant nook, a
little village, largely ruined now by war, still stands
where once stood Cæsarea Philippi.

Could we have gone there closely to inspect the place, we should have seen but little to remind us of the past. The lovely setting, the copious waters, the choked grotto near which the temple stood, a few old votive niches in the rocks, and some Greek inscriptions—"Priest of Pan," "To Pan and the Nymphs . . ."—no more than this, they say, is visible today. What Jesus saw we know well from the records. Because of the beauty of the natural setting and the sacredness of fountains, religion had conspired with love of nature to adorn the spot. Here, where Jordan's head waters pour from their grotto, stood two famous shrines. One was sacred to Pan, the goat god, incarnation of the old paganism with its worship of natural joys. The other was sacred to Augustus. When Jesus was nineteen years old, in Nazareth, the stirring news reached Palestine that the old emperor was dead. For more than fifty years Augustus had been the ruling genius of the world, and the boys of Nazareth doubtless heard eager, anxious discussions about his dying and its probable effect on Palestine. Doubtless, too, they heard with scorn, soon after, that his spirit had been seen rising to heaven from the funeral pyre and that in Rome a splendid temple was to house his worship. A sanctuary for that purpose had been standing here beside the Jordan's springs for many years. So close-knit was the empire, so swift the transfer of new thoughts, new customs, new worships, that Herod the Great had built here a temple to Augustus before the Master's birth. Herod's son Philip refounded and embellished the city,

gave it the name by which the Master knew it, and
raised it to the peak of beauty and sanctity, where it
was when Jesus came.

It was provocative of many thoughts even to stand
afar upon the hills, forbidden by the authorities to
cross the border, and from there to picture the scene
at Cæsarea Philippi.  One naturally thinks of that high
hour, when the disciples recognized the Master
avowedly as Christ and so began the first confession of
Christian faith on which the church was founded, as
set in a Jewish matrix, surrounded by Jewish sights
and sounds, and impregnated with Jewish thoughts
alone.  At the springs of Jordan, however, was no
Judaism, but paganism in its two chief forms: the old
nature-worship of Pan and the new, sophisticated
adoration of the emperor.  The vows of Christ's first
disciples were taken in the presence of the dominant
religions of the Roman Empire.  Who can forbear to
wonder at that strange scene where a Jewish carpenter
gathered his few disciples on the flank of Hermon
within sight of the temple of Augustus?  Here in close
proximity stood two faiths that were soon to battle
for the Roman world.  How certain of success Augustus
seemed! For years he had been addressed as God, not
only in formal temples but in personal discourse, as in
the Odes of Horace:

> As Hercules in Greece, or Castor, may,
>   So thou hast our libations and our prayers;
> Before our Lares we, our debt to pay,
>   Thy godhead blend with theirs.

How incredible it would have seemed then to think that the man from Galilee, sitting there with his few disciples, would gather to himself all the ascriptions of divinity that clothed Augustus and much more besides, until his temples would outstrip the emperor's, and his influence make all that Augustus ever did seem small by comparison!

Many things said to have happened in Galilee during the Master's ministry seem to the modern mind incredible. Yet nothing in advance could have seemed quite so far beyond belief as that which has actually happened since the day when near a temple of the divine Augustus a little group of quite ordinary men rallied to the standard of the divine Christ.

This scene at Cæsarea Philippi emphasizes a truth too little stressed in our thoughts of Jesus' ministry. The civilization of Rome, with its laws and armies, its splendid buildings and incomparable roads, did not simply hold Syria and Palestine in pawn as distant counters in the Roman game, but interpenetrated them and left there some of the most majestic memorials of its greatness. Only sixty miles north of Banias lies Baalbek. We risked the venture of going there, although the French had again bombarded Damascus, irreparably ruining another section of that ancient city, martyring scores of innocent noncombatants, and throwing the whole land into a ferment of suppressed excitement and wrath. We came down over the Lebanons, where we had spent a day among the famous trees, few in number now but still beautiful, and pressed on toward Baalbek. As we progressed we found the stream of traffic flowing unanimously the other way. Laden donkeys, automobiles, and camels passed us, headed toward Beirut and the sea. Curious questions as to the reason rose among us but, happy in our ignorance, we went on. Only when we reached Baalbek itself, to find it utterly disheveled and its few, lingering people badly scared, did we learn that bandits had swept in a few hours before, shot up the town, burned the governor's house, and taken two prominent citizens to the mountains to be held for ransom. Both then and the next day, when going down to Beirut, we met French armored cars and motor lorries full of troops advancing for another try at their endless, futile chase of guerilla foes, I saw sights reminiscent of almost-forgotten days in France.

The ancient ruins of Baalbek are not surpassed, I think, in their impressiveness by anything the Romans left, even in Italy, outside of Rome. They are so well preserved that one can judge their mass and sweep and cumulative effect, as well as the richness and beauty of their decoration in detail. Visited though they were amid the distress of a harried, frightened town, they remain yet in memory one of the most astounding relics of antiquity I have ever seen. Grandiose they are, exaggerated, boastful, and laboriously huge, as though the older Roman chastity of strong and simple line had been forgotten and ambition for bigness had usurped

its place, but, for all that, amazing in their loveliness
and grandeur. In these temples Jupiter, Venus, Mer-
cury, and Bacchus were worshiped in high state, and
every imperial heart-beat at Rome must have made
its pulse felt here.

While, so far as we know, the Master never came to
Baalbek, the Roman life and glory which are represented here were not foreign to his world. He knew
them and estimated their significance. He saw them
with his own eyes in the flourishing cities of the Decapolis across Jordan, in Scythopolis, at the eastern end
of Esdraelon, not many miles from Nazareth, in Tyre
and Sidon, and in Cæsarea Philippi.

His heart was always with unpretentious things—
fields and flowers, vineyards and husbandmen, children,
household tasks, farmers and fishermen—but his mind
knew well the imperial world in which his generation
lived. His sermon on some hillside here in Galilee was
not preached by a visionary speaking to dreamers. He
was enunciating what he believed to be those basic
principles without which no society can be a Kingdom
of God, and before he formulated them he had assayed
the Roman Empire and all its ways. The empire has
departed and other empires, adopting its methods, have
followed and yet will follow it to dissolution, but still
the Galilean sermon haunts the best conscience of mankind. Some day the race will cease calling it visionary.
Even though they do not take it literally, men will take
it seriously, which is another matter. They will discover, as the Master said, that those who act upon these

principles are "like a sensible man who built his house on rock." [1]

## VII

One memorable day a little group of men with a leader whose face was steadfastly set to go to Jerusalem came down from the plateau of Galilee through Esdraelon. Many a conquerer had crossed this plain before him. Here had lain the highroad of all invaders on conquest bent, from the earliest days, when Egypt struck from the south or some caldron boiled over from the north, as Jeremiah said.[2] Let one stand, as I did, on the summit of Megiddo, across the plain from Nazareth, and one will see in visual imagination, on the actual site, the march of the victors from Thutmose III to Allenby. They all have come up by the pass of Megiddo, have been forced to capture that before going farther, until Armageddon has entered the permanent vocabulary of the world as the symbol of a crucial fight.

Here already, in the new excavations, long-hoped-for reminders of the great conquerors have come to light. We saw the broken stele on which Dr. Breasted has found the cartouche of Pharaoh Shishak, who in the days of Rehoboam stole the treasure from the Jewish temple.[3] No confirmation of the Bible story that Shishak came to Palestine had ever been found in the Holy Land before, but his own record of the visit had long

---

[1] Matthew 7:24 M.                    [3] I Kings 14:25-26.
[2] Jeremiah 1:13.

been awaiting excavation at Megiddo. Here we saw, just exhumed, a score of beautiful scarabs of Thutmose III which he, or some officer of his, left behind him fourteen centuries before Christ. Month by month we may expect new findings to illumine the story of the conquerors who have crossed Esdraelon.

Strange irony of history! They came with victorious armies, dangling the destinies of the race in their fingers and deciding with a word the fate of nations, and they all have vanished into items of archeological research. One conqueror, however, crossed this plain, whose living influence grows with every century. He came afoot with a few followers, unheralded, willing to endure two blows rather than give one, going south-ward to be crucified; and "to him be the glory and the dominion for ever and ever." [1]

[1] Revelation 1:6.

# CHAPTER X

## GOING UP TO BE CRUCIFIED

### I

JESUS had doubtless been in Jerusalem many times before the last tragic week of his crucifixion. Having come with his family to the Passover when he was twelve, it is natural to suppose that he accompanied them afterward on their annual pilgrimages. Indeed, according to the Fourth Gospel, it was on his return from a sojourn there after his public ministry began that he encountered the Samaritan woman at Jacob's well.[1]

That well remains one of the most arresting sites in Palestine. Unhappily covered by a partially completed Greek Catholic church, it presents a painful example of ecclesiastical maltreatment of a sacred place; but, even so, one may sit in the open air outside the church and make the events of John's vivid chapter seem visually real. We borrowed a copy of the Greek New Testament from a priest and read together John's picturesque description of the interview. Despite the assurance of scholars that John the Disciple could not have written the Fourth Gospel, it seems incredible that whoever did describe the conversation at the well had not him-

[1] John 4:1-30

self been there.  We found ourselves surprised and fascinated at the correspondences.  As we read the conversation we could put in the very gestures that would fit the words.  An Arab village named 'Askar, commonly regarded as the successor of ancient Sychar, lies up the valley in plain view, ten minutes away, on the rising ground of a hillside.  Sitting by the well, weary with his walking, the Master could have watched his disciples all their way to the village gates and could have seen the woman pass them coming down, jar upon her head, leaving the village spring with its hard water for the softer water of the sacred well.  As for the well itself, choked though it is by fallen stones at the bottom, its seventy-five feet still witness that once it was very deep.[1]  The references in the conversation to local scenery are certainly too pat to be accidental.  "Neither in this mountain, nor in Jerusalem," said Jesus,[2] indicating towering Gerizim, whose steep flanks begin to rise a few hundred yards across the road.  "Lift up your eyes, and look on the fields," he added;[3] and there in the valley grows still some of the fairest grain we saw in Palestine.  Plenty of difficult, perhaps insoluble, problems are associated with the Fourth Gospel, but whoever wrote this chapter had surely been at Jacob's well.

## II

By what route the Master made his final journey to

[1] John 4:11.
[2] John 4:21.
[3] John 4:35.

Jerusalem it is not easy to decide. Mark [1] and
Matthew [2] suggest that he traveled through Trans-
Jordania, called Perea in the Master's day, while Luke
tells us that he went by way of Samaria; [3] but all unite
in picturing his approach to Jerusalem from Jericho,
which would suggest a Trans-Jordan ministry. No necessary conflict is involved, only uncertainty as to the
route he took. Of one thing, however, we are sure:
his journey, apparently leisurely and extending, it may
be, many months, carried him to Perea, across Jordan.

It still is one of the most fertile and sightly portions
of Palestine. The hills are bolder, the valleys more
spacious and productive than even in Samaria, and one
Arab, unwittingly using a phrase of Jesus, told us
gladly that his fields were yielding "sixtyfold." [4] In
the Master's day it was the center of a thriving civilization, the remaining monuments of which are among the
most impressive in the Holy Land.

The more important cities across Jordan originally
were Greek, populated by the Hellenes who followed
in the wake of Alexander's conquering armies. These
cities lost their freedom to the Jews during the age of
the Maccabees and regained it only when Pompey seized
the whole land for Rome and gave Trans-Jordania a
large measure of autonomy. Nevertheless, with a truculent Jewish population on one side and the desert
with its overflow of plundering Arabs on the other,
these foreign towns were in no comfortable place, and

[1] Mark 10:1.
[2] Matthew 19:1.
[3] Luke 9:51-52.
[4] Mark 4:8.

ten of them consolidated their joint interests in a league
called the Decapolis. We hear of it more than once in
the gospels: folk came thence to hear Jesus in Galilee [1]
or returned thither to spread his fame,[2] or welcomed
his coming into their borders.[3] On the chief roads of
Trans-Jordania, southeast of the Sea of Galilee, these
flourishing centers stood, and if the ruins of two of
them, Gerasa and Philadelphia, are typical, they must
have been populous and wealthy towns.

One glorious day in March we went out to Jerash,
old Gerasa, lying some forty miles beyond the Jordan
fords. Trans-Jordania now, as so often in its history,
is in a parlous and uncertain state. Its people nervously
fear the possible extension of Zionism across the river;
they feel still the constant pressure of the Bedouin,
whose long, black tents are seen in all the valleys; they
grow restive at the grip of Britain's hand and watch
with deep concern the military airplanes with their
dreaded bombs. The very tensity of politics, the restless resentment of the people, and the fear of the Jews
make new Trans-Jordania a modern replica of old
Perea. For so too, when Jesus came, the atmosphere
was unquiet. The Greek cities, with Romans over
them, with Jews who hated them on one side and Arabs
on their forays pressing from the other, were never
"safe from the clutches of calamity." [4]

We sped out from the Jordan over military roads, in
building which the British rival Rome, and, having

---

[1] Matthew 4:25.          [3] Mark 7:31.
[2] Mark 5:20.             [4] Habakkuk 2:9 M.

lunched at the fords of Jabbok where, in the old days, Jacob wrestled with the angel,[1] we swung around the noble hills about the picturesque town of es-Salt and came to Jerash, the ancient Gerasa.

For nearly a century before Jesus' ministry the Romans had been masters of Palestine, and under their steady, strong administration, with its relentless policy of consolidating the empire and its ambitious program of lavish building, we may be sure that more than one city in the land had been splendidly embellished. Today, however, even Cæsarea, the Roman capital on the seacoast, where Paul was two years a prisoner,[2] is an unsightly wreck.  Once it was famed for its temples and theaters, its walls and aqueducts, and its hippodrome where twenty thousand spectators could sit, but nothing now is visible save tumbled fragments of masonry and columns strewn along the shore, near an isolated fishing hamlet shut off by bad lands and sand dunes from the rest of Palestine.  So, too, Gaza and Ashkelon were noble towns in Roman days, adorned with splendid buildings, but time and man's destructiveness have ruined even the ruins of their greatness. Here across Jordan, however, in Gerasa, separated from the destructive fury of the crusaders, who spoiled so much Roman grandeur to build their castles, we can see a Greco-Roman city amazingly preserved.  Here we can walk the streets, pause in the colonnades, sit by the public fountain, meet our friends in the forum, worship in the temples, rest on the millstones in the city's bakery,

---

[1] Genesis 32:22-32.          [2] Acts 23:33-35 and 24:27.

sit where the judges sat in the basilica, watch, in imagination, races in the stadium, naval fights on the artificial sea, or comedies of Terence and Plautus in the theater.

A day spent in Jerash supplies one of the most rewarding memories that cluster about a pilgrimage to Palestine. Here one feels in vivid fashion the constructive power of Rome which, from Newcastle-upon-Tyne at the gate of Scotland to this splendid city on the edges of the Arabian Desert, not only conquered but built.

Here, where now only a small settlement survives, once stood a lordly town whose very ruins fairly take one's breath away. Nothing at Pompeii compares with the extensiveness and grandeur of this city. Its little theater, still beautiful and well preserved, could have seated three thousand people. A lovely colonnade, with many columns still erect, made through the city a central artery from the forum, past the Temple of the Sun, and in the midst of it was a fountain. Another temple still is exquisite, although only its façade is well preserved, and its glorious Corinthian columns, prone on every side, await the day of some one's generosity, when they can be reared once more to make the sanctuary almost whole. The Temple of the Sun, an imposing shrine of monumental proportions, crowns the whole community from its height, and everywhere one turns one sees memorials of wealth and artistry which must have made the city a resplendent place.

Did Jesus come here? It is not impossible that he

did. Through this land of Perea, perhaps down the
great trunk road on which such cities stood, he came
on his way to Jerusalem and may well have walked this
colonnade and by this fountain looked and listened even
if he did not teach.

One other city of the Decapolis we visited, 'Amman,
in ancient times the capital of the Ammonites, called
Rabbath Ammon and in Jesus' day known by its
Greek name, Philadelphia. It is nearly thirty miles
from Jericho on the other side of the Jordan. Here one
faces a jumbled potpourri of historical reminiscence so
characteristic of Palestinian towns, for here was the
enormous bedstead or sarcophagus of Og, king of
Bashan, which was fourteen feet long and six feet
broad,[1] at which the Hebrews marveled; under these
walls Uriah died, a victim to the perfidy of David;[2]
here rose, in the Greco-Roman age, a splendid town,
neighbor to Gerasa; and here today the British government centers its military administration, and on the flat
hilltop above the town we saw great bombing planes in
fleets, ready to put the fear of Christendom into Moslem hearts. Here, too, the Master may have come, and
still the visitor can see the ruins of ancient baths, a
Roman temple, and a theater, well preserved, which
once seated six thousand people. Whether to this town
or that of the Decapolis the Master came we cannot
know, but on one point our previous impressions were
abundantly confirmed: he was no stranger to the splendor of the empire where, in giving to Cæsar the things

[1] Deuteronomy 3:11 M.     [2] II Samuel Ch. 11.

that were Cæsar's so many denied God the things that
were God's.

### III

When we came down from Perea to the fords of
Jordan and crossed to Jericho, we were again on certain ground. Here Jesus surely came. Here, where
his forefathers had crossed for conquest, he crossed for
saviorhood, and the town whose inhabitants they had
massacred he made forever memorable by saving
friendship for despised Bartimæus, the beggar, and
Zacchæus, the publican.[1] So desolate is the Jordan
plain, however, despite the palm trees, the banana
plantations, and the orange groves, that I found it
easier to picture the scene when first the Hebrews
sacked the city than when Jesus saw it in all the beauty
with which Herod the Great had clothed it.

Herod made Jericho his winter home and lavished
on it his peculiar care. Josephus must have seen it
much as Jesus did, and even he, the historian, grows
eloquent as he describes its fertile loveliness: "He
would not be mistaken who should pronounce this
place to be divine," "the most fruitful country of Judea,
which produces a great number of palm trees besides
the balsam tree," "a very happy situation, . . . very fit
for producing palm trees and balsam."

Here Jesus saw the aqueducts, the palace, baths,
theater, and fortress which Herod the Great had built,
and walked here, as elsewhere, among the monuments

[1] Mark 10:46-52; Luke 19:1-10.

of Roman engineering and architecture. When Jesus was a child Herod the Great had died here, and we especially were reminded of his long, hard fight for health, his ugly dying, and his gorgeous funeral, when one day at Callirrhoe by the Dead Sea, a few miles from Jericho, we bathed in the hot stream which once fed the famous thermal baths of Herod.

What a strange blend of legend and history encompasses this salt sea! Two days before, far toward the southern end, we had seen Lot's wife.[1] Jebel Usdum, a huge cliff about seven miles long, composed solidly of salt, rises sheer from the Dead Sea. It is one of the marvels of the world. The water, laving constantly this mass of rock salt and absorbing the great fragments that break from its cliffs, is even more saline, they say, than in the north. Here on this mountain of salt, from which our boatmen with pickaxes hacked away great portions for later use, Lot's wife is standing. To be sure, she is rarely twice the same, for, year after year, she too falls into the sea and some new pinnacle is chosen to represent the ancient tale. But with the traditional site of Sodom and Gomorrah near at hand, the Biblical story of the fleeing family and the woman punished for her backward look grows alike easy to explain and vivid to imagine.

Soon, however, we were plunged from tradition into history. Here at Callirrhoe, near the sea's northern end, springs pour from the cliffs so hot that we could not even bear our fingers in them. Once they fed Herod's

[1] Genesis 19:23-26.

baths.   It was a broiling day, I well recall, with the
fierce sun and the steam of the sea's huge caldron con-
spiring to make existence unbearable as we climbed
up from the shore along the streams which, once con-
served in thermal baths, now run loosely to the sea.
Hot as it was, however, we were glad, after three days
in the saline stickiness of that abyss, to find a pool far
enough from the stream's source so that the water had
cooled a little.   Into it we plunged.   It was hardly
bearable but it was refreshing.   I wonder if Herod the
Great, who once sought health in the waters of these
same springs, enjoyed them, for all the grandeur of his
baths, as much as we.

While the ancient works of man in this unique,
weird region are utterly undone, the works of nature
must be much the same.   Perhaps the Master, wandering solitary from the flippant, gay, degenerate populace
of Jericho, sought some evening the Dead Sea's northern shore and walked along it to the mouths of
Jordan, preparing his spirit for the tragic days ahead.
I dreamed of it one evening when I walked there.   The
seashore is a ghastly, barren place, strewn with broken
reeds, the tracks of jackals, spectral logs washed up by
the waves and frosted with the salt, with here and
there unwary fish which, venturing too far down Jordan, have been killed by an unsuspected foe and pickled
in the brine.   Of a sudden, with no inviting green to
herald them, one comes upon the mouths of Jordan.
They thrust their waters out into the sea in the midst
of a dreary wilderness: to the north, slime pits sur-

rounded by clay hillocks, curiously scarped and castellated; on the east the plateau of Moab, purple in the evening light; to the west the dour plain passing into the still wilder Judean wilderness, with the Mount of Olives standing clear in the distance above it; near at hand the drear, dead coast, salt pits, and ghostly, crusted branches of long-perished trees.

In such a landscape Jordan pushes its fresh waters forth into the sea. It is the most impressive symbol of hopeless endeavor I have ever looked upon. These waters came down from the fountains of Lebanon and the snows of Hermon, and here they invade the brine —one can see by the color how far they go—as though Jordan were making a desperate endeavor to sweeten the bitumen sea. It is a useless sacrifice. The tragedy of hopeless striving is here perpetually enacted—fresh water flowing, century after century, into a sea too poisoned ever to be cleansed, too dead ever to be made alive.

Was the Master tempted here so to see his ministry for men? Did he here perhaps renew in prayer his courage and his faith that the human race, not hopeless yet, could still be brought to sanity and peace?

## IV

Many strange processions have gone up from Jericho to Jerusalem—from David, returning after Absalom's rebellion to be king again, to Herod the Great, carried on a golden bier to be buried in high state upon the

ridge.    But no company ever made that journey so
fraught with man's spiritual destinies as Jesus and his
followers.    In memory of them we made the ascent one
unforgetable evening when all heaven and earth conspired to glorify the Judean wilderness.    From the
moment when, climbing up among the intricate and
winding wadies, we came within sight of Olivet again,
the evening shadows so picked out the hills that like
a gorgeous stairway, height beyond height, they rose
to their crest—the Mount of Olives, bearing Bethany,
like a toy town, on its shoulder.    The mystic light that
flooded the scene was silver-white, enveloping the intervening mountains in mysterious sheen and making
Olivet walk among them veiled yet luminous.    Perhaps
the Master saw it so as he came up the path from
Jericho to Jerusalem to be crucified.    Perhaps he
stopped, as we did, to gaze long upon a scene so
glorious in itself and so clothed with memories.    Perhaps that little band instinctively exclaimed as we did,
"O Jerusalem, Jerusalem . . . whither the tribes go up,
even the tribes of Jehovah." [1]

## V

The Jerusalem of Jesus' day was very different from
the old city of David.    Long since, its population had
increased and its walls had been enlarged until within
their compass lay the western hills and the intervening
Tyropœon valley, across which roadways, supported on

[1] Psalm 122:2-4.

great arches, carried the traffic to and from the temple area. In particular, Herod the Great, with his passion for building, had embellished the city in the generation before Jesus, so that his palace on the western hill, his castle near the temple area, and the new temple itself, whose outer colonnades were not completed until after Jesus' death, were the outstanding features of the city. Even a theater Herod had built here to the scandalization of the Jews, and, in the valley below, an amphitheater as well.

The pilgrim to Jerusalem today who wishes to see the Master's city as it was, uncorrupted by the guile of false identifications, faces no easy task. Here the evil work of ignorant piety has done its worst, and many a traveler leaves Jerusalem, not helped to see the days of the Master's passion more vividly, but so dismayed and shocked by superstition and incredible tales as to dare trust no place as a scene of Jesus' ministry and believe nobody as a guide.

Who can blame them? After one has been shown in Jerusalem the very spot where Abraham discovered the ram, the offering of which was substituted for the sacrifice of Isaac; or in the Church of the Holy Sepulcher itself has had pointed out the stone on which the body of our Lord was anointed for burial—although the stone was put there in 1808; after he has been shown the column to which our Lord was bound when he was beaten by the soldiers, which first is mentioned as a relic in 1384 and has changed its size and color frequently since then; when he has seen the Apostles' cave, where the disciples hid during the crucifixion, the house where Dives, the rich man of Jesus' parable, lived, and near at hand a corresponding house for the poor man in his utter penury; when with reverence he has tried to follow the Via Dolorosa, based on a false location of Pilate's court and without a shred of evidence for any spot encountered in its course, he may be excused for utter weariness and disillusionment. Some day one hopes these Christian churches will cease overlaying with their chicanery and ignorance the city of the Master's sacrifice.

In the meantime the intelligent traveler need not rely on guile nor believe in lies in order to walk with the Master in Jerusalem. Let him begin by climbing Olivet and, whether from the crest or from the flanking road that runs past traditional Bethany, look on the city as Jesus did. Here the Master paused and wept [1] as he saw Zion, and even one from Western lands, of cooler temperament, with no such poignant love of Jerusalem as the Master knew, must be deeply moved as he looks down from Olivet upon this city-shrine of many memories.

What the Master saw as he sat on the ass's colt among the multitude that waited with palm branches [2] while he looked, it is not difficult to visualize again. The city wall ran westward from below the present Saint Stephen's gate, past the great Castle of Antonia, which Herod had built not far from the temple, and, swinging around the western hill, took in Herod's massive

[1] Luke 19:41.                    [2] Luke 19:29-44.

palace with its towers; then, rimming the edge of the
valley of Hinnom, crossing the Tyropœon valley eastward to enclose Siloam, swinging northward again to
protect the spring Gihon and the ancient hill Ophel, it
reared itself to a great height from the Kidron valley
at the temple area.  All this circle of Jerusalem was
visible from Olivet, as it is today, and still, supremely
impressive, in the eastern wall, which used to rise
170 feet above the Kidron valley, is the great platform on which the temple stood.

This colossal, artificial stage reared itself up directly
across the Kidron valley from the spot where the
Master waited.  Nearly rectangular, some 400 yards
north and south by 300 east and west, stretched the
stone platform covered with buildings, columns, colonnades,—a fortress, a sanctuary, and an architectural display in one,—and in the midst of it the temple.  When
one reviews upon the spot the elaborate approaches, the
cumulative effects of the many buildings, the delicacy of
the colonnades, the stalwartness of the ramparts, whose
amplitude and beauty still are striking, one can imagine
vividly the scene which greeted the Master.  The whole
circle of Jerusalem lay before him and at the nearest
point, like a pearl in the ring, shone the temple and its
courts.

If the visitor would see the Master's Jerusalem at
close range, let him now come down from Olivet and
wander over the temple area itself.  No recognizable
stones are left of the buildings he knew here, and
a religion whose blend of old Judaism and new Chris-

tianity would be strange to him now is regnant where the temple stood. Only the great platform where he walked and the hills he saw from it remain substantially the same. If, however, one goes down under the Mosque el Aksa, which stands on the esplanade where a church of Justinian once stood, he will find himself in a dark and littered place, to be sure, amid old stone foundations and new concrete buttresses, but, for all that, in one of the most impressive spots in the city. Here one can literally walk in Jesus' footsteps. For here is a Herodian gateway, encompassed by later edifices but still clearly marked by its columns, its enormous lintels, and its steps. This gateway, which led up from Ophel to one of Herod's grand approaches to the temple platform, is one of the few remaining architectural fragments in Jerusalem that have come down from Jesus' day, a remnant to me more striking even than the great stones of the platform's outer wall or the bases of the arched roadways across the Tyropœon valley. By these steps, beneath these lintels, between these columns, Jesus must have passed. Here, where no shrine obscures the facts, we run upon a genuine memorial of the Master's day.

Two places associated with Jesus' ministry, Siloam and the pool of Bethesda, we also can be confident about. Siloam long has been well known—unlovely enough now and needing all the gifts of imagination to reconstruct its meaning to the ancient city. Bethesda has recently been uncovered and seems to be fairly well established. At least, Père Vincent, one of the best archeologists in Palestine, assured me of it. It has, as the gospels say, five porches, for it is a long rectangle—one porch on each of its four sides— divided into two squares by a porch across the middle. Still in process of excavation, it furnishes another link between the modern pilgrim and the Master's city.

Still more interesting are the remnants left us of the Tower of Antonia. One can see yet across the narrow street that leads in from Saint Stephen's gate the upper portion of a Roman arch's central span. The modern street is many feet above the ancient level but, entering a convent close at hand, one can go down to the old grade and see further remnants of the Roman arch and walk upon the very pavement where once the Roman soldiers of the Tower of Antonia idled or prepared to fight. It is a stirring place. To be sure, the sisters who worship and teach here are confident that this is Pilate's court where the Savior stood silent while the crowd cried "Crucify him!" The best archeological opinion disagrees and places Pilate's court in the old palace of Herod on the western hill, but no one doubts that on this pavement we are on authentic ground—the Tower of Antonia.

Under this archway Jesus doubtless walked; here Paul was brought when in the temple court close at hand the mob had seized him, and on some stairway here he turned and addressed his would-be murderers.[1] The grooves worn by old chariot-wheels still run down

[1] Acts 21:27-40.

the neighboring roadway and the pavement stones are marked by the games the soldiers played. One game in particular attracted my attention, played with two rows of seven small holes each, like teacups hollowed in the rock. Strangely enough, a few days later, at the gateway of old Samaria, the city of Omri and Ahab, I saw two Arab shepherds eagerly engaged in this very game which long ago on the pavement of Antonia the Roman soldiers played.

## VI

From the beginning Christian interest in Jerusalem has centered in the sites associated with the Master's crucifixion. The upper chamber, Gethsemane, Golgotha, the tomb—these have been the natural goals of Christian pilgrimage. No one of them can be confidently located except Gethsemane, somewhere on the Mount of Olives.

Throughout his final visit to Jerusalem the Master's customary retreat was Olivet.[1] It remains yet perhaps the most persuasive memorial of him in Jerusalem's vicinity. One comes down through the eastern gate into the Kidron valley and climbs up the Mount of Olives on the other side. Still one can see the whitewashed sepulchers [2] which thickly strew the Kidron's flanks, the Master's symbol for the hypocrites, and many a holy tomb there reminds one yet of his words about those who garnish the prophets' graves

[1] Luke 22:39.          [2] Matthew 23:27.

while they "kill and crucify" the prophets of their own time.[1]

Today on Olivet the olive trees are present still, but man and locusts have diminished them and Christian churches have crowded them.  It is not easy to find quiet and solitude here.  On the night of Maundy Thursday, when one would gladly be alone upon the hill, crowds throng up, the automobile horns honk in merciless confusion and headlights flash unwelcome brilliance into the densest shade.  No longer is it easy to imagine that here

> Into the woods my Master went,
> Clean forspent, forspent.[2]

But as the night crept on and the sermons, which had seemed an intrusion on the rights of silence, were long finished and the songs in many tongues were stilled, it became peaceful in Gethsemane.  The exact spot is quite unknown, but somewhere on this hillside the Master faced his agonizing spiritual travail beneath the olive trees.  Yonder, across the Kidron below him, he could look on Jerusalem.  The Bible's phrase, "on the Hill of Olives opposite the temple," [3] correctly draws the scene.  The evening lights were shining from the temple area and tower while he was praying.  There on the morrow they would crucify him,

[1] Matthew 23:29,34.
[2] Sidney Lanier: A Ballad of Trees and the Master.
[3] Mark 13:3 M.

and within view of the city that betrayed him he said, "Thy will be done."

The site of Pilate's Prætorium is fairly sure but to call it impressive would be untruthful. One goes in the Jaffa gate, and there in a little plaza where David Street pours out its motley throngs and the foreign business of banks and tourist agencies has its center, one sees the massive remains of an ancient citadel. In its present form it dates from the fourteenth century, with later additions, but the great rocks of its lower foundation are Herodian. Here Herod built his famous Phasael Tower, often reconstructed, which in its present form affords the tourist the best reminder of the ancient wall-towers of Jerusalem. Here, in connection with the towers and palace, stood the king's judgment-hall and here, so far as our evidence indicates, Pilate released Jesus Bar-Abbas and sentenced Jesus Christ.[1] Nothing remains to lend either atmosphere or detail to the picture. One would do well to fall back on Munkacsy's painting, Christ Before Pilate, and let that kindle his imagination, because this Tower of Phasael is empty of suggestiveness. As I passed it repeatedly, amid the jostling crowds, I used to marvel that all this eager chaffering, this sweating toil of laden men and beasts, was going on where once the walls echoed "Crucify," and where the Son of Man, bowed beneath his Cross, passed through the throngs toward Golgotha.

[1] Matthew 27:15-26 M.

## VII

The traditional site of the Cross and the tomb has been hallowed for over fifteen centuries in the Church of the Holy Sepulcher. Let the visitor go there as to one of the most interesting places in Christendom, with a continuous tradition from the days of Constantine the Great, and made sacred by the prayers and vows of innumerable pilgrims, but let him not go there as to the assured site of either crucifixion or resurrection. No one knows where that site is, and doubtless no one ever will.

Eusebius, a Christian historian of the fourth century, tells us that in 134 A.D. Hadrian, having sacked the city and wishing to force pagan worship on it, reared a great terrace over Golgotha and built an altar there; and that when in Constantine the Great's time, three hundred years after the crucifixion, Christians demolished the terrace, they found Golgotha and the empty tomb beneath. Three centuries of paganism are so long a span, and the evidence of a historian in the fourth century A.D. is dated so far after the event, that one's confidence cannot be assured.

Apart from tradition, the archeological argument has been associated with the position of the city's second wall, outside of which the crucifixion was consummated. Where that ran the scholars have debated for years, some thinking it just inside the present sacred site, some sure that it was outside. Just now the debate has been fired with new fuel because the apparent line of the third wall has been exhumed approximately where long ago Dr. Edward Robinson conjectured it should be. While we were in Jerusalem, a congress of archeologists debated the question and left the matter, with good authorities on both sides, uncertain still. Since then Dr. Albright, of the American School of Oriental Research in Jerusalem, has informed me that there is no longer any doubt that the new excavations have uncovered the third wall, but he thinks the authenticity of the Holy Sepulcher is not settled by the fresh discoveries.

Some doubtless will regret this uncertainty about sites to Christians the most sacred in the world, but, for myself, the more often I visited the Church of the Holy Sepulcher the more grateful I was that we are not compelled to think of the Master's Cross and tomb as being there. Let the visitor, some high day in Lent, go himself and see! Five services are on at once —the Greek Orthodox, the Roman Catholic, the Armenian, the Jacobite Syrian, and the Coptic. These five possess monopoly of the church and no others are allowed to hold public worship there. So jealous are they of their rights in this carefully districted sanctuary, where none may overstep his privileges by a single inch, that within the memory of my friends in Jerusalem a riot broke out and two men were killed because a Greek had swept one more step of an outer stairway than it was his right to sweep. Even under British rule, while there have been no deaths, there has been bloodshed, and Moslem soldiers still keep guard over the competing Christians.

Disturbances are frequent. On Good Friday night, while we were in the city, an Armenian Christian who brought a Jewess in his party to the church was set upon by Moslems and Christians alike and thoroughly beaten. Here is the very crux and center of all the rampant prejudices and bitter rivalries that rend Jerusalem asunder. After the miracle of the sacred fire, that very Easter, a three-page foolscap letter came from one of the patriarchs to the government. A responsible British official narrated to me the incident. The patriarch was in great mental distress; sacred immemorial rights had been invaded; the government was implored to save the situation and protect the church from further wrong; and the trouble was that during the service of worship the Jacobite Syrian kavass had stood on a step of the stairway where only the Armenian kavass had a right to stand, while the Syrian should have stood upon the floor.

Such is the atmosphere of the Church of the Holy Sepulcher today and public worship is an unhappy advertisement of it. In gorgeous, ecclesiastical vestments the five sets of churchmen parade around the sanctuary, chanting, genuflecting, ringing bells. The groups proceed, each in its appointed course and order, about the rambling, meticulously apportioned church, to swing censers before the holy places. The spot where Constantine's mother found the "true Cross," Golgotha itself, the stone of anointing for the burial.

the place where Mary stood when she saw where they
laid him, the Master's tomb, and Joseph of Arimathæa's
own sepulcher as well—such holy places within the
sanctuary are venerated with swinging censers twice a
day by every one of the five churches, and no one of
them dares omit a single occasion lest it lose forever the prized privilege of sharing in the fivefold
monopoly.

The church itself is bedlam to the eye and ear.  The
garish, gawdy decorations, the competing din of five
simultaneous services, the hideous, dissonant gongs,
the very lamps which hang in multitudes from the roof,
their differences advertising their fivefold sectarianism
—all this represents a type of religion that Jesus dis-
liked most and represents nothing that he pleaded for
and for which he died.

What will they not show you in this place?  The
spot where Adam was buried, the cleft in the rock
which the earthquake opened at the crucifixion [1] and
through which Christ's blood, dripping, fell on Adam's
skull so that he revived and walked the streets of
Jerusalem, [2] the pillar of scourging [3]—you may thrust
a stick through a hole to touch it and then kiss the
stick; even the stocks into which the Master's feet
were put while the Cross was being reared, two impressions of his footsteps on the solid rock, and the very
hole into which the Cross was thrust—such chicanery
and superstition shock the eyes while the ears are filled

[1] Matthew 27:50-51.                [3] Mark 15:15.
[2] Cf. Matthew 27:52-53.

with the hideous dissonance of five kinds of Christians venerating their sacred sites.

Was Jesus really crucified and buried here?   Was this the place where Easter morning broke in glory?   For myself, I hope not.   Let his sacrifice and his victory find their memorial anywhere rather than here.   This pretentious and ugly paganism mingled with disgraceful imposture is utterly alien to his spirit.   Was it not enough that he was crucified?   Must the reputed place of his sacrifice be thus profaned by his followers?

If we must have a site for the crucifixion, let us go to "Gordon's Calvary"; at least that is decent and quiet. If we must see an empty sepulcher, let us go to the "Garden Tomb"; at least the place is reverent and beautiful.   But, best of all, let us climb Olivet again and lose, in the farther view of the city, the sight of man's folly and the noise of his discords.   Thence, if we climb high enough, we can see Bethlehem shining on its noble hill.   There, five miles to the south, cluster the happy memories of Christ's nativity; below us somewhere among the northern suburbs of the city gather the recollections of his sacrifice.   From Bethlehem to Golgotha—where so vividly as on the crest of Olivet can one ponder the significance of the life that lay between?

# CHAPTER XI

## CHRIST AND CHRISTIANITY IN PALESTINE

### I

THE contrast between the spirit of Jesus on one side and historic Christianity on the other is sufficiently appalling in any country, but it is natural that the disharmony between the two especially should shock the pilgrim in Palestine. Here the life of Jesus seems in many a place so vivid and so close at hand that one keenly feels the jar in passing from memories of him to the churches, creeds, and rituals which are supposed to represent him.

When one has lived for even a few weeks in Palestine intent on following the Master's steps, every landscape becomes vocal with some news of him, and one understands the meaning of that Syrian Christian in America who says that whenever he opens his Bible it reads like a letter from home. The vineyards with their watch towers, such as Jesus saw, still are here; [1] public, noisy mourning when death befalls still is a familiar scene; [2] donkeys frequent the roads, piled high with grass which tomorrow will be "cast into the oven;" [3] stones and flowers, grapes, thorns, figs, and

[1] Matthew 21:33.　　　　　　[3] Luke 12:28.
[2] Matthew 9:23.

thistles, which he used in teaching, are everywhere; and in innumerable, small, revealing ways the land lights up the gospels. As for the Master himself, he looms impressively real and commanding against the background of his native land, at the same time more human in the circumstances of his life and more divine in his quality of character.

The same land, however, which deepens faith in Christ awakens shame for Christianity. A more appalling contrast does not exist in history than the antithesis between these two, and a Christian, often shocked and penitent, must face here the undeniable evidence of historic Christianity's three chief exhibitions in the Master's land—monasticism, militarism, and mummery.

## II

It was natural that in the days when asceticism was in its ascendency hermits and monks should flock to the Holy Land. Even before Constantine made Christianity the imperial religion and crowned with churches the sacred sites of Jerusalem, the story of Palestinian anchorites began. Sometime in the latter half of the second century Narcissus, Christian bishop of Jerusalem, unable longer to sustain the struggle against rancor and malevolence, left his see and retired to a solitary life in the wilderness, and Hilarion of Gaza, born about 291 A.D., made a great name for himself by his austerities in a hut of "chips and broken tiles." This movement toward the ascetic life, whether in the lonely sufferings of hermits or the communal severity of monks and nuns, swept into its current the whole church, and Egypt, Palestine, and Syria became, in particular, the habitat of those venerated "athletes of piety." All over Palestine today one sees the memorials of their presence, sometimes in solitary caves high in the cliffs of arid wadies, sometimes in monasteries once famous and populous but now tended by a few bedraggled monks.

The sort of life which these hermits' caves and monasteries represent was too highly honored in its time to escape detailed description, and he who can endure the gruesome record may fill with vivid pictures the framework which still remains. One hermit passed ten years in a suspended tub; one lived in a cistern on five figs a day; one passed sixty years without seeing or speaking to a human being; one lived for thirty years on one meal a week; one by desperate devices kept himself awake twenty-one hours daily; one habitually practised standing like a crane upon one leg until he fainted—such was the Christian asceticism which reigned throughout the East.

Indeed, it was but a few miles from Palestine's northern border in Syria that the most venerated of the anchorites, Simeon Stylites, lived upon his pillar, and the ruined pillar and the church afterwards built round it are said to be visible still. He long had practised the most rigorous austerities until, as one adoring disciple cried, "When he walks vermin drops from his body," but that was not enough. He tried burying himself up to his neck in the ground, but after a summer of that he mounted his pillar, gradually raised its height from four to forty cubits, stayed there for over thirty years, and became one of the most venerated figures in Christian history—"that great miracle of the world," as one admirer wrote of him, "that angel upon earth," as another said. Such was the Christianity which reigned for centuries in Syria and Palestine. As many as were minded practised this ideal life of the ascetic, and all the rest adored them, made pilgrimages to see them, and prayed before the sites of their immolation.

The most famous of them all in Palestine proper were Jerome and Paula. They came from Rome and they lived in Bethlehem. In 385 Jerome, having failed to secure the papacy, retired to the monastic life and for thirty-four years made the town of our Lord's nativity the scene of his ruthless austerity and energetic toil. For, ascetic though he was, he was a scholar too, and his literary labors, from writing the praise of asceticism to translating the Scriptures into Latin, were immense and varied. Paula was a wealthy Roman matron who, stirred by Jerome's example and teaching, left her family and, coming to Bethlehem, lived the ascetic life and used her wealth to build monasteries there. An impressive picture of her farewell to her broken-hearted and protesting children has been preserved for us: "She raised dry eyes to heaven, and overcame her love of her children by her love of God. She knew herself no longer a mother."

If one would reconstruct in imagination a vivid picture of that ancient day when countless thousands— monks, nuns, anchorites, and hermits—peopled these cliffs and barren wilderness stretches of Palestine and made the world ring with tales of their austerities, one would do best to visit Mar Saba.

It lies between eight and nine miles from Jerusalem in the wilderness and can best be reached by donkey. We rode out one lovely April morning by way of the Kidron valley into a land utterly baked and sterile. True to the intention of its founders, this famous monastery, with its rambling buildings plastered against the sheer wall of a precipitous cliff, stands in the midst of a dreary, arid waste. Nearly six hundred feet below runs the so-called Wady of Fire—a blazing trench leading down seven miles to the Dead Sea. Here in the fifth century Saint Euthymius gathered a settlement of monks and called his favorite pupil, Sabbas, to join him in the wilderness. Sabbas organ-ized a monastery, and his sanctity, as famous as it was austere, together with his reputation as a lusty defender of orthodoxy against contemporary heretics, established it in the veneration of the people. Thousands of monks are said to have been here. These dens and caverns, with which the cliffs of the wady still are riddled, were peopled with them when the allies of Chosroes, the Persian, in 614 A.D. swept in on their furious raid. Here, still, in this wobegone and desic-cated place thirty-five monks of the Greek Church pro-long the old idea of a "holy" life.

They are an ill-omened group. Misfits in the outer

world, they have retreated here to live decadent lives. The long-haired, long-bearded, frowzy member who opened the door turned out to be a naturalized citizen of the United States who for ten years had been a fireman in New York and Chicago hotels. That strenuous occupation proving too absorbing to admit of fasting and prayer, so he said, he had, for his soul's sake, retired to this place where he need attend to nothing else. The rest of the brotherhood are from Greece proper and the islands of its archipelago, but I found one who had kept a fruit store for three years in Salem, Massachusetts.

Here these men live, their only privation abstinence from meat, and their hardest duty maintaining the rituals of the church. Twice daily, for long hours at a time, and every night for five hours beginning at 2:30 A.M., they rehearse the ponderous liturgies of the Greek service. They were at their prayers when we arrived; a droning voice was sleepily intoning a ritual in a dark, incense-laden chapel, while blinking, indolent forms lounged in the stalls, peering curiously at us, talking audibly with one another and obviously thinking of anything but prayer.

When I asked the ex-fruitseller from Salem what good it all did, I could get no certain answer except that, whether he would or not, he must somehow keep awake those five hours every night. Nevertheless, both English-speaking monks agreed that it was easier to be Christians here than at their former tasks, and if hard and honest work interfere with Christianity they should indeed be saintly now. Food in plenty is sent down to them weekly from Jerusalem and they need do nothing save bake a little bread and cleanse the dishes. No service can be rendered to any human being. No one is within reach whom they could help even if they so desired. They eat and sleep and drone their prayers and let the poor world wag—a dowdy brood of decadent men as eager for a few piasters bestowed by a visitor as any beggar by the roadside asking bakshish.

Here in this ancient monastery these left-overs of a bygone age guard their relics: the grotto and grave of Saint Sabbas, whose body long ago was taken to Venice; the tomb of Saint John of Damascus, whose body has been transported to Moscow; the skulls of martyrs slain by Chosroes, with three laid out to kiss, and kissed so often that they shine. One hymn which still is in our hymn books came from this monastery:

> Art thou weary, art thou languid?
> Art thou sore distressed?

Having been there, I have no desire to sing it again.

When one considers the amazing strides with which, when once it started, Islam stalked across western Asia and northern Africa, defeating a decrepit Christianity with ease, one must recall that not in military strength alone but in moral virility Islam was the superior. It was not Christ that Islam crushed but a Christianity which had become an organized denial of Christ. Multitudes of monks lived throughout the land daring in only one channel to let their balked emotions flow.   They hated heretics.   That passion they could freely indulge and they gave loose rein to it.   They acted, as another put it, "only according to the dictates of their rage."   In 530 one could have seen in Constantinople noble matrons and virgins raised in the air by pulleys, their feet heavily weighted while their naked bodies were torn by whips and burned with red hot irons.   Indeed, it is said that a patriarch of Alexandria in a rage so kicked and trampled a patriarch of Constantinople that the latter died of his wounds.   This was the Christianity which Islam conquered.   The enmity of Christians toward each other, said Ammianus, an early historian, surpassed the fury of savage beasts against man.

One does not mean that no grace and beauty ever grew, like water-flowers from the mud, out of this morass of dogmatic monkishness.   We read of one monk who kept a hospital and called his patients his jewels.   This spirit of human service, however, which characterized wide areas of Western monasticism, was exceptional then, as it is today, in the indigenous Christianity of Palestine.   One who walks here must feel with poignant shame that Christ, indeed, is glorious but that Christianity is sick unto death.   Never was a religion's founder more tragically misrepresented than Jesus has been in his home country.

### III

The second impressive exhibition of itself which Christianity gave in the Holy Land was militarism.

That began early.   Constantine the Great became the first Christian emperor because when he was hard pressed in war a vision of the Cross in heaven promised him military victory.   An untoward beginning in the East, therefore, Constantine gave Christianity when he made it the imperial religion.   An ungoverned, barbarous Serbian, his life was a succession of battle-fields from York in England to the shores of the Black Sea.   To the day of his death he was really a pagan in religion.   As for his personal character, it may suffice to note that he murdered his wife, his son, and a considerable number of more remote and insignificant relatives.   The story of Christianity in the Near East is in no small measure a lamentable continuance of this unholy start.

The supreme example of Christian militarism in the Holy Land is, of course, the crusades.   One runs on the memorials of them all over Palestine.   In view of their meaning to this land and the disastrous consequences which they wrought it is not easy to write of them with cool reserve.   Individual men went into them from high motives.   Sincere piety marked the knightly vow "to avenge the shame done to Jesus Christ, and to reconquer Jerusalem, if so be that God will suffer it."   High-minded men went out from their homes with poignant self-sacrifice as did Joinville, who wrote: "Never while I went to Blécourt and Saint-Urbain would I turn my eyes towards Joinville for fear my heart should melt within me at thought of the fair castle I was leaving behind, and my two children." They exhibited also such fortitude in their sufferings and courage in their attacks that the story of the exploits which, with a handful of knights, they wrought against myriads is one of the most astounding chapters in the military annals of the world.

Despite fair vows, brave deeds, and high purposes, however, the crusades degenerated into a selfish, jealous, murderous orgy. Personal character collapsed before the allurements of license and plunder, and things were done in the name of Christ that make Saracens like the great Saladin seem comparatively tolerant and merciful. When at last the crusaders were driven disastrously from the Holy Land, the best of them rightly felt that God had not let them keep it because they had not deserved it.

Indeed, the very motive for the crusades was not so high as has been advertised. Pope Urban put it frankly when he summoned Christendom to undertake them. He appeared before feudal lords who were engaged in endless wars among themselves and said, "If you must have blood, bathe your hands in the blood of the infidels. I speak to you with harshness, because my ministry obliges me to do so: Soldiers of hell, become soldiers of the living God!" They were to fight Saracens, that is, in order not to fight each other, and in the end they did both with lamentable consequence. No high results could come from such a motive and from such a cause. We need not wonder, therefore, that the crusaders in Antioch made one of the worst records known to history for ungovernable and prolonged drunkenness and debauchery; that putting Moslems on spits and roasting them over the fire was the great Bohemond's manner of dealing with spies; that, treating their enemies so, they did not scruple at the slaughter of their fellow-Christians, so that in Constantinople hatred ran high until Greek churchmen martyred thousands of Latin churchmen, sold four thousand more into perpetual slavery to the Saracens, and chanted thanksgiving to the Lord when a Latin cardinal's dissevered head was dragged through the streets fastened to a dog's tail. As for their treatment of a conquered Moslem stronghold, when the crusaders seized Jerusalem on July 15, 1099, they indulged in promiscuous massacre, respecting neither age nor sex for three days, and estimated gratefully that they killed seventy thousand Moslems before their rage was satisfied. One cannot forbear the recollection that when Saladin retook the city he made terms which spared the lives of the Christians within it.

With mingled feelings, therefore, one travels among the memorials of the crusaders in Palestine. How tremendously they wrought in the few years they held this land! Under the massive porticoes they reared in Jerusalem to shelter pilgrims, the markets of the city still are thronged today. In out-of-the-way places like little Kiriath-jearim, ten miles from Jerusalem, one comes on lovely crusader churches with a stalwart dignity and grace that make one sure of high quality in the men who so could build. Sometimes in utterly unsuspected places, as in a dirty, unkempt khan in

Tyre, a traveler finds himself in an old crusader church once fragrant with the altar's incense, now noisome with the stable's smell, where near at hand the great Frederick Barbarossa of thrilling history and endless legend is said to have been buried in 1190. Crusader names—Belfort, Belvoir, Mirabel, Blanchegarde, Sinjil—strangely commingled with Semitic place-names all about them, recall the ineffaceable impress of the invaders. Especially along the coast north from Beirut in Syria, one sees great ruins of crusader castles, marvelous yet in their massive strength, with walls that have sustained the shock of war and weather and the quarrying of centuries.

In some ways the most impressive memorial of the crusaders that I saw was something which not they but nature made—"the horns of Hattin." They are the twin summits of an elongated hill rising some two hundred feet above the barren moor by which the plateau slopes down toward the Sea of Galilee, between Tiberias and Mejdel. The hill is visible from a large part of the sea, and repeatedly from the water or the shore, looking on these memorable horns, I was disturbed by painful recollections of their meaning. Here, within view of them, Christ had taught. Here his gospel of good-will had its first enunciation, and somewhere on these hills he preached his Sermon on the Mount. Legend even has it that the scrub-covered, arid plain at the foot of Hattin is the wilderness where the hungry multitude followed him on foot. And here in 1187 of his era a religious piratical expedition which called itself by his name went down in ruin. The Christian army had come from Sepphoris with a piece of the "true Cross" carried into battle as the ancient Hebrews bore the Ark, and, on a hot July day, with the terrible sirocco blowing from the east, they met the Saracens. Fire flaming through the scrub into their faces proved a foe as difficult to meet as Saladin. The knights were smothered in their armor, lost heart, gave way, died or surrendered, and the ill-starred crusades, while lingering on for many years, were broken in strength and doomed to failure. What a travesty of Christ is such truculent Christianity, and where could the travesty be so keenly felt as beside the Sea of Galilee?

Let the traveler go a few miles south from Haifa and he will find the ruins of 'Athlit. They thrust themselves splendidly out into the Mediterranean with great walls still menacing in their wreckage. The crusaders built the castle to protect Christian pilgrims and they defended it until it fell before the Moslems in 1291. It was the last fortress held in Palestine by the crusaders. I walked the shore among the ruins, where the blue sea now peacefully laps the sand, and saw those valiant but sorely mistaken cavaliers of the Cross driven from their last refuge. From the day the crusaders started with a massacre of eight hundred Jews at Worms and one thousand more at Mayence, as an initial baptism of blood upon their enterprise, to the day they took Jerusalem and, driving the city's Jews into a synagogue, burned them alive, the story of their unmitigated brutality against non-Christians and fellow-Christians alike is one of the most appalling portions of humanity's record.

To us it is ancient history, but in Palestine and Syria yet it symbolizes to multitudes the nature of Christianity. Even in universities where the best youths of Islam are gathering today, the traveler finds a view of Christianity which at first astounds and then shames him. We have called Moslems bloody; they think of us as holding a religion of the sword. We have accused them of massacres; they have vivid memories of multitudinous massacres perpetrated on their forefathers by Christians and they see Christianity represented among them still by French guns bombarding Damascus and British airplanes menacing Arab villages. We have claimed for ourselves a gospel of peace; they see us red-handed with history's most colossal wars, while of themselves they say, as one said to me, "I am a man of religion and therefore a man of peace." These students are young, free of spirit, their faces forward, as lovable and hopeful as any youths in America. The best of them hate their own race's shameful deeds, like the massacres of the Armenians, and in their hands lie the best hopes of their race and their religion. They honor Christ; he is one of the accepted prophets of their faith; and an appeal to Christ meets always their reverent respect. But they do not honor Christianity. They hate and fear it. They have experienced too long and too bitterly its bloodthirsty militarism.

## IV

Mummery, if it be used to express, not a mood of scorn, but a matter of fact, is not too strong a word for the third exhibition which Christianity has given of itself in Palestine. It is not easy to judge with impartial fairness the Eastern churches,—Greek, Syrian, Coptic, Armenian,—whose religious life so largely has degenerated here into outward form with small ethical result. One surely does not mean to sweep into the discard as spiritually futile the elaborate symbolism of Eastern worship, which, fitted to the temperament of the people, has nourished genuine piety and devotion through the centuries. But in Palestine the traveler is shocked at the lack of those fruits of religion for which Jesus would be looking. Philanthropy, education, individual charity, and public service—such things are largely absent in the face of terrific need for them; and, as for personal character, a Christian himself confessed to us that, as between a Moslem and a Christian village, there was no discernible difference except that the Moslems were probably more truthful. Meanwhile, with endless, gorgeous ceremonial, with the pomp of fabulously valuable robes and miters, the liturgies of the churches are performed in honor of the Galilean.

One who endeavors truly to estimate the situation must always bear in mind one major fact: these Eastern churches, since the coming of Islam and especially since the arrival of the Turk, have been subjected to a withering persecution so sustained that the very fact of their survival testifies to an inward vigor and fidelity which deserve our uttermost respect. We who come from lands where Christianity has triumphed should walk cautiously in judgment in lands where for many centuries Christians have been outlaws and pariahs, forbidden to proselytize, forced by law and violence to become self-contained, unmissionary communities, stripped of privilege and opportunity, subject to periodic outbursts of popular fury, sometimes exiled and massacred. No wonder that the marks of such prolonged suppression should be visible upon the Eastern churches. Moreover, today, the Greek Church in Palestine, with all its revenues from Russia stopped, with the stream of innumerable Russian pilgrims dried at its source, is hard put to it to survive, so that the desire to educate and serve its people, even were it alive and ardent, would be checkmated by lack of means. Nowhere is a more obvious or pressing need and opportunity for service presented to Western Christians than in the Eastern churches.

Nevertheless, if one is to write truly what his eyes have seen in Palestine, he must describe scenes in Christian churches which are plainly mummery.

Most famous of them all is the miracle of the sacred fire. On the Saturday before the Greek Easter, at the hour set, the Church of the Holy Sepulcher in Jerusalem is given over to the Greeks, Armenians, and Copts. The premises are jammed with an eager, excited throng. Windows, arcades, vaults, and domes—wherever human beings possibly can cling—are occu-

pied. For today the holy fire comes down from heaven
—a glorious annual miracle—and blessings await the
fortunate folk whose tapers are lighted and whose
household fires are set ablaze with the sacred flame.
Hours before the event the crowds gather, fill the
adjoining streets, roofs, and windows, throng the
courtyards of the church, and assail its entrances, cover
its terraces, line its balustrades, and fill its interior.
The expectancy is intense. From far above, on a bal-
cony about the dome, we look down upon the throng
milling around the Chapel of the Sepulcher, from two
apertures in which the sacred fire will come. Those
nearest the apertures already are holding their places
with fierce earnestness, with pugilistic violence when
needful, for will not those be specially blessed whose
tapers first are lighted by the fire, when it is fresh from
God and has not passed through intervening human
mediums?

When at last those who have secured admittance
through special entrances have found their places, the
main doorway is thrown open and a shouting, singing
mob surges into the church—already apparently filled
—carrying cheer-leaders on their shoulders and both
acting and sounding like nothing so much as college
students celebrating a football victory. It is a wild
scene to begin with; it becomes a mad tumult of song,
shout, and violence as the crowd shoulders its way
as close as may be to the Holy Sepulcher. As for the
religious spirit of it, that may be judged by the song
the crowd sings as it comes in:

O Jew! O Jew! Yours is the feast of the
devil but ours is the feast of the Lord.

Then the procession of gorgeously arrayed priests,
clad in golden-yellow robes, begins its laborious march
about the Sepulcher. Chanting their liturgy, they make
their way three times about the tomb, but only with the
aid of the constabulary which forces a slender pathway
through the throng. At last the procession is ended.
The aged high priest is divested of his outer robes and
is led into the Chapel of the Sepulcher.

Then one can feel the excited tensity deepen. In a
moment the sacred fire will come. The crowds strain
about the apertures. Individuals lose control of themselves and fight for better places only to be mauled by
their neighbors or thrown out by the police. Let a
man have what opinion he may as to the quality of
religion represented here, it is surely one of the best
mob scenes he ever witnessed. Suddenly, amid the
frantic pealing of great bells, the sacred fire comes.
A Copt seizes it first, doubles up over his flaming
bundle of tapers, and, protected by a well-organized
interference, makes a dash through the crowd worthy
of a champion half-back. He carries his captured flame
to the Copt shrine behind the Sepulcher and at once
rapidly multiplying scores of tapers, lighted there,
twinkle in the shadows of the church. Man after man
of picked strength and speed lights his torch from the
Sepulcher's continuing flame and makes his flying dash
through the crowd despite strenuous tackling in the
endeavor to steal his light. It is now a mad scene.

of our Lord's nativity at Bethlehem.  Only two years ago, when the Greek Easter came, which falls upon a different date from the Roman, the Latins obtrusively came into the church to hang a picture so that they might not seem to surrender right to the sanctuary even on a rival's holy day.  A free-for-all fight ensued. A hurried call was sent for the constabulary.  The combatants were unceremoniously pitched from the church and even a gray-haired bishop, fighting like the best of them, was included in the forcible ejection.

Typical alike of the bad temper and triviality of these Christian fanatics is the affair of the three nails. A pillar divides the Greek portion from the Latin in the Church of the Nativity and in the pillar are three nails.  On one the Greeks may hang the end of their tapestry; on another the Latins may hang theirs; but the central nail is neutral, from which is supposed to depend a candlestick.  One day the Latins in intense excitement complained to the government that the Greeks had hung their tapestry upon the central nail. This intolerable invasion of sacred rights became a matter of serious governmental investigation.  Witnesses were sworn; the traditional use of the nails was traced and verified; and at last, under compulsion, pledges for the future were legally drawn up and signed.

For many years we have heard of Islam's impervious obduracy against the persuasions of the Christian Gospel.  But why should Moslems desire to accept Christianity?  What is there in the Christianity they best have known to tempt their minds or challenge their consciences?

Moreover, this unethical religion repeatedly slips over into venal mendacity.   Travelers now are shown in a monastery near the ancient Tower of Antonia what the monks call the "prison of Christ."   The monks had a real treasure in their monastery—bona fide portions of the lower rooms, storage places, it may be, or stables of the tower.   But these tradi- tionally unembellished relics were not drawing visitors enough.   The monks, therefore, closed the monastery for repairs, brought in a mason to bore holes like stocks and otherwise rearrange the stonework to make the place appear a prison, and now they advertise it as the site where Jesus was incarcerated.   It is a deliber- ate fraud like many another in this Holy Land.   Not only can that be proved from drawings made on the spot by an archeologist before the alterations had been thought of, but the mason who did the work explained to friends of mine just how it had been done.

## VI

No Western disciple of Jesus can regard such Chris- tian monasticism, militarism, and mummery in Pales- tine with any sustained feeling of superiority.   This appalling contrast between Christ and Christianity, which smites the conscience of the traveler in the Mas- ter's land, is the crucial problem of Christians in every land.   Even in the Church of the Holy Sepulcher no these knightly pilgrims once engaged upon this very spot. From the Knights of Saint John sacking Jerusalem to the Knights of Saint John building ophthalmic hospitals in the Holy City for Moslems, Jews, and Christians alike is a great advance. Perhaps our children's children yet may see Christ genuinely honored in this city that he loved, where for centuries he has been crucified.

## CHAPTER XII

## PALESTINE TOMORROW

### I

No observant traveler can visit Palestine today
without being sure that the country has a future. The
days of its living importance to humanity are far from
ended and in it movements are afoot which may either
contribute signally to man's welfare or land the world
in fresh confusions and alarms. When the archeologists, the historians, and the Biblical scholars have
seen in Palestine all that their specialties reveal, the
student of contemporary affairs has a large and lively
residue to handle.

For weal or woe the new day was launched in the
Holy Land by the famous Balfour Declaration:

His Majesty's Government view with favor the establish-
ment in Palestine of a national home for the Jewish people,
and will use their best endeavours to facilitate the achievement of this object, it being clearly understood that nothing
shall be done which may prejudice the civil and religious
rights of existing non-Jewish communities in Palestine or the
rights and political status enjoyed by Jews in any other
country.

The reading of that is brief and easy, its purport seems
generous and laudable, but its results are visibly excit-

ing, offering alike spectacles of heroic adventure and possibilities of tragic failure.

Come down, for example, to Dilb in the Shephelah hills, a few miles below Jerusalem, where a hardy band of Jewish colonists is establishing its homes and farms. The story of folk like this is one of the romances of modern times and one hopes that, whether they win or lose in their venture, they may sometime find a historian worthy to record their exploits. The tale of this group begins in Odessa in the Ukraine in 1917. There local Zionists founded an agricultural school and for two years the future colonists attended it. Like most Jews, they knew nothing of agriculture. Ten university graduates, a printer, a druggist, a bookstore keeper, a carpenter, small merchants—such was the constitution of the group. After two years of preparation an advance section came to Palestine and were assigned this rough, rocky, untilled valley, treeless and largely soilless, where from the ground up they had to create the very elements on which agriculture depends. They cleared the land, terraced the hillsides to make soil, constructed a water system in an arid and hitherto unwatered land, built barns, houses, a school, and when I was there had 160 acres under cultivation. This is pioneering with a vengeance. Almost any Western country would reward such toil with far greater returns, but these Jews have come from patriotic motives to help rebuild Zion.

The meagerness of living in a colony like Dilb, the grim struggle against a niggardly land, the paucity of

the results, and the terrific cost of work and money
to achieve them, add glamour to the courageous ideal-
ism of the colonists. The £22,500 required to pur-
chase the land, prepare it for cultivation, build barns,
houses, and waterworks, buy farming instruments and
animals, came from the Zionist central funds. In 1926,
with one-third of their vineyards just coming to fruitage, they paid sixty per cent of their running expenses;
they hoped two years later to pay all; but only in 1929
do they expect to start paying a small interest on the
capital which they have borrowed. The adventure is
not only moral but economic. One wonders how it
will turn out.

Meanwhile, at the time of our visit, a hardy group
of seventy-five men and women were endeavoring here
to make their ancient land bloom again. Already they
had a flourishing forest nursery with sixty different
kinds of eucalyptus trees. Granted the colony's success, in a few years these hills will be wooded and
green once more. The oldest colonist was aged forty.
Fifteen young children were in a school which the
colony maintains. The manner of life is communistic;
no private property is held; and the moving ideal which
has brought the settlers here combines the love of
Palestine with the desire to create a cooperative fel-
lowship where each shall give according to his strength
and receive according to his need.

This is Zionism in the concrete. This is its cutting
edge and crucial exhibition. Here its enthusiasm meets
the test of barren, unwatered land and poor soil, cost-

ing immense expenditure of toil and means to transform into fertility. And here, too, are the lure and thrill of Zionism, where pioneers dedicate life to the rebuilding of the Holy Land.

## II

The motives which have made this new movement toward the homeland so kindling to Jewish imagination are not difficult even for a non-Jew to understand. The patriotism of Jews for Palestine has a long tradition. In the days when Nineveh and Babylon practised the cruel policy of exile, many peoples were absorbed and lost in the populations among which they forcibly were settled, but the Jews survived. Out of the midst of that supreme temptation to assimilation in Babylon came the passionate cry,

> If I forget thee, O Jerusalem,
> Let my right hand forget her skill.
> Let my tongue cleave to the roof of my mouth,
> If I remember thee not;
> If I prefer not Jerusalem
> Above my chief joy.[1]

We ate the Passover supper in Jerusalem with a Jewish family of the humbler sort. They came from forefathers who had fled out of Spain when the Jews there were persecuted in the sixteenth century. Three

[1] Psalm 137:5-6.

generations were at the table, from an aged grandsire
past ninety to a brisk youth who had come down from
the American University in Beirut to keep Passover
with his family. It was a remerable occasion for
a Christian, both because one cannot often eat Passover in Jerusalem, where the Master kept it with his
disciples, and because this fine-spirited and friendly
family of the Master's race made us feel anew the
depth and warmth of Hebrew loyalty to Zion. In particular I recall the old man's commenting on those
words of the ritual which Jews have used for centuries when keeping Passover in any other country:
"This year we celebrate it here; but we hope next
year to celebrate it in the land of Israel; this year we
are bondsmen, but next year we hope to be freemen."

This long-cherished dream of restoration to their
ancient land has become the more alluring to Jewish
people as the hardships of their life elsewhere, their
confinement in European ghettos, their persecutions
and pogroms, have shut against them other doors of
hope. The treatment of Jews in Christendom makes
one of the most appalling stories of truculence and
bigotry that history knows. Even now for millions
of Jews in eastern Europe life is hardly tolerable. A
weak folk long since would have collapsed but the
Jews, vigorous, persistent, imperturbable, with physical and intellectual vitality which nothing can dampen,
much less extinguish, have not collapsed. Hated,
ostracized, hemmed in, fretting for an outlet, a great

people without a national home—no wonder their aspirations have turned increasingly to their ancient land.

Multitudes of Jews today, even in countries where they are not persecuted, feel continually that they are aliens; their natural loyalties are outraged and their sensitiveness is hurt. As one put it to me: if in Belgium a Jew rises to great distinction he is heralded as an eminent Belgian; if he falls into disgrace he is called an accursed Jew. Can this be God's intention for his people? the religious Jew asks. I have sat in the chambers of one of the eminent members of the Supreme Court of the United States and in the home of the leading British jurist in Palestine, and from these two eminent Jewish lawyers have heard stirring pleas for Zionism, based on the argument that Providence could not mean to leave a nation so able to contribute spiritual gifts to humankind without a land and a culture of its own through which to channel the contribution.

Such motives lie behind Zionism, mingled with pity on the part of prosperous Jews for their unfortunate fellows and with desire to open in Palestine a place of refuge from the pogroms of eastern Europe. The United States sent only 166 Jewish immigrants to Palestine in 1922 and only 125 in 1923. From such a land there is no lure for Jews in the exhausting toil and small reward of Zionist colonies in Palestine. But America furnishes from two-thirds to three-quarters of the funds which bring Jews from Poland, the

Ukraine, and Russia as fast as the immigration authorities will allow.

### III

What, then, is the truth about Zionism as it appears
to a non-Jew who, neither Zionist nor anti-Zionist, is
interested without prejudice to observe the facts? For
myself, I found my mind swaying like a pendulum
between two positions: first, sympathy with the ideals
of the moderate Zionists, mingled with profound
admiration for their devotion to their cause, their daring confidence in its success, and many of their practical achievements up to date; second, clear percep-
tion that before this courageous venture can succeed
it must face serious problems whose solutions are not
easy to see.

The economic problem is colossal. Everything
hinges upon that. Here is a people famous for its
financial shrewdness and yet plunging, on the basis
of emotional loyalties, sacred memories, patriotic sentiment, and racial altruism, into an enterprise which
obviously flies in the face of economic fact. The
rehabilitation of Palestine is not a task that any one
would dream of undertaking for economic reasons.
Dr. Weizmann, the supremely influential figure in Zionism, said to me in Jerusalem that for the movement
to succeed it was necessary both to remake the people
and to remake the land. That is the succinct truth.
To make Jews into farmers, which is alien to all their
history, and to make Palestine profitably arable—these

Insecure in Egypt, she wished from the Palestinian side to control the Suez Canal, an essential artery of her empire's life. This selfish aim in taking Palestine was carried further in Zionism. By introducing Jews she divided the country into two mutually suspicious groups and so secured her power by playing off one against the other. As for the Jews themselves, our host hated them. They had no more right in the land, he said, because of previous occupation, than the American Indians had in New York City. There was no possibility of working out a common Palestinian civilization between Arab and Jew. To him the future looked dark and perilous.

The second dinner gave opportunity for conversation with aristocratic Arabs of the ruling class. Here was the Grand Mufti of all the Moslems in Palestine and a group of leaders from chief families of the land. They were clean-cut and relentless in their attitude. They foresaw violence and they minced no words in saying so. The triumph of Zionism did not mean in their eyes simply a numerous addition of Jews to the population. It meant the supersession of their Arab culture and civilization by another culture and civilization altogether. They saw clearly that Zionism involved a new economic life built on Western models, a new, progressive type of agriculture with which they could not compete, new applications of scientific method such as would oust from power all who would not adopt them, new Western types of relationship between men and women brought in by Jews and unutterably scandalous to Arabs, and, finally, new aggressiveness on the part of the Jews as their numbers mount until at last wild Zionist dreams, already publicly expressed, of rebuilding Solomon's temple where the Mosque of Omar stands, might come true. They said frankly that they would fight before they would suffer this supersession of their culture, and that all Islam around them, in Syria, Arabia, Egypt, like a sea around the enisled Zionism of Palestine, would rise in fury.

These two conversations, while typical, are not exhaustive of the Arabs' attitude. Arabs are an accommodating folk, long experienced in adjusting themselves to such relationships as promise enough to eat, and many of them, finding that money comes with the Jews, are making friends with this mammon of unrighteousness, and some are even learning to speak Hebrew. The scale of living has risen, wages are higher, opportunities greater, economic movements swifter. Indeed, hostility to Zionism on the part of city Arabs of the upper class may be partially explained by the fact that they are losing their grip upon the poor fellahin of the villages, who are better off with Zionism than they were without it. What the end will be only a predictive prophet of the first class could foresee. Many are sure that the interracial relationships are improving. Of this, however, I am certain: the situation still is loaded with dynamite. If the generous ideals of a moderate Zionism become dominant, coupling Arab and Jew alike in the plans for a rejuvenated Palestine, were getting on comfortably with the Arabs and who now are vexed with the new Zionists, whose coming has stirred up contention.  Some are pro-British, trusting England's conservative endeavor to make haste slowly; some are "revisionists," trying to force Britain's hand and compel aggressive action toward making Jews the dominant political power.  They come from all lands with all conceivable economic and political theories, with every imaginable shade of faith and skepticism, with innumerable differences of custom, costume, language, and education.  They are bound together by one tie only—they are Jews by race, speaking here the classic Hebrew as their common tongue, and wishing a national home.

This infinite variety presents at once a fascinating spectacle and an ominous problem.  One does not mean that it is insuperable.  The Jews differ no more than Christians do.  But here in Palestine they are engaged in a hazardous adventure beset with many perils, where success in any case must be won despite staggering obstacles and where coherence and unity are critically demanded.  As one watches the situation, one wonders whether in the end the greater difficulties will lie in external circumstances or within the Jewish communities themselves.

## VI

Meanwhile, no one does justice to the situation who does not fairly estimate the positive achievements already won in the first few, experimental years of this venture. One who knows the apparently exhaustless vitality of the Jewish race would expect its energies, released by the ardent hope of a national home, to flow into Palestine in multiplying streams. That such is the case any one who stays here long enough to see must testify.

Wherever the Jews go, education goes, and schools are flourishing in all the Zionist colonies, with higher schools of advanced standing in Jerusalem already crowned by a university. Illuminating statistics make plain the superior standards which the Jews are introducing into Palestine and show how difficult will be the competition of the Arabs, whether Christian or Moslem, with the education-loving Zionists. According to official figures in 1923, of the children of Palestine from five through fourteen years of age, seventeen per cent of the Moslems, eighty-one per cent of the Christians, and ninety-six per cent of the Jews were in school. Of children from fifteen through eighteen years of age, three per cent of the Moslems were still proceeding with their education, thirty-seven per cent of the Christians, and forty-two per cent of the Jews.

As they bring with them their passion for education, so they bring their Western ideas of medicine and philanthropy, and one sees in Jerusalem the beginnings of hospital service, public clinics, child welfare work, under the direction of thoroughly trained British and American Hebrews who are putting expert knowledge at the disposal of their people. Typical of this gether different from the new Zionist settlements. Here religious faith is ardent, experienced German farmers have succeeded in achieving self-support from the first, and each individual owns his own property.

Most visitors do not see these little settlements which are the real evidence of Zionism's vitality and the ultimate test of its success. Most travelers visit Tel-Aviv, an amazing town near Jaffa which since the war has grown from nothing to sixty thousand folk. Tel-Aviv, however, is rather an excrescence on Zionism than its normal fruit. It looks like a boom town in the Middle West with its raw newness, its paved streets, modern buildings, electric light plant, Western stores. Like the Zionism which it represents, it stands for the aggressive invasion of a new civilization. The contrast is vivid as one turns to Jaffa's neighboring bazaars and streets so Orientally picturesque. Not here in Tel-Aviv, but out in the colonies where pioneers invest life itself in the reclamation of the Holy Land, are alike the lure and hardship, the test and the possible tragedy of Zionism.

While tragedy is obviously possible, I personally hope that Zionism may succeed. What other fortunate outlook there is for Palestine I do not see. The Arabs, in the present stage of their development, would doubtless leave it as it is. Under their sway it has been stripped and impoverished, and they lack, at least at present, the ability swiftly to change either themselves or their environment. In time, these Arabs, who are a great race, will be compelled to achieve a synthesis of their ancient culture and modern life, but the time for that seems distant. Meanwhile, the present hope of a rejuvenated Palestine lies in Zionism under British guidance.

The hope of Zionism, however, lies in its own moderation and wisdom. If it would be successful it must be unselfish. It must count Arab welfare as precious as its own. It must center its efforts on creating in the Holy Land a cultural expression of world-wide Judaism. It must forego grasping ambition for political dominance and turn its back on chauvinistic nationalism. It must cease its absurd pretense that into this poor land as a place of refuge millions of persecuted Jews from southeastern Europe can be poured when the plain fact is that the country can do no more than absorb with difficulty a few thousand each year. If Zionism will thus clean house of wild extravagances and lay hold on a few immediate and obtainable objectives that can be reached with profit to all Palestinians and with wrong to none, then success may come. But if the partisans of political Zionism, as now seems probable, are allowed to force the issue, I am willing to risk my reputation on prophecy: Zionism will end in tragedy.

A Christian who, like a Jew, loves the Holy Land as the homestead of his faith, will regard the progress of events with eager, sympathetic interest. This is not the first time the Jews have undertaken a desperate venture in Palestine. Going north one day from Haifa, along the Mediterranean shore, we saw a great field of cucumber vines and in the midst of it a torn and tattered booth where, before the fruit was gathered, a guard had watched. The booth, made of a few bare poles and interlaced with faded vines, was now deserted—a perfect picture of lonely desolation. We recalled as we saw it Isaiah's description of Jerusalem in his day left "as a lodge in a garden of cucumbers." [1] More than once the Jews have thus seen their sacred land desolate or have lost it altogether and yet have rewon it by the very power of their passionate loyalty.

One who knows what happened when the little band of returning exiles from Babylonia long ago refounded on Zion their struggling commonwealth amid the ruins of their sacred city and the scornful antagonism of their neighbors will not be so much impressed by difficulties now as to be certain that the Jews cannot win again. Perhaps they can. The whole world is debtor to them for having won before. By that victory they set the stage for all that followed of tremendous import alike to them and to mankind. One hopes, although sometimes against hope, that they may so handle their present penetration of their ancient land that future generations with good cause may be grateful for another contribution to mankind's enrichment.

[1] Isaiah 1:8.

# A SELECTED BIBLIOGRAPHY FOR THE TRAVELER

GENERAL WORKS:

> Smith, George Adam—The Historical Geography of the Holy Land; A. C. Armstrong & Son.
> Conder, Claude Reignier—Tent Work in Palestine: A Record of Discovery and Adventure; Richard Bentley & Son.

HISTORY:

> Smith, Henry Preserved—Old Testament History; Chas. Scribner's Sons.
> Macalister, R. A. Stewart—The Philistines: Their History and Civilization; Oxford University Press, published for British Academy.
> Peters, John Punnett—The Religion of the Hebrews; Ginn & Co.
> Bewer, Julius A.—The Literature of the Old Testament in its Historical Development; Columbia University Press.
> Barton, George A.—Jesus of Nazareth: A Biography; The Macmillan Company.
> Warschauer, J.—The Historical Life of Christ; The Macmillan Company.
> Rihbany, Abraham Mitrie—The Syrian Christ; Houghton Mifflin Company.
> Margoliuth, D. F.—Mohammed and the Rise of Islam; G. P. Putnam's Sons.
> Mott, John R., editor—The Moslem World of To-day; George H. Doran Company.

295

Workman, Herbert B.—The Evolution of the Monastic Ideal; Charles H. Kelly.

Archer, T. A. and Kingsford, Charles L.—The Crusades: The Story of the Latin Kingdom of Jerusalem; G. P. Putnam's Sons.

Adeney, Walter F.—The Greek and Eastern Churches; Charles Scribner's Sons.

Macalister, R. A. Stewart—A History of Civilization in Palestine; Cambridge University Press.

Lawrence, T. E.—Revolt in the Desert; George H. Doran Company.

Graves, Philip—Palestine, the Land of Three Faiths; George H. Doran Company.

POPULAR TREATISES:

Kelman, John—The Holy Land; A. & C. Black.

Van Dyke, Henry—Out-of-Doors in the Holy Land: Impressions of Travel in Body and Spirit; Charles Scribner's Sons.

Bell, Archie—The Spell of the Holy Land; The Page Company.

Hichens, Robert Smythe—Holy Land; The Century Company.

Harrison, Paul W.—The Arab at Home; Thomas Y. Crowell Company.

ARCHEOLOGY:

Smith, George Adam—Jerusalem: The Topography, Economics and History from the Earliest Times to A.D. 70; A. C. Armstrong & Son.

Barton, George A.—Archæology and the Bible; American Sunday-School Union.

Driver, S. R.—Modern Research as Illustrating the Bible; Oxford University Press, published for the British Academy.

GUIDE-BOOKS:
  Baedeker, Meistermann, Cook, etc.

# INDEX OF SCRIPTURAL REFERENCES [1]

[1] Note that the references are to the American Standard Revised Bible, published by Thomas Nelson & Sons, except those indicated by M, which are to the New Translation by Dr. James Moffatt, published by George H. Doran Company.

# INDEX OF SUBJECTS AND PROPER NAMES

305